To Rosemarie,
Listen
Be Still.
God loves you
Peace.
Fr. Joe.

The Eternal Mystic

The Eternal Mystic

St. Teresa of Avila, The First Woman Doctor of the Church

by
Joseph Glynn, O.C.D.

VANTAGE PRESS
New York / Washington / Atlanta
Los Angeles / Chicago

FIRST EDITION

All rights reserved, including the right of reproduction in whole or in part in any form.

Copyright © 1982 by Joseph Glynn, O.C.D.

Published by Vantage Press, Inc.

516 West 34th Street, New York, New York 10001

Manufactured in the United States of America

ISBN: 533-05407-9

Library of Congress Catalog Card No.: 82-90304

Nihil Obstat: Patrick Sugrue, O.C.D., Regional Vicar
Imprimatur: †Timothy, Cardinal Manning
Archbishop of Los Angeles

To all the people who come to my
retreats and days of prayer

The Flaming Heart

O thou undaunted daughter of desires!
By all thy dower of lights and fires;
By all the eagle in thee, all the dove;
By all thy lives and deaths of love;
By thy larg draughts of intellectual day,
And by thy thirsts of love more large than they:
By all thy brim-filled bowles of fierce desire;
By thy last morning's draught of liquid fire;
By the full kingdome of that finall kisse
That seiz'd thy parting soul, and sealed thee his;
By all the heavn's thou hast in him;
(Fair sister of the seraphim);
By all of him we have in thee
Leave nothing of myself in me;
Let me so read thy life, that I
Unto all life of mine may dy.

                                              Crashaw

Contents

Acknowledgments   xi
Introduction   xiii

Part One
St. Teresa Becomes a Doctor

Chapter 1.   *What Makes a Doctor of the Church?*   3
                Lofty doctrine; woman of genius; writings; holiness of Teresa; contemporaries speak out; reading Teresa's writings; relevance; the Carmelite school of spirituality.

Part Two
The Life of St. Teresa

Chapter 2.   *God in Search of Teresa*   35
                Birth; childhood; the Heart, a lonely hunter; Our Lady of Grace School; Monastery of the Incarnation; The bewitched priest and the quack doctor of Becedas; breakdown; St. Joseph; a lax middle-aged nun; death of Teresa's father.

Chapter 3.   *The New Book of Life*   55
                The Jesuits; first rapture; first vision; St. Peter Alacantara; visions of the demonic world.

Chapter 4.	*The Reform of an Order*	75
	Doña Luisa de la Cerda; St. Joseph's Avila; persecution.	
Chapter 5.	*The Foundress*	92
	Medina del Campó; reform of the friars; Malagon; Valladolid; Duruelo; Toledo; Pastrana; Salamanca; Alba de Tormes.	
Chapter 6.	*Light and Darkness*	109
	Prioress of the Incarnation; Mystical marriage; Segovia, Princess of Eboli; Beas; Gracian; Seville; misunderstanding among superiors; Caravaca.	
Chapter 7.	*The Storm Breaks*	123
	Election at the Incarnation; Light at the end of the tunnel; Villanueva de la Jara; Palencia; separate provinces; Soria; Princess of St. Joseph's; Burgos.	
Chapter 8.	*Death and Glory*	135
	Cold Medina; Alba; death; burial; honored after death.	

Part Three
Prayer Life Within

Chapter 9.	*The Castle Within*	145
Chapter 10.	*Prayer*	173
Chapter 11.	*Contemplation*	184
Chapter 12.	*Prayer of Recollection*	199
Chapter 13.	*The Prayer of Quiet*	214
Chapter 14.	*Prayer of Simple Union*	229
Chapter 15.	*Spiritual Betrothal*	236
Chapter 16.	*Spiritual Marriage*	257

Bibliography   271

Acknowledgments

I wish to thank Sr. Ellen Muldoon, S.S.C., Mary Lou Petrie, Mary Frances Magaña, and Betty Pecharich, who helped type this book. I also wish to thank Fr. Patrick Sugrue, O.C.D., for his fraternal support.

New English Translation

Although I have been using the Allison Peers translation myself for some thirty years, I highly recommend the new English translation of the writings of St. Teresa, *The Collected Works of St. Teresa of Avila*, by Kieran Kavanaugh, O.C.D., and Otilio Rodriquez, O.C.D./I.C.S. Publications, Institute of Carmelite Studies, Washington, D.C., 1980.

Introduction

History was made on September 27, 1970, when Pope Paul VI declared St. Teresa of Jesus, the great saint, mystic, foundress, and writer, a doctor of the church. She was the first woman to be given this title, and so it is an honor for this extraordinary woman herself, an honor for all women, especially religious women, an honor for the Order of Discalced Carmelites, which she founded, an honor for the church, which has once again raised a woman to so high a pedestal, an honor for Spain and Avila, her native country and city, and an honor for Vatican II, which declared that, "women claim for themselves an equity with men before the law and in fact" (*Church Today*, par. 9); "Women are now employed in almost every area of life. It is appropriate that they should be able to assume their full, proper role in accordance with their own nature." (Ibid., par. 60.) For too long a time, women have been denied this equality and role, especially when it came to teaching and preaching. Today, a woman has broken through this barrier of prejudice, and proves that women can equal and surpass men in the loftiest form of human knowledge, the science of contemplation, prayer, and mysticism. Teresa of Avila has been hailed as the "Mater Spiritualium," the mother and master of spiritual men and women, and a mother and master in spiritual and mystical doctrine. She is also called the "Mysticae theologiae doctrix seraphica," the seraphic doctor of mystical theology.

St. Teresa is a charismatic figure called by the Holy Spirit to clarify, simplify, and spread the science of the saints. She stands equal, if not above, St. John of the Cross, St. Bernard, St. Bonaventure, Blessed Suso, Tauler and Ruysbroeck. And she has had far more influence than all these men on modern men, as can be seen by studying the bibliography. The influence of Teresa in mystical theology is comparable with that of St. Thomas Aquinas in dogmatic theology. Several Popes and eminent doctors have affirmed this fact: She treated the most difficult and mysterious problems on grace, the Trinity, Christology, theological virtues, the gifts of the Holy Spirit, and the mystery of the church with ease and clarity. Nobody has explained the stages in the life of prayer and cast so much light on the relationship of the soul with God at the heights of Union, Spiritual Betrothal, and Spiritual Marriage, as this humble virgin from Avila. She is like a mighty reservoir that contains within herself all the riches, the wisdom, knowledge, experience on prayer and mystical matters stored up within the bosom of Mother Church for almost 2,000 years. The fountain of living water has certainly sprung up within the heart of Teresa, and from that great and loving heart, wisdom and knowledge have come to all of us, to enrich our lives and inspire our ideals. She is a sun in the sky giving light and life to all who seek it.

To the rest of us who travel our pilgrim way to heaven guided by the dim light of faith, the writings, and experiences of Teresa hold out a beacon of hope. We know that everything promised by Our Lord in the Gospel is possible. The incredible gifts of God's love and presence are available. God does make His home in man; we are the shrines of His presence; God does speak to men still as a friend speaks to a friend; man can look on the face of God and live; a human being can live all day long in union and communion with the Blessed Trinity. Miracles of grace are still possible; the science of angels is available to man. We are really children of God, brothers of Christ, heirs to heaven. We do share God's nature. We are divinised. We have a wonderful dignity and an awesome destiny. We are a royal priesthood, a consecrated people, a race set aside for the worship of God, a people of priests whom God wants for His own. We can be holy, we can be great; we can be fulfilled, we can be perfect. The paradise lost can be restored within our souls. Heaven is possible on earth for those who love God. Teresa of Jesus proves the heights to which all of us can ascend. She shows the way, and teaches how the greatness of man and woman is not in external possessions, physical statistics, or mental ability but in his power to know and love God, his fellow man, himself and the world all around him and to leave all these latter things a little bit better, just because he has passed that way hand in hand with God, building up the wonderful world we live in and cooperating with the Creator in the work of creation.

The Eternal Mystic

Part One
St. Teresa Becomes a Doctor

1.
What Makes a Doctor of the Church?

Prosper Lambertini states there are three requirements to become a Doctor of the Church:

1. Lofty doctrine
2. Great holiness of life
3. The declaration by a General Council or the Pope. In the case of Teresa, this was granted by Pope Paul VI on September 27, 1970.

(De Servorum Dei Beatifactione, in Concessionis Tituli Doctoris S. Teresiae Abulensis, Roma, 1969, p.3)

Lofty doctrine

Every Doctor of the Church must teach lofty doctrine. It must be free from every taint of error, give a clear, lucid explanation of the faith and be based on Sacred Scripture. All this is true of the writings of our Doctor. (*Concessionis Tituli Doctoris, Informatio Patroni,* p. 7.)

St. Teresa studies the deep mystery of the Christian life, the life of grace, our incorporation into the Mystical Body of Christ, the life and indwelling of the Three Persons of the Blessed Trinity, prayer, mystical experiences, and difficult moral problems.

She treats these matters in an "existential manner," based on her own personal, lived experience. She gives us a profound theological study and a psychological description of what happens within the deified Christian soul sanctified through the merits of Christ, by the Holy Spirit on its way to perfection to the Father. The life of union and communion and dialogue of the soul with the Trinity is at the heart of Teresian teaching.

The spiritual life is the mystery and work of Christ in us. He is our Brother from whom all good things come. Christ has the fullness of grace. He is our model, the Way, the Truth, the Life. Teresa had a very special devotion to the Sacred Humanity, and recommended meditation on the mysteries of Christ; even at the loftiest peaks of prayer, Christ is our Mediator to the Father. We shall study this in greater detail later, when we take up her teaching on prayer.

St. Teresa loved the church. She died in peace, proudly praying, "Thank God I die a daughter of the church." Her life and foundations were spent and consecrated to the building up of the church. The Protestant schism hurt her terribly, and she did everything in her power to restore charity and unity once more to the heart of the church. She did not pray for herself, but for the church, priests, preachers, theologians, and missionaries.

Another remarkable feature in the case of Teresa is that she has not fallen foul of heresy or erroneous doctrine, although she never studied theology and her knowledge of Scripture was limited. In fact, she illumines us on doctrine and life. The Inquisition could never accuse her, and her writings have passed the test of the closest scrutiny at the time of her beatification and canonization. At a period of history, when confusion abounded, Teresa taught a clear, lucid doctrine of Scripture, the teaching authority of the church, grace, Theological virtues, the Humanity of Christ, Our Lady, St. Joseph, and the close relation between virtue and contemplation, asceticism, and mysticism. She never fell into the error of Quietism or Jansenism.

Moreover, nobody has done more to clarify the mysterious world of the mystics. She has chartered the depths of the human spirit with a dexterity and simplicity that can only be termed charismatic and divine. The rich sources of her knowledge were faith and her experience of grace.

For four centuries now St. Teresa of Jesus has been influencing the lives of people, learned and unlearned, saint and sinner alike. Several Popes have acclaimed her as a great teacher. The faith of the people, the "sensus fidelium," the unerring instinct of the People of God, has already titled Teresa a doctor, before finally being sealed with the official stamp of the church.

St. John of the Cross (1542–1591) praises the doctrine of St. Teresa in these words, "The Blessed Teresa of Jesus, our mother, left notes admirably written upon these things of the Spirit, which notes I hope in God will speedily be printed and brought to light." (*Spiritual Canticle*, St. XIII,par.7,p.234; Allison Peers, *The Complete Works of St. John of the Cross*, vol.II, London, Burns, Oates and Washbourne.)

St. Francis de Sales (1567–1622) in his "Treatise on the Love of God" praises Teresa of Jesus for her words on divine love written with such humility and simplicity. This woman of little learning makes the great men of letters appear ignorant as she discourses on the beauty of holy love. (*Concessionis Tituli Doctoris, De Convenientia*, p.17.)

Modern critics admit that the Doctor of Avila had much influence on St. Francis de Sales, the Bishop of Geneva. His doctrine on prayer has been coloured by his reading of the books of St. Teresa.

St. Alphonsus Liguori was directly influenced by Teresa.

> Among the Saints, Teresa is the one he quotes most. St. Teresa was his teacher in writing about spiritual life, just as she was his teacher in living it. Many saints, we may say, instructed St. Alphonsus in spirituality, in various ways and in different degrees, but one saint constructed him—she whose name he added to those of Jesus, Mary and Joseph at the head of his letters up to the time of his consecration as bishop . . . He called her 'my holy seraph, St. Teresa of Jesus' . . . He concludes his 'Short Way,' with the words, 'Long live Jesus, Mary, and Teresa, now and throughout all ages. Amen.' So be it. (*The Influence of St. Teresa of Avila on St. Alphonsus Liquori*, by Sean O'Riordan in *Saint Teresa of Avila*, ed. Frs. Thomas and Gabriel, O.D.C. Dublin, Clonmore and Reynolds, Ltd. 1963.)

Three Doctors of the Church, John of the Cross, Francis de Sales, and Alphonsus, acknowledge their enlightenment by the first woman doctor of the church, Teresa of Jesus.

Many other canonized saints have admitted how they have been helped by St. Teresa. The quotations may be read in the work "De Convenientia Declarandi S. Teresiam a Jesus Virginem Ecclesiae Doctorem," written by the Pontifical Theological Faculty of St. Teresa and St. John of the Cross (Teresianum) in Rome, pp.21–28.

Mentioned among others are Joseph Oriol, Antonio Claret, Joan de Lestonnac, the Ursuline Mary of the Incarnation, Charles de Foucauld, Charles A. Sezze, O.V.M., Leonard of Port Maurice, Paul of the Cross, Vincent Palotti.

St. Teresa of the Child Jesus, the Little Flower of Lisieux is the spiritual daughter of the great Doctor of Avila.

Works of Art

The feeling of the faithful as regards St. Teresa has been manifested in many works of art down the centuries. She is depicted as holding a pen, writing a book, overshadowed by a dove. Some writers and artists like Gottfried Eichler have placed her in the company of St. Thomas Aquinas. Other artists have dressed her in the cap and gown of a doctor.

Woman of Genius

Kate O'Brien in her book, *Teresa of Avila*, examines her heroine as a woman of genius.

> Women of genius are few. If there have been some female stars in science, medicine or the plastics arts, I must be forgiven if I ignore them here, where I pursue only the idea of genius expressed in the word and in action arising from the power of the word. Reducing then, for purposes of convenience, our discussion of genius in woman to her power in and because of words—which is the most probable way for the expressive to reach the inexpressive—and searching for examples of it we find very few . . . I say, with great regret, that within the thousand or so years that my very poorly trained vision can take in, genius has hardly ever flowered in woman. We can jump back beyond those two thousand years and boast of Sappho. But we have only fragments, rumours of her—and in any case we have to wait for a woman to match her until England and the nineteenth century . . . there was still no tracking down of a woman who could

> be called genius until Emily Bronte's burning shadow flung out. Not as broken, not as indefinable as Sappho's, but strangely sympathetic to her legend, and just as unsatisfactory. And they are the only female geniuses of our recorded knowledge in literature. . . .
>
> Now we must face my complicated exception. Teresa of Avila was not a great poet. But she was a formidable writer of prose. Indeed, in certain difficult passages of expression, passages luminously, miraculously great, as I shall try to show, we hear a great poet, who had to be used in another field of genius. Even so, her prose, for all its marvellous accidental beauties, does not, qua writing, entitle her to be called "genius" . . . Wherefore, I claim for her that through the power of the word—since her words have left us what she was—Teresa was a woman of genius. On lonely terms, her own; a minor poet; an easy, fluent, careless writer of prose, who, compelled again and again by high necessity, could say in plain words—because she had to—what greater writers could never say. That is why literature must half-accept, and life wherein we seek for God—must wholly embrace Teresa as a genius. (Kate O'Brien, *Teresa of Avila*, The Mercier Press, Cork, reprint; 1967, pp.12–13.)

Teresa of Avila was a genius, by human standards. She was also the mysterious instrument of the Holy Spirit in explaining to modern man the great secrets of grace and the spirit. She confesses in her "Life" that she was not a woman of letters. She did not receive a scientific training as a writer. Her grammar is at times incorrect and faulty, and yet, as Allison Peers has pointed out:

> Her works are read and re-read by Spaniards today and translated again and again into foreign languages. Probably no other book by a Spanish author is as widely known in Spain as the *Life* or the *Interior Castle*, with the single exception of Cervantes' immortal *Don Quixote*. It is surely amazing that a woman who lived in the sixteenth century, who never studied in the Schools or poured over tomes of profound learning, still less aspired to any kind or degree of renown, should have won such a reputation, both among scholars and among the people. We cannot expect to find the reason for this in the purely scientific or literary merits of her writings: we must look for it by going deeper. (Allison Peers, *Complete Works of St. Teresa of Jesus*, Vol 1, p.38.)

Teresa wrote of the loftiest and most complex matters and

mysteries with a simplicity that amazes us, because she spoke from her own personal experience, and it flows out in conversational language. We cannot, therefore, expect her to be logical, or orderly in textbook fashion. Very often she did not reread her notes, and she took up her pen after a lapse of time, distracted by business, headaches, troublesome sisters, and demanding prelates.

She enjoyed writing, which is obvious, but she never began a book unless commanded by a confessor. All her books had the blessing of obedience. Teresa never expected to win an immortal niche for herself on the shelves of literature and spiritual theology. She was one of the humblest writers that ever lived. She believed her work at the spinning wheel was more effective.

> The authority of persons so learned and serious as my confessors suffices for the approval of any good thing that I may say, if the Lord gives me the grace to say it, in which case it will not be mine but His: for I have no learning, nor have I led a good life, nor do I get my information from a learned man or from any other person whatsoever. Only those who have commanded me to write this know that I am doing so, and at the moment they are not here. I am almost stealing the time for writing, and that with great difficulty, for it hinders me from spinning and I am living in a poor house and have numerous things to do. (L.C. 10,p.61.)

Genius cannot be contained. Teresa of Avila is modern already in the sixteenth century. She broke through convention. She was a revolutionary in her own time, a woman who broke through the barricades that confined the women of her century. Her initiative, courage, prayerfulness, and tremendous organizational capacities could never be blocked by the wiles and guiles and customs of lesser men and women. She is a woman to be admired and loved. Women today who clamor for the rights and equality of women everywhere would well be advised to study the life and works of the Saint from Avila, just as any student who wants to master English must study the life and writings of William Shakespeare. The life and writings of Teresa are works of art, touched by the finger of God's right hand. The word "saint" must not frighten us. As a young woman, she appeared a poor candidate for sanctity. She was made of flesh and blood like the rest of us, with powerful passions but determined spirit.

All life long she lived patiently with a sickly body, a body perhaps showing the psychosomatic signs of neurosis. Teresa overcame many obstacles.

Some people may still say she was mad, as they calumniated her when she lived. Perhaps, she was, but it was a charming madness. Christ was called a madman. Teresa was a fool for Christ, and yet this fool or madwoman wrote some of the most beautiful and charming and sane literature ever penned by the feather of man. Gracious, witty, humorous, she charms us still. Her holiness remains human, yet her vision is divine. Christ lived in her; Teresa lived in Christ. She was Teresa of Jesus: Christ was "Jesus of Teresa." This identification may explain the human and the mysterious in the writings of our Saint.

Lover of Learned Men and Books

As a child, Teresa became a lover of books. She read the tales of chivalry enjoyed by her mother. Afterwards, as a foundress and superior, she consulted learned men. She appreciated more the judgment of the learned to that of the pious.

> Learning is a great thing, for it teaches those of us who have little knowledge, and gives us light, so that, when we are faced with the truth of Holy Scripture, we act as we should. From foolish devotions may God deliver us . . . Every Christian should try to consult some learned person, if he can, and the more learned this person, the better. Those who walk in the way of prayer have the greater need of learning; and the more spiritual they are, the greater is their need . . . I think the devils are very much afraid of learned men, knowing that they will find them out and defeat them. (*Life*. Ch.13,pp.80–81.)

Teresa appreciated and loved the Jesuit and Dominican fathers, because they were learned. With their approval, she felt safe. God speaks through the light of human reason. She wrote her sisters:

> You, daughters, must always consult persons of learning, for they will show you the way of perfection with sincerity and discretion. If superiors wish to do their work well, it is necessary for them to have learned men as their confessors; otherwise, though

believing themselves to be acting in a holy way, they will commit many flagrant errors, they should also see that their nuns have learned men as confessors. (*Foundations*, Ch.19,p.92.)

Teresa herself read many books. "I have read many spiritual books . . . (Life Ch.14,p.85) I have spent a good many years doing a great deal of reading." (*Life*, Ch.12,p.73)

Her father and Uncle Pedro passed on to this precocious child the love for books. She read the *Tercer Abecederio Espiritual* of Francis de Osuna, (*Life* Ch.4), *Vita Christi*, of Ludolph of Saxony, a Carthusian, the *Letters of St. Jerome*, (*Life*, Ch.3,7), and *Conferences* of Cassian. (*Way of Perfection*,19,13), *The Morals of St. Gregory*, (*Life*, Ch.5,p.30), the *Ascent of Mt. Sion* by Bernardino de Laredo, (*Life*, Ch.23,p.149) *The Art of Serving God*, by Alonso de Madrid. She was also acquainted with the writings of St. Bernard, St. Francis, and St. Catherine of Siena. (*Life*, Ch.22) The Confessions of St. Augustine had tremendous influence on her life. (*Life*, Ch.9) Teresa loved the Word of God in Sacred Scriptures. In page after page of her writings we find references. She wrote a short mystical commentary on the Canticle of Canticles, entitled "Conceptions of the Love of God."

In the *Way of Perfection*" she writes, "I have always been fond of the words of the Gospel and have found more recollection in them than in the most carefully planned books." (*Way of Perfection*, Ch.21,p.90.)

There is a wonderful balance between the human and the divine, the natural and the supernatural running through the books of our Doctor of the Church. This makes her unique. "I shall speak of nothing of which I have no experience, either in my own life or in the observation of others, or which the Lord has not taught me in prayer." (*Way of Perfection*, Prologue,p.2.)

A. Major Works

1. Life

This is the autobiography of the saint. Teresa gave it no title, but called it "mi alma": it is the story of her soul. Fr. García de Toledo, O.P., commanded her to write the book at Toledo,

1562. At the time she was founding the convent of St. Joseph at Avila. The book was finished by the month of June, and then she was asked to add the story of the foundation of St. Joseph's. In 1565, Dominic Bañez told her to rewrite the book and divide it into chapters. This latter is the redaction that has come down to us.

The autograph is to be found in the Escorial.

The book is divided into forty chapters. We cannot call it a history in the strict sense of the word. It is rather a confession, like that of St. Augustine. Teresa lets us look into her soul: she narrates, prays, cries, confesses her sins, sings of the mercies of God, and describes her mystical experiences. She wanted to obtain light from the learned on the state of her soul and God's ways with her.

Part I—chapters 1–10. This section is mainly historical. It tells the story of her childhood, her sins, her vocations, graces, prayer.

Part II—chapters 11–22. Teresa treats of prayer telling the story of her own experience, the nature, degrees, and effects of prayer. She makes use of the allegory of the garden, the four ways of irrigating, meditation, recollection, the prayer of Quiet, Sleep of the Powers and Prayer of Union.

Part III—chapters 23–31. This is an historical-doctrinal part mainly on her interior life, her third conversion, mystical experiences, sufferings, ecstacies, locutions, transverberation of the heart, growth in virtue.

Part IV—chapters 32–40. The story of the foundation of the convent of Saint Joseph at Avila, the purpose, difficulties, and success.

2. *The Way of Perfection*

Teresa wrote this didactic book for her nuns. It is the more ascetical of her books, and teaches the nuns what virtues they must practice, and how they are to live their lives for the greatest benefit of the church.

She wrote the first draft, which is now to be found at the Escorial, probably in 1566. This codex is in the Carmelite convent at Valladolid.

In this book, Teresa speaks in a conversational manner with her sisters. She points out the road to God, how to prepare for contemplation, advice on community life, and how to practice virtue.

Introduction—chapters 1–4. Teresa treats of the purpose of the Carmelite way of life, the Ecclesial nature of the vocation, how prayer helps to build up the Mystical Body of Christ.

Part I—chapters 5–15. The virtues necessary for a spiritual life, charity, detachment, humility: these prepare us for a life of union with God.

Part II—chapters 16–22. Treats of the life of prayer. She makes a commentary on the "Pater Noster." She teaches how a life of prayer and virtue go together. Contemplation and life are intimately connected: Life is an adventure in communion with God.

3. The Interior Castle

This is the most ordered, most mature, most spiritual and mystical of all St. Teresa's books. She offers us here a systematic synthesis of the entire course of the spiritual life. It is a masterpiece. Gracian commanded her to write. She apologizes:

> Few tasks which I have been commanded to undertake by obedience have been so difficult as this present one of writing about matters relating to prayer: for this reason, because I do not feel that the Lord has given me either the spirituality or the desire for it; for another, because for the last three months I have been suffering from such noises and weakness in the head that I find it troublesome to write even about necessary business. But, I

know that strength arising from obedience has a way of simplifying things which seem impossible. (*Interior Castle,* Prologue,p.199.)

She began her book on Trinity Sunday, 1577. It was a time of terrible suffering. Her friend the Nuncio Ormaneto had died; she had so much traveling to do, persecution broke out against the Fathers; she had to stop writing for five months after she had already finished chapter three of the fifth Mansion. St. Joseph's, Avila, was transferred from the jurisdiction of the Ordinary to that of the Order. There was the stormy scene at the Incarnation, when the nuns tried in vain to elect Teresa, their Prioress, once again. Divine and human inspiration, the fruits of many years experience, some mystical phenomena, and tremendous determination of spirit brought the best out of Teresa and produced this gem in spiritual literature.

The autograph is to be found in the convent of the Discalced Carmelite nuns in Seville.

The synopsis of the doctrine will be found in the section of this book on prayer.

4. *Book of the Foundations*

When Teresa was at Salamanca in 1573, her spiritual director, Jerome Ripalda,S.J., commanded her to continue the story of her foundations. She began there and then, wrote the first ten chapters, continued the work in Avila to chapter nineteen. She was no longer under the guidance of Ripalda, but in 1576, while at Toledo, Gracian commanded her to finish the history. She came as far as chapter twenty-seven. When and where she wrote the last four chapters we do not know, but she had ended in any case before July 26, 1582.

The book tells the story of the various foundations.

The Book of Foundations is not a strictly scientific-historical work. A mother tells her daughters the edifying story of the foundations, little moral lessons on the virtues, God's Providence, and prayer.

5. *Conceptions of the Love of God*

This is a short book of meditations on the Canticle of Canticles. Gracian gave it this title for the Brussels edition, 1611. We do not know the exact date of the composition, probably between 1571 and 1573, at Avila, Alba de Tormes, or Salamanca.

When she took her manuscript to her confessor, Fr. Yanguas, O.P., at Segovia, he told her to destroy it. This she did, but fortunately, her sisters had made some secret copies.

The books contain lofty matters on mystical theology and the place of Sacred Scripture.

6. Constitutions

When the General of the Order Rossi visited Avila, 1567, Teresa showed him her *Constitutions*. The autograph has been lost. One of the best known copies is to be found in the Discalced Carmelite convent at Alcala de Henares.

In this booklet, she lays down the fundamental spirit, virtues, and laws for her convents.

7. Method for the Visitation of Convents

At the suggestion of Gracian, Teresa wrote this little book to help visitators. The booklet is marked by its prudence, balance, psychology, and pedogogy so that the visitator may understand the problems of cloistered nuns.

B. Minor Works

1. Spiritual Relations

In sixty-seven short writings, Teresa narrates her method of prayer and her spiritual graces to her confessors.

2. Exclamations of the Soul of God

These are prayers written by Teresa after communion. They reveal Teresa's love for Jesus. Allison Peers describes them as "white hot embers from the fire of the Saint's love." The probable date is 1569.

3. Poems

These are some thirty-one religious verses full of feeling and joy, written for special occasions. They are not all of equal value and authenticity.

4. Maxims

Teresa wrote them for her nuns.

5. Answer of Saint Teresa of Jesus to a spiritual challenge

6. Judgment given by Saint Teresa upon various writings on the words "Seek thyself in me."

7. Thoughts and maxims of Saint Teresa of Jesus
8. Four hundred fifty-eight letters

Holiness of Teresa

A doctor of the church must have led a life of remarkable virtue and holiness before being given the title. Principle must be proved by practice.

As Vatican II teaches us, the church is holy. She is the bride of Christ. Christ died for the church so that she might be sanctified. He united her to Himself as His own body, crowned her with the gift of the Holy Spirit, for the glory of the Father. It is the will of God that we should all be holy.

The holiness has always been manifest in the church, especially in so many members, who have striven for the perfection of charity through the practice of the evangelical counsels, of poverty, chastity, and obedience. Jesus Christ, the Model and Teacher of perfection, preached holiness of life to all His disciples, irrespective of race, sex, color, profession, or situation. Nobody has a monopoly.

"You therefore are to be perfect, even as your heavenly Father is perfect." (Mt.5:48.) He has sent His Holy Spirit to all of us, to be the vital principle of life and love and truth within us. The Spirit of Love, the Paraclete teaches us to love God with all our heart, and soul and mind and strength (Mk.12:30) and to love one another as Christ loved us. (Jn. 13:34,15:12.)

We are holy not by our own merits and talents but by the grace and plan of God. None of us can glory before God. We are beggars. We are justified through baptism and faith. We must hold on to God's gifts by our holiness of life, live as God's chosen people,

> In sincere compassion, in kindness, and humility, gentleness, and patience; bear with one another, forgive each other . . . be thankful . . . teach each other, advise each other . . . sing psalms and hymns and inspired songs of God. (Col. 2,12: 17.)

We must put all self-indulgence to death through fruits of the spirit, "love, joy, peace, patience, kindness, goodness, trustfulness, gentleness and self-control." (Gal.5,22:23) (Lumen Gentium Par.39,40) As we shall see from the following pages, Teresa of Jesus had all these virtues. She practiced what she preached.

Teresa was very fortunate to have met so many learned and holy advisors. It was the golden era of Spain, and St. Francis Borgia, St. Peter of Alcantara, St. John of the Cross, St. John of Avila, John de Ribera, Blessed Anne of St. Bartholomew all knew, advised, and counseled her. Never before has a saint been the recipient of such providential coincidence. Jesuit saints, Carmelite saints, Franciscan saints, a secular priest who was a saint, St. Augustine's writings, and learned and holy Dominicans all helped to educate the seraphic doctor. Teresa was a woman of destiny. The loving and learned Gracian was there, Dominic Bañez, Jerome Ripalda, Diego de Cetena, Baltasar Álvarez, Doctor Velásquez, Bishop of Osma, men great and glorious by any standards.

As we read the accounts written by her contemporaries, when her cause of beatification was being prepared, we see how outstanding Teresa was in virtue. They all mention her simplicity, her prudence, her justice, her spirit of mortification, her humility and prayer, her fraternal charity, her obedience, poverty, and patience in the midst of trials and sufferings. She was zealous for the church, sacrificed herself for souls, had a great veneration for Sacred Scripture and the teaching of the church.

Contemporaries of Teresa Speak

The Carmel of Flemington, New Jersey, has printed in mimeograph form "Depositions Given by Those Who Knew St. Teresa," translated by Elvira Sarmiento and a Carmelite of Grand Rapids, Michigan. I take some passages out of this important document, so that the good reader may know what the people who knew and lived with Teresa thought about her.

Padre Bañez, of the Dominican Order, knew her for twenty years; he taught her, defended her, acted as her director and persuaded her to write.

> Greater simplicity and humility he has never seen in anyone else. In everything Madre Teresa did he saw her exercising both natural and supernatural virtue. . . . She had great courage to undertake great things for the service of God; her foundations are a tangible proof of this virtue.
>
> Fray Pedro Fernández, Provincial of the Spanish Dominican Province, a legally minded man, very chary of false mystics, began to examine her even more cautiously than the witness himself had, but in the end he came around and said that after all Teresa de Jesus was a holy woman which, in the mouth of this Master, was praise indeed. He even went so far as to say that she and her nuns had shown the world that it was possible for women to follow the evangelical perfection. . . .
>
> Another master of the same order of St. Dominic, called Fray Juan de Salinas, who was also provincial, once tried to warn this witness, saying: 'Who is this Teresa of Jesus, whom I gather is a friend of yours? One cannot trust women's virtue, you know, meaning by this to put me on my guard, as if I were not already so even more than he.' He went to Toledo and heard her confessions nearly every day and tested her quite severely. When this witness next met him, Fray Juan answered jokingly: 'Oh, you had deceived me for you said she was a woman; upon my word she is a man, a real strong man.'
>
> By this he was referring to her determination and discretion in her own behaviour and her rule over her nuns. (p.8–9.)

Mother Ana de la Encarnacion

Mother Ana de la Encarnacion knew Teresa for thirty years and had this to say:

> She always saw great simplicity and humility in Madre Teresa de Jesus and in spite of being the foundress of all these monasteries she did not wish to exercise any authority in any house she happened to be in. On the contrary she would serve in the refectory, cook in the kitchen, and perform mortifications in the refectory. She was fond of taking advice and would take it from the youngest in the house.
>
> She was very kind to the sick and fond of poverty. In spite of being sick she would go on the fast and did not want any delicacies. She wore a torn and mended habit. If she saw anyone with a vocation for the order, she received her even if she had no dowry saying that as they were God's servant, His Majesty would provide so that the rest would eat. She had great trust in Providence.
>
> She had a great devotion to the Saints and in particular to Our Lady and the glorious St. Joseph and always celebrated their feasts with all the solemnity possible. . . .
>
> She was pleasant and very grateful and treated people tactfully and graciously for indeed she was gracious and people liked to talk to her. However, this did not lessen her hours of prayer nor prevent her from confessing frequently. Although she knew she was criticised for all she did she never complained.
>
> On another occasion it happened that a Provincial took exception to her, sent her a command under pain of excommunication that she would leave the monastery in Medina with the Prioress who was there. This order arrived very late, round about Christmas time on a very cold night and they left straightaway, for the sake of obeying. She suffered very much on the way owing to the extreme cold and because she had paralysis and other ailments. Yet, with all she went happily and cheerfully.
>
> She saw her suffer many illnesses, fevers, paralysis, and serious heart trouble so that at times nuns had to support her so that she would not hurt herself. She frequently fainted and vomited, but she bore everything cheerfully and when she revived she would thank the Lord for she was glad to suffer for His Majesty's sake. She also bore persecution, great troubles and pains happily. (pp.12–13.)

Juana de Jesus

Juana de Jesus knew her twelve years.

Once when a sister asked her to teach her how to become a saint she said: "I will do so my daughter for I am going to make a foundation and I will take you and there I will teach you this." She did indeed take her. Later when this sister had some troubles which she complained to her, the Mother answered her: "Sister, didn't you ask me to teach you how to become a Saint?" Well, you will indeed become a saint; implying by these words that sanctity consisted in suffering for God. This witness is convinced that she suffered for the greater glory of God, for she showed this both by word and deed. (p. 23.)

Anne of St. Bartholomew

She knew her for twenty years.

Her charity was so great that if ever she were given generous alms, she would share them, leaving none for herself, as liberally as if she had a great income and funds, . . .

Just before she died Our Lord was at the foot of the bed . . . . The glorious splendour emanating from Our Lord formed a kind of canopy and this witness came to herself with so great a sense of consolation and so remarkable fortitude which she had been devoid of, that she never felt any grief then or now for the death of the Holy Mother, who then died leaving a strong and pleasant fragrance in the whole room. All the sisters who were in Alba were in the Mother's cell at her death with Padre Fray Antonio de Jesus and another companion he had with him noticed this fragrance. . . .

The body of the holy Mother had turned so transparent and shining that it seemed as if one could see oneself in her hands . . . What this witness has to declare is that two days before her death the holy Mother told her that she was going to die . . . She believes that what finally caused her death was that her ardent and fervent desire and love for Our Lord and God and her anxiety to be with Him and enjoy Him weakened and enfeebled her . . . When the Blessed Sacrament was brought to her, so great was her joy and happiness when she saw Him, that if she had not been prevented she would have thrown herself out of bed with so much fervour and desire that it seemed as if her soul were rushing out after his Divine Majesty . . . She died in this witness' arms. (pp.27–29 passim.)

Saint Julian of Avila

He knew Teresa more than twenty years and accompanied her on several foundations.

> On the journeys I gave Holy Communion daily, whenever possible; for so long as it was possible I never failed to say Mass on the journeys and I very frequently heard her confessions. I could see that their rule was adhered to on the journeys as if they were in the enclosure as far as possible. . . .
>
> So great and continuous was her prayer and her realization of the presence of God that to be able to stand it she had to be absorbed and attend to external affairs pertaining to the Rule and increase of the houses of the Order. Moreover, she used to communicate to God her business affairs and He used to talk to her and tell her many things concerning her foundations, with far more familiarity than one reads of in the case of other Saints.
>
> This used to take place ususally just after she received Holy Communion . . . She used to tell me that she was conscious of God's presence in her soul; that neither the journey nor business transactions distracted her from it. So it is obvious that although she still lived here below her ordinary converse was in heaven. We can also see that she lived more where her love was rather than where she dwelt . . .
>
> She was so busy, as the whole day was taken with business affairs and she never failed writing letters and doing other things she could do at home; usually it was not till after midnight that she was able to recollect herself. Had she done all this in perfect health it would not be so amazing, but her health was so poor . . .
>
> She was also very grateful to anyone who did anything for her. From this we may surmise how grateful she was to God who did so much for her. (pp.43–69 passim.)

Fray Diego de Yepes

He knew her fourteen years.

> This witness believes that the Mother's converse with God was great and continual . . . She replied that she was in perpetual prayer and was never out of the presence of God and all that she wished for was the fulfillment of His will. Our Lord had put her in that state fourteen years before. Since then she had no more ecstasies, for if they had continued she would have died; but she received the same joy without ecstasy.

The Mother suffered severely because it was not the persecution of people who were of no account and still less of authority, it was the persecution by people in religious and serious-minded people and prelates to whom one had to pay attention or insult them seriously in not believing them. So many were the false testimonies raised against the aforesaid Mother . . . They attacked her chastity, saying the worst that could be said against a woman of ill repute, and withal she was cheerful and of admirable composure.

"Even the Nuncio at the time, owing to the sinister stories he had been told, said that she was a restless gadabout and ordered her to go to the Monastery of the Discalced in Avila and stay there for good." (pp. 72–79 passim.)

Ana de Jesus

She knew her for eighteen years.

This Bishop of Avila, Don Alvaro de Mendoza used to say, "I swear to you that I don't understand the Mother, but I believe her because she always achieves what she puts her hand to." Whenever there was something seemingly impossible the Bishop used to ask us if we had heard the Mother say that it would happen and if we said yes, he would reply, "Well, then I know it will be!"

If she saw us inclined to receive some applicants because of their large dowry she was very sorry and would say, "Look, that is not what is going to support us, but only our trust in God. That is why I prefer the houses I founded without any human aid. Remember this when I am dead and gone.

She loved greatly the humble and she found it difficult to deal with those who did not consider themselves small and of no importance. She was very sorry for those with interior trials. When their trials were due to scruples and depressions she pitied them and grieved over them and told us to beg God to remedy these things for she said she experienced some of them and so knew what a trial it was to suffer them and how much loss of time and progress it cost the souls. She worried about them until she knew they recovered from these trials. . . .

She was always very kind to us whenever we were ill or in need. When owing to poverty she could not give us anything, she used to make up for it by telling us some amusing things or she went to find some little flowers or herbs to refresh us or whenever she could she gave us some dainty prepared by her own hand. When we were travelling, she wanted to cook what we were to eat and did so. In the convents she often served us in the refectory and infirmary and by this means she satisfied her desire to exercise her charity.

She was very courteous. She treated everyone courteously, treating no one as an inferior, but with so much consideration that she made us laugh, for she would seem to the very person with whom she showed it that her humility raised rather than degraded her. She took humility really to heart. (p.85 passim.)

Madre Maria de San Jose

She knew her for 20 years.

She was most obedient to the Holy Apostolic See, having great respect and veneration for the name of His Holiness; and instructing the nuns to do the same by obeying all Apostolic commands. The Madre was also very respectful to Bishops . . . It is perfectly true that Madre Teresa de Jesus observed completely the ceremonies of the Holy Roman Church. . . .

Madre Teresa always used to read spiritual books . . . she exhorted them not to neglect reading spiritual books however devout and recollected they thought they were. . . .

She was always very humble as could be seen in her words and deeds; she used to perform lowly tasks with great care . . . She implored the superiors with tears that the office of Prioress should be lifted from her at the beginning of the foundation of the first convent. It turned out that the one who was Prioress mortified Madre Teresa very much, she suffered it with great joy and humility, and she gave orders to the superior in all the convents not to call her foundress but just her name, Madre Teresa de Jesus. On the very day that the said Mother founded any monastery, she named one of the nuns Prioress. At times to teach her nuns the reverence with which they were to treat their Prioress the aforesaid Mother was the first to stand when the Prioress passed, although she was the foundress of all. (p.108 passim.)

Reading St. Teresa

At this stage the good reader may be tempted to go to the nearest bookstore and order, if available, a copy of the works of the Santa Madre. The reader may be in for a disappointment, trying to wade through those pages. The many visions, ecstasies, and supernatural phenomena, which no longer appeal to our modern sensibility may be repellent and secondly the mildewed conventions of religious life in sixteenth-century Spain may not be attractive to modern tastes.

If we are to enjoy reading St. Teresa, we must try to imagine her in the historical context in which she wrote. Women were bound by stuffy conventions, chaperoned through life. They had no option outside marriage and the religious life.

Today, a woman with the ability of Teresa could be a prime minister, president of the UNO, a journalist, university professor, television director, doctor, missionary, or a member of some peace corps. We might well ask, if Teresa were alive today and wanted to help the church in the post-Vatican II era, what would she have done? I am sure, she would have done essentially the same as she did in the Tridentine times. She had a charisma to be a teacher of prayer. But she would certainly have got rid with a smile many of the stuffy conventions that haunt convents and still smell of the sixteenth century. No sane woman of the twentieth century should be a slave of sixteenth-century convention. Unfortunately some are.

Teresa would have come up-to-date with her ideas about obedience, humility, penance, the function of the body, psychology, and the habit. Her libraries would be well stocked with good books. She would be a person far more physically fit and psychologically mature at a far earlier age. In all probability, her books would have less visions and fewer ecstasies. In any case, these were all eliminated during the last twelve years of her life. They are not essential to the beautiful work of art, which is the life of Teresa of Avila, the woman who lived by faith and trust. But, then, we would be poorer, because we would not have had the fruit and comment of her experiences. We have learned a lot at the cost of her suffering and ignorance. The strange phenomena are there; Teresa did not take them too seriously; neither should we.

As we read through Teresa, let us concentrate on her more modern appeal, her courage, determination, business acumen, initiative, her diplomacy with men whom she could twist around her little finger and who could never resist her human charm, her prayer and her charity. She was alive and involved in the world and the church of her today. She knew what was going on.

For Teresa, God was alive and near. There was for her a Providence that guided the fate of man. She cast all her care on Him and He sustained her. She walked with God, and helped build up His Kingdom on earth.

And so the life and writings of Teresa may very well help the modern atheist. Atheism is spreading. It is no longer the cult of a few privileged rationalists or avant-garde philosophers. Spreading from the intellectuals to the bourgeoisie, it has now penetrated the masses, and as Vatican II states, "Atheism must be counted among the most serious problems of this age." (*Constitution on the Church in the Modern World*, par. 19.)

Some people expressly deny the existence of God; some believe that we can assert absolutely nothing about Him; others teach that positive science can tell us nothing about God; the question and the very word "God" have no meaning; others exaggerate the place and importance of man, that they leave no time or page for God. Some never mention God or think of God—and others still spend their time destroying the God created by their own imaginations. They have not outgrown childish images. Modern materialism and civilization complicate the problem, and the Christian indifference to the moral, social, and political evils in the world drive many to the camp of the communists and atheists. The amounting pile of evil in our world makes many question the very existence of the good Christian God.

Teresa could never understand how faith in God could lessen the dignity, the power, and the talents of man. Her prayer and her communion with God perfected her. The greatest woman of history was a firm believer in God. Her life, her writings, and her achievements, purified and perfected by the Holy Spirit, help to convince us that women of prayer can do more than philosophers dream of.

Relevance

A doctor of the church must be relevant to man and his problems today. A doctor is a light that shines within the church and for the church at a time when some truth needs special focussing, so that we may see more clearly our way and understand revelation better.

The teaching of Teresa is perennial and relevant today, when, after Vatican II, there is still a certain amount of confusion. Too much dust came out, when John XXIII opened the windows. In spite of the dust, the air is now healthier. New values are being stressed, but old values must not be forgotten. Teresa is the doctor of prayer and common sense. She is as fresh today as when she wrote four centuries ago.

This is proved by the number of books written on her, the record number of editions of her work, and the several authors who quote her. Fr. Simeon, O.C.D. (Concessionis Tituli Doctoris, Bibliographia) in his bibliography on the Saint, numbers 1,212 books on Teresa in Spanish, English, French, German, Hungraian, Italian, Yugoslav, Latin, Portuguese, Dutch, Polish, Arabic, Japanese, Bengalese, Korean, Danish, Ukrainian, Greek, Malayan, and Chinese. There are at least twenty editions of her *Complete Works* in Spanish and forty-eight editions of the *Major Works*. Seventy-eight editions are available in the four main European languages—English, French, German, and Italian.

Movies, documentaries, television, radio, magazines, and new books continue to spread the teaching of Teresa of Avila.

Teresa is an ecumenical figure. She gave her life to undo the harm caused by the Protestant schism. Today, Protestants read her avidly.

The Anglican, E. Allison Peers, a professor in Liverpool, England, translated all the works of Teresa into English. He has also written five books on the life, times, and teaching of the Saint. (*Spanish Mysticism;* a Preliminary Survey, London, 1924; *Mother of Carmel, a Portrait of St. Teresa of Jesus,* New York: 1946; London: 1946; New York: 1943; London: 1951; *Saint Teresa of Jesus, and other Essays and Addresses,* London: 1951; *Handbook to the Life and Times of St. Teresa and St. John of the Cross,* London: 1954; and *Studies of the Spanish Mystics,* III, London: 1960, pp.1–80.)

In 1962, Dr. Ramsey, the Anglican Primate, acknowledged his debt and admiration for Teresa, and the Anglican pastor, E.W. Trueman. Dicken has written one of the most beautiful books written in English on the two Carmelite Saints, Teresa and John of the Cross, *The Crucible of Love.* He writes:

No one doubts that the Christian faith in this country today is in a period of comparative recession . . . Curiously, the one remedy which Our Lord has promised to crown with success, although not necessarily in any wordly sense, has yet to be seriously put to the test—prayer! The generality of English Christians frankly give very little time or energy to prayer, have little real confidence in its power, and are pitifully ignorant of what it really entails.

This book is written in the belief that whatever else we may do to recall our nation to God, prayer is the ultimately indispensable key to the situation. Further, it is axiomatic that if we are to pray, we must know how to pray; and we cannot reasonably demand the help and guidance of the Holy Spirit in this if we neglect the obvious aid he has already given us in the writings of the spiritual masters. By a continuous tradition all down the centuries these teachers of prayer built up, tested and handed on the accumulated experience of millions of prayerful and saintly Christians, and it is widely acknowledged among scholars at the present day that in Teresa of Jesus and St. John of the Cross this tradition came uniquely into flower.

The venerable Patriarch Athanagoras of the Byzantine church confessed to a group of Spanish pilgrims at Constantinople his devotion to the two Carmelite doctors. He read them in the original, and they were his most frequent books for spiritual reading.

Roger Schutz, the superior of the Calvinist religious community in France, was often seen reading the writings of St. Teresa as he attended the Vatican Council.

Evelyn Underhill writes:

> Like St. Catherine of Siena, these three mystics (St. Ignatius Loyola, St. Teresa, Peter of Alcantara), and to them we must add St. Teresa's greatest disciple, the poet and contemplative St. John of the Cross, seems to have arisen in direct response to the need created by the corrupt and disordered religious life of their time. They are the "saints of the counter-Reformation," and in a period of ecclesiastical chaos, flung the weight of their genius and their sanctity into the orthodox Catholic scale . . . St. Teresa working against heavy odds, infused new vitality into a great religious order and restored it to its duty of direct communion with the transcendental world . . . All three practical organizers and profound contemplatives, exhibit in its splendour the dual character of the mystic way. They left behind them in their literary work

and abiding influence, which has guided the footsteps and explained the discoveries of succeeding generations in the transcendental world. (Evelyn Underhill, *Mysticism; a Study in the Nature and Development of Man's Spiritual Consciousness*, New York: pp.341–342, quoted CTD.)

Edith Stein was a German Jewess (1891–1942). She studied psychology and history and worked under Edmund Husserl, the philosopher, founder of the phenomenological school. As a young woman, she was an athiest, until once, by chance, she took down and read the *Life of St. Teresa*. Struck by God's grace, she exclaimed, "This is true." She was baptized a Catholic in 1922. From 1922 to 1933, she published *Psychic Causality, Individual and Community, the State,* and a translation of St. Thomas Aquinas's *Investigation of Truth*. In 1933, she entered the Carmelite Order at Cologne. One of her more famous books is *The Science of the Cross*, a study on St. John of the Cross. This book has also many references to St. Teresa. She was arrested by the gestapo in 1938 and died in the gas chamber at Auschwitz.

Dr. John C. H. Wu passed from Confucianism, through Buddhism and Protestantism and is now a Catholic. He wrote in 1953, the beautiful book, *The Interior Carmel,* (John C. H. Wu *The Interior Carmel, the Threefold Way of Love,* Sheed and Ward, New York, 1953), which has already been translated into many languages. As the title suggests, St. Teresa and St. John have influenced this Chinese writer, as he shows what the great mystics of the East and West have in common. In Teresa, we have a common link between East and West, between Lao Tsu, Confucius, and the writer from Castile. Today many people are interested in the religious mysticism of the East. They may find their way back to Teresa of Avila.

Marxists, such as the learned R. Garaudy, admit their admiration as humanists of the great Spanish mystics. At the Salzburg conferences in 1965, he said, "For us Marxists the Spanish mystics, St. Teresa and St. John of the Cross are noble examples of human love." (Quoted in *Concessionis Tituli Doctoris, de Convenientia,* p.109)

The mystic's experience of God is a challenge to the atheistic Marxist. The life, writings, and achievement of a woman like Teresa inspire curiosity and demand study.

May they be fed with the food of her heavenly doctrine. May they grow in loving devotion to God.

Carmelite School of Spirituality

St. Teresa and St. John of the Cross began the Carmelite School of Spirituality, but this school had its roots in a long history and living tradition. The church has been enriched by many great schools of spirituality centered around the old religious orders. Different in the means, the goal remains the same—the sanctification of the human person. We expect the sons of St. Benedict to instruct us on the liturgy; the sons of St. Dominic to teach us Catholic doctrine; the sons of St. Francis to exemplify the poverty of Jesus; and the Carmelites to lead us in prayer.

St. Teresa is a deep reservoir of wisdom fed by three streams of medieval mysticism. First came the Franciscan Spanish school of mystics, Bernardino de Laredo and Francisco de Osuna. The Rhineland mystics were mostly Dominicans. Finally she was nourished by the great river of her own Carmelite tradition. The Carmelites, a group of Crusaders or pilgrims began their simple eremitical life of prayer on the slopes of Mount Carmel at the time of the first crusades.

James of Vitry, Bishop of Acre, 1216–1228, wrote of these early Carmelites:

> Some lived a solitary life in the beehive monasteries of simple rooms, like bees of the Lord bringing forth honey of spiritual sweetness. Their model was the holy and solitary man, the prophet Elia. (*Historia Orientalis*, Ch. 52, ed. J. Bongars, Gesta Dei per Francos, *Hanover*:1611, 1075.)

Albert Vercelli, the Latin Patriarch of Jerusalem (1206–14), gave them a rule. The essential aim of these Carmelites was "To live for the sake of Jesus Christ and to serve him with purity of heart and good conscience."

They were to be called the Brothers of the Blessed Virgin Mary of Mount Carmel, fostering a very special devotion to the Mother of Jesus and modeling their lives on her. The atmosphere of Carmel was one of silence, solitude, solitary prayer, a simple liturgy, community chapter of faults, the vows of poverty, chastity, obedience, the practice of the theological virtues of faith, hope, and charity, manual labour, the armor of the moral virtues and a spirit of joy. This basically spiritual rule of life is not legalistic; it is practical and simple.

When they moved to Europe, harassed by the Saracens, their way of life had to change and Pope Innocent IV, by the Apostolic letter *Quae Honorem Conditoris,* Oct. 1, 1247, introduced four significant changes: 1. a common refectory, 2. choral office, 3. permission to live in urban areas, and 4. have their cells all in one house. Carmelites now combined the contemplative and active lives. To retain the balance between the contemplative and apostolic life has been a perennial battle and source of conflict among Carmelites ever since.

The book *De Institutione Primorum Monachorum,* which first appeared in 1370, had immense influence on medieval Carmel. The author taught the importance of the virtues, the mastering of the passions, interior silence, perfect charity, and the need to live in the presence of God.

Although the Carmelite Order fell afoul of the general decay that permeated the religious life after the Black Death and during the Renaissance period, men like Bl. Bautista of Mantua (1447 to 1516) and Bl. John Soreth (d. 1471) kept the contemplative flame alight.

The *devotio moderna* movement, fathered by Gerard Groote, found its way into Carmelite cloisters in the fifteenth century. In contrast to the Thomastic and Scotist speculative approach to spirituality, this devotion stressed the affective way, the humanity of Christ, the passion, the Eucharist, asceticism, retirement, reading of Scripture, and interior fervor. *The Imitation of Christ,* by Thomas à Kempis, is the best known book from this school.

As we read through the writings and life of Teresa, we can easily perceive the influence of these various schools and traditions, but the fruit that was born from the rich, receptive, creative spiritual womb of our writer was something new, Teresian, very original and personal. Teresa is the mother of modern Carmelite spirituality.

Historical Background

St. Teresa was a woman of sixteenth-century Spain and some knowledge of the historical background is indispensable for a fuller understanding of her life, work, writings, reform, and style.

By the year 1515, when Teresa was born, the modern world of Western Europe, with its materialism, science, printing, discoveries, expansionism, and culture, was also in its birth pangs. The middle ages, with its feudalism and political system of sacerdotium and imperium, priesthood and empire, was swiftly coming to an end, and before she died Teresa had witnessed the dissolution of the medieval order that embraced the political, intellectual, and religious life of the times. The world that she was born into fell apart. The Europe she was born into fell apart, too. She lived through an age of revolution and counter-revolution, an age of reformation and counter-reformation in many ways similar to our own post-Vatican II world. The new uprising nations would not accept the authority and unity of Europe under pope and emperor. Some renaissance Popes had not inspired their people, as they became more interested in politics and pleasure than in theology or reform. The dominance of medieval clericalism suffered the inroad of renaissance and Erasminian humanism. The new scholars were antischolastic and anticlerical, and poked fun at the lax and ignorant lives of so many of the clergy. Religious life in monastery and convent was lax and dissolute, too. Bishops and pastors did not regard themselves primarily as shepherds of souls, but as privileged people who held benefices. Many Abbacies were open only to the nobility. Simony, nepotism, and favoritism were rampant.

The Curia sought to fill its coffers with all kinds of financial fees, taxes, and even indulgence offerings. This latter roused the wrath of an Augustinian Monk called Martin Luther, who decided to do something about the scandal. Zwingli, too, exploited the dissatisfaction in Switzerland. Then Calvin added fuel to the fire, which ended with the whole of Europe in schismatic and heretical conflagration. Henry VIII availed of all the turmoil on the Continent to declare himself head of the Church in England, and by the Acts of Supremacy and Succession to make himself virtually the Pope of the British Isles. The rich and extensive monastic lands was the bait that lured the nobles to follow him. The three Cathusian priors, the Lord Chancillor Thomas More, the brave bishop John Fisher were the victims of Henry's anger and died as martyrs.

An active militant and sometimes ruthless Calvin carried

his Calvinism from Geneva to France, the Netherlands, Scotland, and England. The Huguenots became a political power in France, and under the leadership of Prince de Conde and Coligny convulsed France in wars and massacres that devastated France for thirty years. Ever since the reign of Ferdinand and Isabella, there was a close tie between church and state in Spain. Religious unity was the excuse of expelling the Jews from Spain in 1492. There were mass conversions of the Moriscos in 1502, and Teresa's own grandfather was among them. The Inquisition was established to root out ruthlessly all the heretics from Spain. Although the spirit of the new humanism and renaissance entered Spain, it did not cause the harm charasteristic of Italy and Europe. Reform was introduced gradually into Spain, and scholars like the Dominicans Cano, de Soto, and Bañez retained a high intellectual level. The spiritual movement led by St. Ignatius, Bernardino of Loredo, Francis of Osuna, Luis de Leon, Thomas of Villanueva and Peter of Alcantara kept the Spanish church on a level keel. Charles V and Philip II, in spite of political differences with the papacy, held Spain as the bastion of Catholic orthodoxy.

The defeat of the Turks at Lepanto, 1571, halted the Mohammedan threat, for the Moriscos in Spain were constantly conspiring with the Turks. Nevertheless, Spain was the most powerful state in the sixteenth century, and during the lifetime of Teresa had expanded her conquests to the new world. The gold and merchandise flowed into Spain, and Teresa was to benefit from her friendship and business relationships with these traders, merchants, soldiers, and sailors.

The Catholic Reform

By the middle of the century the Catholic Church decided on reform. This reform has been called the Counter Reformation, because the church inwardly renewed and reinvigorated after the Council of Trent proceeded to counterattack and recover lost territory. The Popes and bishops began the reform. The old mendicant order began a spiritual renewal, and new ones like the Jesuits were formed. The objective of the council was the order and clarification of Catholic doctrine and to pass laws that would thoroughly reform the church. The council passed decrees on the doctrine of Scripture on the jurisdiction and residency of bishops, the sacrifice of the Mass, the establishment of seminaries, the sacraments, religious formation, and indulgences.

Pope Pius V carried out the decrees, published the Roman Catechism for pastors, the Breviary, Roman Missal, and a revised edition of the Vulgate. Provincial and diocesan synods, often under the eyes of Papal representatives, implemented the council decrees at a local level. Then such great saints as Teresa arose to carry the spirit of renewal and reform into the hearts of convents, seminaries, and villages.

Part Two
The Life of St. Teresa

2.
God in Search of Teresa

Birth and Early Years of the Saint

Saint Teresa of Jesus, better known as St. Teresa of Avila, came into the world in that old city of saints, stones, and knights at the heart of the Castile at the dawn of the day on Wednesday, March 28, 1515. Her parents, Don Alonso Sánchez de Cepeda and Doña Beatriz D'Ávila y Ahumada, were well to do and of a lesser noble-class family. She was baptized on April 4, the day of the inauguration of the Carmelite convent of the Incarnation, where she would begin her religious life.

Her grandfather, Juan Sánchez de Toledo, was a cloth merchant from Toledo and was a *converso*, or "convert" from Judaism. He had to accuse himself before the inquisition for Judaizing, and was compelled to wear the humiliating *sanbenito* in procession for seven days as a penance. (Kieran Kavanaugh, O.C.D., and Otilio Rodriquez, O.C.D.; *Collected Works of St. Teresa of Avila*, vol. 1, p.1.) He later moved to Avila with his wife Ines de Cepeda, who was originally from Tordesillas. His son Alonso was fourteen when they arrived in Avila. The cloth merchant succeeded in having his children marry into the noble families. In 1505, Alonso married Catalina del Peso, who died two years later, leaving him with two children, Juan and Maria. In 1509, the young widower married the beautiful and wealthy fifteen-year-old Dona Beatriz de Ahumada from an illustrious Avilan family. She became the mother of ten children, Hernándo, Rodrigo, Teresa, Lorenzo, Antonio, Pedro, Jerónimo, Agustín, Juana, and another child of whom we know nothing.

Teresa herself leaves us a picture of the home:

> My father was fond of reading good books, and he also had books in Spanish for his children to read. These good books together with the care my mother took to have us pray and be devoted to Our Lady and to some of the saints began to awaken me, when I was six or seven years old, to the practise of virtue. It was a help to me to see that my parents favored nothing but virtue. They possessed many.
>
> My father was a man very charitable with the poor and compassionate toward the sick and servants. Nobody was ever able to convince him to accept slaves . . . He was very honest. No one ever saw him swear or engage in faultfinding. He was an upright man.
>
> My mother had many virtues and she suffered much sickness during her life. She was extremely modest. Although very beautiful, she never gave occasion to anyone to think she paid attention to her beauty. (*Life,* Ch.1,p.33.)

Her memory, as she wrote fifty years later, would take Teresa back to the books, prayers, devotion to Our Lady, St. Joseph, the saints, and family virtues and values. The great saint and mystic was cradled in the atmosphere of a good, powerful Catholic home.

At an early age, religious scenes and the hope of martyrdom stirred the vivid imagination and precocious mind of Teresa de Ahumada. At the age of six, she already showed her talent for leadership and used that tremendous asset of hers . . . her power to charm and love. She persuaded her favorite brother, Rodrigo, to go off together to the country of the Moors, to prove her love for God and be with Him—"forever-ever-ever" (*Life,* Ch.1,p.11) and where martyrdom awaited them. The idea of eternity already haunted her. Every earthly pleasure would pass away. There was only one joy that would last *para siempre, para siempre.* Teresa and her brother, Rodrigo, stole out of the house to begin their long journey on foot to Africa and crossed over the old bridge that would leave Avila behind them. Providentially, their paternal uncle, Don Francisco Álvarez de Cepeda, came along and, recognizing them, brought them back home.

Denied the palm of martyrdom, Teresa's child imagination worked up and invented other worlds of make believe. She lived out her fantasies, acted the part of a hermit, prayed alone, recited her rosary, built little convents, forced her cousins to observe the rules, sing her songs, dream her dreams, and follow her visions.

Life in this fairyland world was soon shattered by the harsh reality of her mother's death in 1528, when Teresa was thirteen years old, and she was forced to face the sensitive and difficult days of adolescence all alone. In her loneliness, she turned to Our Blessed Mother.

> When I began to realise what I had lost I went in my distress to an image of Our Lady and with many tears besought her to be a mother to me. Though I did this in my simplicity, I believe it was of some avail to me, whenever I recommended myself to this Sovereign Virgin, I have been conscious of her aid; and eventually she has brought me back to herself. (*Life* Ch. 1, p.12.)

Her childhood was over. Devotion to Our Lady was to absorb her entire life.

The Heart, a Lonely Hunter

Teresa de Ahumada y Cepeda was an attractive young lady.

> Biographers have given posterity a detailed description of her. She was of medium height, tended to be more plump than thin. Her unusual face could not be described as either round or aquiline: the skin was white and the cheeks flesh-coloured. Her forehead was broad, her eyebrows somewhat thick, their dark brown colour having a reddish tinge. Her eyes were black, lively and round, not very large, but well placed, protruding a little. The nose was small, the mouth—medium in size and delicately shaped and her chin was well-proportioned. The white teeth sparkled and were equal in size. Three tiny moles, considered highly ornamental in those days, added further grace to her appearance . . . one below the center of the nose, the second over the left side of her mouth, the third beneath the mouth on the same side. Her hair was a shining black and gently curled. (*Collected Works of St. Teresa of Avila*, vol. 1, p.12, Kieran Kavanaugh, O.C.D. and Otilio Rodriquez, O.C.D.)

The romantic heart of Teresa opened at an early age. Her mother had been an avid reader of books on medieval chivalry, and her precocious young daughter read them on the quiet. Looking back, she was to write:

> My mother was fond of books on chivalry; and this pastime had not the ill effects on her that it had on me, because she never allowed them to interfere with her work. But we were always trying to make time to read them. She permitted this in order to stop herself from thinking of the great trials she suffered. . . . This annoyed my father so much that we had to be careful lest he should see us reading these books. (*Life*, Ch.2,p.13.)

Teresa, at fifteen, was as vain as she was vivacious and beautiful. Friendly, passionate, and loving by nature herself, she craved attention as he felt the first stirrings of womanhood within her. She took extra care of her hands and hair, used perfume, dressed fastidiously, and wore the best gown and finery. Teresa was no saint, as she apologizes:

> There was nothing wrong with my intentions. I should never have wanted anyone to offend God because of me. This great and excessive fastidiousness about personal appearance, together with other practises which I thought were in no way sinful, lasted for many years. I see now how wrong they must have been. (*Life*, Ch. 2,p.13.)

Some of her father's own young nieces and nephews were frivolous and worldly. Although her good father supervised the family, his favorite daughter, Teresa, was led along paths that were perilous and sinful. We can easily imagine the conversations and stories of intrigue and romance that filled the days and minds of Teresa and her idle and older cousins. We know the names of her Uncle Francisco's children, who lived next door . . . the boys were Pedro, Francisco, Diego, and Vincent; the daughters, Beatriz, Ana, Jeronima, and Inés. One of these young men adored Teresa, and she loved him. She reveals no names. One of the older daughters was the chief villian in the drama that led Teresa into devilment. Our Saint had her regrets and warnings.

> I learned every kind of evil. . . . I became fond of meeting this woman. I talked and gossiped with her frequently. . . . My father and sister were very sorry about this friendship of mine

and reproved me for it. They could not prevent my friend from coming to the house, and when it came to doing wrong I was very clever. . . . I lost nearly all my soul's natural inclination to virtue. . . . I was greatly influenced by her and by another person who indulged in the same kinds of pastime. . . . When I thought that nobody would ever know, I was rash enough to do many things which servants, too, were quite ready to encourage me in all kinds of wrongdoing. (*Life*, Ch. 2, pp. 14,15.)

The one virtue that saved Teresa at this time was her sense of Spanish honor. She mentions this virtue often. Her sense of honor at times was a greater deterrent from sin than her fear of God. "All that I was seriously concerned about was that I should not be lost altogether." (*Life*, Ch.2,p.14.)

Temptation was strong and serious. Teresa was now at an age when her mother had been married, and was introduced herself to the high society of Avila—its fiestas, dances, bullfights, and parties. Like other Castilian ladies, she rode on the back of a mule as she travelled from place to place. She played her games of chess; learned to spin, sew, and embroider; dressed in her mother's velvet and silken gowns; wore her golden jewels, rings, bracelets, and earrings as she, with her vivacious and warm beauty, dreamed of marriage.

During an epidemic in the south, an historic event took place in Avila. The Empress Isabel, with her daughter, Maria, and her son who was to become Philip II (and who was to play no little part in the later life of Teresa), made Avila her capital. The Emperor, Charles V was engaged in the religious and political wars in Germany. More likely Teresa was one of the young Avilan ladies who welcomed the royal visitors.

Our Lady of Grace Convent School

The good father, and her more mature sister, Maria, worried over their precious, gifted, and precocious Teresa. The father felt it was best to nip the danger in the bud. When Maria married and moved to Castellanos de la Cañada, the opportunity arose for an excuse to send Teresa to the convent school, Our Lady of Grace, run by the Augustinian nuns. Teresa knew that the real reason was to protect her from her wordly companions. This family secret was shared by only a few relatives. This troublesome teenager could not be trusted alone in the house; yet she adds:

> So excessive was my father's love for me and so complete was the deception which I practised on him, that he could never believe all the ill of me that I deserved, and thus I never fell into disgrace with him. (*Life*, Ch.2,p.15.)

The father loved her too much!

The little company of Augustinian nuns edified Teresa as they followed their rule in practicing austerity of life. After a restless and suspicious start, this determined young lady settled down and accepted the inevitable. Her charm and intelligence won many friends.

"All the nuns were pleased with me, for the Lord had given me grace, wherever I was to please people, and so I became a great favourite." (*Life*, Ch.2,p.15.) Wherever she went, Teresa made friends. She went to confession, confessed her sins (which her biographers agree were never very serious), made her peace with God, and settled down to study.

Teresa stayed in this convent school some eighteen months from July 1531 to the end of 1532. This was the same school at which St. Thomas of Villanova had been director from 1520 to 1526, and as Augustinian provincial visited the convent in 1531, at a time when another Augustinian, called Martin Luther, was shaking and shocking the church in Germany.

Her outside friends still communicated with Teresa, and went so far as to smuggle in letters to the convent. Can you imagine her reading those love notes? The chapter in her autobiography that speaks of letters smuggled to her ends with an ambiguous statement that has baffled translators and biographers:

> My intimacy with this person was of such a kind that I thought it might end satisfactorily in her (for my) marriage: and both my confessor and other persons told me that in many respects I was not offending God. (*Life*, Ch.2,p.18.)

Teresa loved her maestra, Sister Maria Briceño, a Castillian lady descended from the most illustrious family of Avila. This humble and holy sister slept in the dormitory with the boarders and had many intimate conversations with Teresa. Maria had been struck by the Gospel "many are called but few are chosen" and discussed the mystery of a vocation with Teresa as they shared their similar backgrounds.

In this peaceful environment Teresa felt the first call to the religious life, but she resisted and battled.

"I had a great dislike to being a nun . . . and this had become deeply ingrained in me." (*Life*, Ch.2,p.17.) A terrible tug of war wrenched the heart of Teresa as she decided whether to give her life and love to a human husband or a divine spouse. Her motives were not lofty, since her criterion in weighing one against the other was that which seemed to serve to her advantage more.

Teresa's heart was so hard and worldly at this time that prayer was difficult, and even the story of the passion that Holy Week could not stir a tear. The future doctor of prayer envied the prayer life of the girls around her. She was afraid to marry and yet not anxious to be a nun. Some of her friends encouraged religious vocation, while others told her to marry. The nuns in the convent doubted her readiness for religious life. Her past still worried her, as her future was in no way clear. She still was sensual and vain and not very spiritual, as she confesses: "Good thoughts about being a nun came to me from time to time, but they left me and I could not persuade myself to become one." (*Life*, Ch.3,p.18.) The tug o' war went on, . . . "I was still anxious not to be a nun, for God had not as yet been pleased to give me this desire, although I was afraid of marriage." (*Life*, Ch.3,p.17.)

The rigorous and vigorous life of the good Augustinian nuns was a bit too much for a lukewarm Teresa. Besides, her Carmelite friend, Doña Juana Suarez, influenced our doubltful young lady with the "pleasures of sense and vanity," which she hoped to find in the Carmelite convent that appealed to her.

The Lord continued to call gently and the anxiety grew to compromise. "By the end of my time there, I was much more reconciled to being a nun, but not in that house."

The conflict that went on inside Teresa must have been very deep and difficult indeed, for she broke down under the pressure, and she became seriously sick. The sickness freed her to leave the convent, return to her father's home, and later recuperate at her sister Maria's home out in the country at Castellanos de la Cañada.

On her journey to Maria's house she and her father visited

with her uncle, Don Pedro de Cepeda, at his *palacio* in Hortigosa. Catalina, Don Pedro's wife, was dead, and had left him with a son, Pedro.

This old widower who was "very shrewd and full of virtues," as our author says, had a library of books, and persuaded his eighteen-year-old niece to read them to him. Although obviously bored by this renaissance relative, she was too polite to refuse. The old man, his books, and how he lived influenced Teresa greatly:

> The impression made on my heart by the words of God, both as read and heard, and the excellence of my uncle's company made me understand that all things are nothing, and that the world is vanity and will soon pass away. I began to fear that, if I had died of my illness, I should have gone to hell. (*Life*, Ch. 3, p.18.)

In having to read for her uncle, she was forced to ponder.

She continued her journey to the home of Maria and her husband, Don Martín Guzmán y Barrientos. There, in the clear air of the countryside of Castellanos de la Cañada, and amid the sheep and the shepherds and the serene, pastoral setting, the struggle went on. Whether or not to become a Carmelite nun was the problem, and trying to resolve it made her literally vomit and faint.

Lavished with love and affection by the members of her family, she contemplated her future in the springtime of 1533.

Our young student read the letters of St. Jerome, and these are persuasive indeed. Gradually it dawned on her that the only way to save her soul was behind a convent wall.

> I could not incline my will to being a nun, I saw that this was the best and safest state, and so, little by little, I determined to force myself to embrace it. . . . The trials and distresses of being a nun could not be greater than those of purgatory and I had fully deserved to be in hell. ... . This decision to enter the religious life seems to have been inspired by servile fear more than by love. (*Life*, Ch.3, p.19.)

We can barely expect words like this to have been written by a saint who wrote so ideally later on religious life and persuaded so many to join her. She had so many temptations herself, and the devil did everything possible to destroy her vocation. He knows his worst enemies.

The greatest obstacle, however, was to come not from the devil or her own personal weakness, but from her good father. It is amazing how good, devout parents might prevent, hinder, and halt a good religious vocation. It is very understandable that Don Alonso expected Teresa to take the place of María in the home. She was his favorite, and one by one his sons were departing to seek fame and fortune in the Americas. Her beloved brother, Rodrigo, sailed for Buenos Aires and was killed in 1557. Five of Teresa's brothers fought side by side at the Battle of Inaquito in 1546. While her brothers were engaged in conquering the outer world, Teresa was about to begin her journey into the inner world—the endless voyage to God.

Once Teresa had made the decision to become a nun, nothing could stop her, not even her father's love.

> He was so fond of me that I was never able to get his consent, nor did the requests of persons whom I asked to speak with him about it succeed in doing so. The most I could obtain from him was permission to do as I liked after his death. (*Life,* Ch.3,p.19.)

Monastery of the Incarnation
November, 1535

Teresa had no alternative, but to run away from home. She had already persuaded her younger brother, Antonio, to become a Dominican at the Monastery of St. Thomas. At early dawn on one cold November morning, two hooded figures could be seen walking the streets of Avila. The Dominicans sent young Antonio back home, but the Carmelites accepted the twenty-year-old Teresa. She leaves us a most moving account:

> I remember—and I really believe this is true—that when I left my father's house my distress was so great that I do not think it will be greater when I die. It seemed to me as if every bone in my body were being wrenched asunder for as I had no love of God, to subdue my love for my father and kinsfolk, everything was such a strain to me that, if the Lord had not helped me, no reflection of my own would have sufficed to keep me true to my purpose. But the Lord gave me courage to fight against myself and so I carried out my intention. (*Life,* Ch.4,p. 20.)

The Convent of the Incarnation in Avila had been founded some fifty-six years before the entry of Teresa de Ahumada. It began in a very humble way as the residence of some members of the Third Order of Carmel. In 1512 fourteen *beatas* had formed a small community in honor of Jesus Christ, His Blessed Mother, and the twelve Apostles, and had dedicated themselves to a simple life of prayer. These good women took simple vows, and under the prioress, Doña Beatriz de Higuera, adopted the mitigated rule of the Order of Our Lady of Mount Carmel. This was the convent destined by divine providence to form and shape the early years in religion of our saint—one of the greatest women of all time.

The community at the Incarnation, like so many others at the renaissance and prereformation times, had lost its pristine idealism and fervor. The sisters who were not strictly cloistered were allowed visitors at any time; some still owned property; and certain ladies of honor from the fashionable Castilian families had their own special privileges and prerogatives. Doña Teresa de Ahumada enjoyed her own apartment, while others from a lower social class had to share rooms. The silence was not maintained, and it is difficult to imagine any form of disciplined, contemplative life in a community of 180 women.

Doña Teresa de Ahumada received the Carmelite habit on the probable date of November 2, 1536. As a novice, she followed a regular religious life—fasted, abstained, took the discipline on Monday, Wednesday, and Friday, confessed regularly, attended daily Mass, received Communion on the First Sunday of Advent, Christmas Day, First Sunday of Lent, Holy Thursday, Easter, Ascension, Pentecost, Corpus Christi, All Saints, Feasts of Our Lady, and the Anniversary of her Profession. The office was recited daily, and silence reigned between Compline and Prime. In the chapter of faults, the novices had to accuse themselves to any shortcomings. At least, as a novice, Teresa had to follow this routine.

Teresa sings of her first fervor in terms of favors, joys, tenderness, and delight. The novitiate year seems to have been one blessed by God. Menial manual labor was not beneath her dignity. "When I was spending time in sweeping floors which I had previously spent on my own indulgence and adornment, I realised that I was now free from all those things and there came to me a new joy." (*Life*, Ch.4,p.21.)

Teresa was professed at the end of her novitiate year on November 3, 1537. She was twenty-two. Determined to be a good Carmelite, she pronounced her vows of poverty, chastity, and obedience with great fervor, determined to be the betrothed of the Lord.

Love is not easy, and fervor does not last. There were dark days of depression and discontent. Everything did not go her way. . . .

> I was very often blamed when the fault was not mine. This I bore very imperfectly and with great distress of mind. . . . When they saw me alone weeping for my sins, they thought that I was discontented. . . . I could not hear anything which seemed to make me ridiculous. I delighted in being thought well of. . . . I knew how to get pleasure for myself out of everything. . . . I followed what I knew to be wrong and neglected what was good. (*Life*, Ch.5, p.26.)

Happy to be a nun, she did not shun the painful side of life. There was a nun in the convent who suffered from open sores in the stomach, that forced her to reject all food. Although the others feared her, Teresa spent time with her and envied her patience in pain. The incident was providentially to prepare her mind for her own suffering.

Her health of body did not match her determination of will. The diet, lifestyle, and the religious rigor soon undermined her health, and within six months, she was suffering from fainting fits, heart trouble, and the frequent loss of consciousness. Her father, doctors, and community decided that it would be better for her to leave the convent and to seek help in the countryside.

During that time, there was a famed woman in Becedas who had the gift of healing, and so Teresa with her good friend Sister Juan Suárez set out for Becedas sometime in the autumn of 1538.

On her way, she visited her uncle, Don Pedro, in Hortigosa. The good uncle introduced her to the *Tercer Abecedario* by Francisco de Osuna, a saintly Franciscan, who published ten years earlier in Toledo. This book, the third volume on the ABC's of Prayer, was to introduce Teresa into the lofty world of contemplative prayer. Very soon she could write:

> The Lord granted me the favour of leading me to the Prayer

> of Quiet and occasionally even to Union. . . . It is true my experience of Union lasted only a short time. . . . I am not sure that it can have been for as long as an Ave Maria. . . . But the results were considerable. I seemed to have trampled the world beneath by feet. . . . I used to think of Jesus Christ as present within me, and it was in this way I prayed. . . . I liked to read good books. (*Life*, Ch.4,p.23.)

Our great doctor of the mystical world favors reading a good book when preparing for prayer and when distractions and aridity strike:

> Anyone unable to meditate should occupy himself frequently in reading. . . . During all those eighteen years (of trials and aridity), except after communicating, I never dared to begin a prayer without a book. My soul was as much afraid to engage in prayer without a book, as if it were having to go and fight against a host of enemies. . . . aridity only came when I had no book. . . . provided I had books and could be alone, there was no risk of my being deprived of that great blessing. (*Life*, Ch.4,p.24.)

She found a book and silence good companions in prayer, and there was no better place to pass that winter than at the home of her sister Maria among the fields, woods, rivers, and blue skies in the Village of Castellanos de la Cañada.

The Bewitched Priest and the Quack Doctor of Becedas
April to July, 1539

Throughout her life, Teresa appreciated learned priests. She was to suffer so much from ignorant ones. Prayer and scholarship seemingly go together. She wrote: "I have always been attracted by learning. Confessors with a little of it have done my soul great harm . . . a truly learned man has never led me astray. Not that these others had meant to lead me astray; it is simply that they have known no better." (*Life*, Ch.5,p.27.)

While at Becedas, her appreciation for learned and intelligent priests led Teresa into a romantic and rather dramatic situation. This was a very delicate relationship needing to be handled with reverence and care, and Teresa herself leaves a lot to our imagination. She makes us read between the lines, and some biographers have read more between the lines than Teresa ever wrote, while others pass over the incident as something that could never have possibly happened to our saint. But saints are human and have moments of weakness and blindness out of which the Lord draws good. St. Paul, in spite of many revelations, visions, gifts, and virtues, was given a thorn in the flesh to keep him from becoming too proud, so that he could cry in victory, "My grace is enough for you; my power is at its best in weakness. . . . For it is when I am weak that I am strong." (2 Cor. 12,9–10.)

Our saint was strong, but for this moment she was weak. The devil was there to trouble her soul.

The local priest in the village came from a good family. He was very intelligent and of some learning. Teresa chose him as confessor and this somewhat worldly but compassionate man took "an extreme liking to her." She adds: "There is nothing wrong in his affection for me, but it ceased to be good because there was too much of it." (*Life,* Ch. 5,p.28.)

The two spent a lot of time together and spoke a good deal. There was danger but no serious sin, and as his love and admiration for this good and innocent young woman grew, the priest gradually opened up his heart to Teresa and revealed the perilous and sinful situation in which he lived with a rather immoral woman in the village who had "bewitched" him. This sinful relationship had gone on for seven years. It was no longer a secret, and although he continued to celebrate the Eucharist, he had lost his good name and honor. No one dared reprove or correct him. Teresa loved him and she was determined to save him. Love risks! She wrote: "I was sorry for him because I liked him very much. At that time I was so frivolous and blind that I thought it a virtue to be grateful and loyal to anyone who liked me." (*Life,* Ch.5,p.28.)

She gradually wooed the priest away from the other woman, persuaded him to surrender a copper figure that held this spell, which he carried around his neck. She commented: "When I heard about this spell I began to show the priest greater affection—my intentions were good, but my action was wrong." (Ibid, p.29.) Teresa gave him little sermons on God, but she comments, "I believe his liking for me did more."

Once she got her hands on the charm, Teresa had it thrown

into the river. The priest awoke as from a swoon, realized his danger, left the woman, and turned to the Blessed Mother. A year later he died a holy death. Our saint adds her own epilogue to this dramatic episode:

> I never thought there was anything wrong in the great affection he had for me, although it might have been purer . . . I would not at that time have done anything which I believed to be a mortal sin. And I think his realisation that that was so increased his affection for me. . . . Women can get more from men in this way. (Ibid.p.29.)

How true!

Breakdown—1539

Teresa remained at Becedas for three months, but instead of helping her, the treatment made her worse. The curandera was a quack. The pain must have been terrible.

> I feared I was going mad. . . . I could take nothing but liquid . . . I was in a continual fever . . . my nerves began to shrink . . . pain gave me no rest by night or day . . . I was consumptive . . . nervous pains are intolerable." (*Life,* Ch.5,pp.29,30.)

In her misery, our saint turned to prayer and the story of Job in the *Morals* of St. Gregory, but her pain increased, and finally, on August 15, 1539, when she was just twenty-four, a fit of catalepsy was to incapacitate her for eight months. She desired to go to confession: She had many things on her mind. "If I had died then, my salvation would have been very uncertain." (Ibid. p.31.) But her father, fearing that she was about to die, would not hear of it. She condemned this excessive human love.

A fit left her unconscious and apparently dead for four days. When she woke up she found some candle wax on her eyelids. It was customary for eyelids to be sealed with candle wax at death. Her friends recited the Credo, gave her the Sacrament of the dying, and Ribera tells us that her grave had been dug at the Incarnation and another monastery had performed the last rites for her. But the Lord of life had something more beautiful than death in store for Teresa, and she gradually recuperated. Her first act was to go to confession and gratefully receive communion.

The agony went on, and she leaves a detailed account of her Calvary.

> My tongue was bitten to pieces . . . my throat was choking. . . . I could not even take water . . . my bones seemed to be out of joint. . . . I was all doubled up like a ball. . . . I was no more able to move arm, foot, hand or head than if I had been dead. . . . I could move only one finger of my right hand. . . . They used to move me in a sheet. . . . The paralysis lasted three years. . . . When I began to get about on my hands and knees, I praised God. (*Life*, Ch.6,pp.32,33.)

In spite of her physical pain, these months proved to be fruitful for her moral and spiritual growth. Forced to practice heroic virtue, she prayed, read good books, resigned herself to the will of God, and enjoyed solitude.

St. Joseph

In April, 1540, Teresa was taken back to the Convent of the Incarnation, and when no doctor or medicine could relieve her pain, she turned in faith to her heavenly doctor, St. Joseph, and she now pens one of the greatest passages in Catholic literature on that great and glorious saint.

> I took for my advocate and lord the glorious Saint Joseph and commended myself earnestly to him. And I found that this father and lord delivered me both from this trouble and greater troubles concerning my honour and the loss of my soul. He gave me greater blessings than I could ask of him. I do not remember even now that I have ever asked anything of him which he has failed to grant.
>
> I am astonished at the great favours which God bestowed on me through this blessed saint, and at the perils from which he has freed me, both in body and soul.
>
> To other saints the Lord seems to have given grace to succour us in some of our necessities, but of this glorious saint my experience is that he succours us in them all. The Lord wished to teach us that He was himself subject to him on earth, just so in Heaven He still does all that he asks.

This has also been the experience of other persons whom I have advised to commend themselves to him. And even today there are many who have great devotion to him through having newly experienced this truth. (*Life,* Ch.6,pp.34,35.)

The mystical doctor encourages all of us to have devotion to St. Joseph, especially if we are interested in a life of prayer and purity. She was to dedicate her first convent to St. Joseph, and all her monasteries had a statue of Our Lady of Mount Carmel and St. Joseph outside to greet the visitor. Teresa revived devotion to St. Joseph in the church. He cured her of her paralysis.

A Lax Middle-Aged Nun

Many nuns are tested in their thirties. The days of initial fervor, the completion of training, and the lifting of restrictions are behind them, as they work for a career. If the proverbial three-score and ten years are granted her, the thirties mark the halfway span of the nun's career. From these turbulent years emerges the more mature and spiritual woman, one who has passed through a physical, psychological, moral, and spiritual crisis. These years comprise the phase of the Dark Night.

Teresa of Jesus did not come through these turbulent years unscathed. It was a time of deep inner war, and she lost many battles before eventually winning the campaign.

Teresa grew lax and careless. As her health gradually returned, she returned to her worldly and vain ways. This human frailty warms our hearts and gives us courage. Mental prayer was no longer a joy! The old tendency to vanity and frivolity returned; her desire to be loved, admired, and popular led her into many distractions, and the devil filled her with the poison of false humility. She wrote: "Seeing that I was utterly lost, I began to be afraid to pray . . . I was one of the worst people alive." (*Life,* Ch.7,p.37.)

She gave up mental prayer and followed the external routine of community vocal prayer in order to make sure the others had a good opinion of her. However, this made her feel like a hypocrite.

Teresa does not try to exonerate herself, but she subtly gives herself a pat on the back, too, as she lets us know that she did not go to the extremes of some of her fellow sisters. There were some young women who didn't have a vocation but were simply locked up by their parents to keep them out of trouble. These parents preferred to see them suffer behind convent walls rather than suffer the indignity of a marriage beneath their family station. But the walls were never too high and never too thick for some of these passionate and daring young ladies. Teresa boasts that she never took the liberty "to talk to people through crevices or over the walls or by night." (*Life*, Ch.7,p.38.)

Our saint here condemns the mores of the time that sent so many unworthy candidates to the nunneries. They should have been kept at home. In the convent they could hide their wickedness, do harm to others, and corrupt community life and them.

> If the friar and the nun are to begin to follow their vocation truly, they need to be more afraid of the religious in their own house than of all the devils, . . . Youth, sensuality and the devil invite and incline them to do things which are completely worldly. (Ibid. pp.40,39.)

Back to Doña Teresa de Ahumada herself—beautiful, charming, affectionate, thirty years old. The Incarnation depended on the good will of the noble families of Avila, and many of them visited the parlors of the convent to be entertained by our brilliant conversationalist. One such señor called her "the world's magnet."

> All day long with her without noticing the time, and all night long in the hope of seeing her again next day, for her way of speaking was delightful—and the word *gracioso* in Spanish adds a touch of wit to the delightfulness, and her conversation pleasant and at the same time serious, simple and full of good sense and absolutely sincere. She was so much on fire with the love of God. The warmth radiating from her words was so gently persuasive that it melted the hearts of all who came in contact with her without causing them pain; for among her qualities she possessed gratia sermonis, graciousness of speech, and drew to her, as she wanted them and for whatever purpose she wanted them, all who heard her. It might have been said that she held in her hand the helm that steers all hearts. (Marcelle Auclair, *St. Teresa of Avila*, p.65.)

No doubt, Teresa may have had her favorites among her visitors, and one friendship may have caused her qualms of conscience and regret. It cannot be ascertained whether she speaks of a man or woman, but it is believable that it may have been Don Francisco de Guzman, described by Marcelle Auclair as, "young, well endowed with worldly goods and belonging to one of the noblest families of Castile." (Ibid,p.70)

We do not know how long this friendship lasted, or how dangerous it really was, but the Lord kept a jealous eye on his bride and was to intervene in a very extraordinary manner. She had a vision.

> Christ revealed Himself to me, in an attitude of great sternness, and showed me what there was in this friendship that displeased Him. I saw Him with the eyes of the soul more clearly than I could ever have seen Him with those of the body. It made such an impression upon me that although it is now more than twenty-six years ago, I seem to have Him present with me still. I was greatly astonished and upset about it and I never wanted to see that person again. (*Life,* Ch.7,p.40.)

Teresa soon forgot the warning and began to rationalize her way out. She argued that the vision was not real or authentic, and was just an hallucination of the imagination. (She was so human.)

She wrote: "Because the vision did not please me, I forced myself to give the lie to my own instinct. . . . I entered into relations with that person once again." (Ibid. p.41.)

She admits that she was very fond of this person and found it hard to break off the relationship that had become "a pestilential pastime."

She further states that she saw a crawling toad coming toward them in broad daylight, frightening her out of her wits and rationalizations. She got a message with a deeper meaning from the Lord. His Majesty had to resort to some extraordinary tactics to wake Teresa up.

While failing herself, Teresa at the same time was trying to take care of others and to lead them into the ocean of mental prayer. It was embarrassing not to practice what she was teaching. One of her better students was her own father, whom she so dearly loved. During the last seven years of his life, the good

Don Alonso spent a generous amount of time with his favorite daughter. Very much alone now, with his other daughters married and his sons fighting and dying in the New World, his daughter, the Carmelite, was his sole comfort. She gave him books on prayer, spoke to him on God, and led him into the deep waters of contemplation.

One sad day, Teresa had to confess to him that she herself was no longer giving time in communing with God, and although she offered her poor health as an excuse, she knew deep down in her heart that this was a lie. She had wasted time on vanities. Don Alonso was compassionate. She said: "My father holding the opinion of me that he had, and loving me as he did, believed everything I told him and in fact was sorry for me." (*Life*, Ch.7,p.43.)

Death of Her Father

Toward the end of 1543, when he was fifty-eight-years old, Don Alonso's health and financial affairs declined. He had his troubles. His favorite daughter hurried to her father's bedside to comfort and console him, for he was the person she loved most in the world. "In losing him, I lost my greatest blessing and comfort. . . . So deeply did I love him that, when I saw his life was ending, I felt as if my very soul were being torn from me." (*Life*, Ch.7,p.44.)

He died a glorious death, having received the last Sacraments. On the day of his death, the Lord restored his consciousness, and he died while reciting the Credo. "He looked like an angel."

The death of Don Alonso was to be a graceful event to Teresa. She was introduced to his confessor, the Dominican, Vicente Barrón. Fr. Barrón persuaded her to make a good confession, recieve Holy Communion once a fortnight, and return to a regular life of mental prayer. She decided to resolve the conflict within herself. Prayer was not easy. The spirit was not master in me, but slave. I could not shut myself up within myself, without at the same time shutting in a thousand vanities." (*Life*, Ch. 7,p.45.)

The battle continued for twenty years, but she adds triumphantly: "I never again abandoned prayer, . . . It was no longer in my power to give up prayer, because He who desired me for His own in order to show me greater favours held me in His hand." (Ibid.p.45.)

From the school of experience, Teresa gives us some sound advice. When we begin a life of prayer, we must surround ourselves with a support group of resurrection friends, people who encourage and enlighten us. False humility must not deter us. "This scruple is an invention of the devil; Charity grows when it is communicated to others." (Ibid.p.47.)

The next fifteen chapters of her *Life* are dedicated to her teaching on prayer, and if the gentle reader has patience with me, I will put it all together as best I can in the second part of this book. Prayer saved Teresa!

3.
The New Book of Life

CONVERSION 1553

Sometime in 1553, His Majesty touched the strings of Teresa's heart in a stirring manner. It happened as she entered the oratory one day. Since this is a turning point in her life, let her speak for herself:

> I saw an image of Christ sorely wounded. . . . I was deeply moved to see Him thus, so well did it picture what He suffered for us. . . . I felt as if my heart were breaking, and I threw down beside Him, shedding floods of tears and begging Him to give me strength once for all so that I might not offend Him, . . . I believe I told Him that I would not rise from that spot until He had granted me what I was beseeching Him. I feel sure that this did me good for from that time onward I began to improve.

After this a change came over Teresa. Her conversion had really begun, for she was now singleminded and determined. Her prayer life improved and her self-confidence was restored. She read more books and experienced her first, fleeting elementary mystical experiences. Teresa decreased and the Lord increased.

> I am speaking of another and a new book—I mean another and new life. Until now, the life I was describing was my own; but the life I have been living since I began to expound these matters concerning prayer is the life which God has been living in me." (*Life*, Ch. 23, p. 145.)

His Majesty frequently granted her the favor of the Prayer of Quiet, and the Prayer of Union that lasted quite a time. The devil, however, returned to the attack, and she went through years of doubt and fear. Although she was inwardly sure of the authenticity of her experience, her spiritual friends cast dispersions and doubt upon them. Fear, fear, fear—the favorite tool of Satan is printed many times on these pages of the book of her life.

The elderly Don Francisco de Salcedo entered her life about 1554. He was to play an important role in helping and confusing her. Teresa recognized him as a gentleman, saintly, virtuous, intelligent, charitable, gracious, and a good conversationalist. Don Francisco, although married, was far advanced in the life of prayer. For twenty years he had been attending lectures in theology at the Dominican Monastery of St. Thomas. Related to Teresa by marriage, he was a frequent visitor at the Incarnation. After his wife's death in 1570, he took Holy Orders. Teresa was to write of him, "I might almost go so far as to term him the person to whom . . . I owe most in the world, for he was the first who seriously enlightened me." (Letter 128.)

Teresa was fortunate to have this layman friend to enlighten her, for the hounds of the Inquisition were once more around seeking to devour any suspect they could find, and Teresa was one of the suspects.

The story of the Poor Clare nun, Magdalena de la Cruz, had put fear into all Spain. She lived for forty years at the convent of St. Isabel of the Angels in Córdoba, and had such a name for holiness and healing power that pilgrims came to her from all over Spain. The Empress Isabel, wife of Charles V, sent her as a gift the very robes in which her son Philip II was baptized at Valladolid in 1527. Her body bore the marks of the Stigma; she lived on the consecrated host, took no food, and underwent terrible penances.

Gradually, she fell under suspicion, was arrested, and confessed that she was not a Catholic, but an Alumbrada, a secret sect that was anti-Christian. She was a secret devil worshiper, who at the age of seven was induced by the evil one to pretend to be holy and simulate the Crucifixion. At the age of eleven, she made a pact with two incubus demons who came to her at night, inflicted the wounds on her body, imitating those of

Christ, and gave her the powers she wielded. (Cf. Walsh, *St. Teresa of Avila*, pp. 110–115.)

There are real mystics and there are psuedomystics. And when the authentic abound, the false do more to cast the shadow of confusion on the truth. Satan, the Lucifer, is the father of lies; and now the shadow of suspicion fell over the beata at the Incarnation.

> When I found that my fear was getting such a hold over me because I was progressing in prayer, it seemed to me that there must either be something very good about this or something terribly bad. (*Life,* Ch. 23, p. 146.)

In her confusion, Teresa opened her heart to Francisco de Salcedo and the good man could not reconcile the lofty graces of the Lord with the weaknesses of the woman. He could not believe they were from God, so he called on the local priest, Don Pedro Gaspar Daza, a maestro in theology who was well known and highly respected.

Teresa chose him as confessor. She was not very happy with the choice, for Don Pedro treated her with severity, handled her as if she were a novice in the spiritual life, returning her to the purgative way of mortification and virtue.

"Though he was a person with a particular gift for leading beginners to God, it was not God's will that he should understand my soul or desire to take it into his charge." (*Life,* Ch. 23, p. 148.)

Since her friends could not enlighten her, Teresa searched for knowledge once more in books, and the Franciscan laybrother, Bernardino de Laredo's book, *The Ascent of Mount Sion*, came to her rescue as it spoke about a prayer without words and above thought. "When I was experiencing that type of prayer I could think of nothing." (Ibid, p. 148.)

Her spiritual friends did not understand such a way of communing with the all-silent God, and told her she was deluded by the devil. Twenty years of prayer down the drain. To make matters worse, her friends discussed her case publicly among themselves, and Teresa condemns their indiscretion and lack of reverence for secrecy.

The final blow fell when Salecedo came to the Incarnation with the verdict:

> When this gentleman came to me, it was to tell me with great distress that to the best of their belief my trouble came from the devil. . . . This caused me such distress and fear that I did not know what to do. I could only weep. (Ibid. p. 151.)

Part of the medicine suggested was a general confession of her entire life to a Jesuit. The experts were to be called in. In her fear and embarrassment Teresa turned to prayer. She entered the oratory, and words of St. Paul consoled her: "God is very faithful and never allows people who love Him to be deluded by the devil." (Ibid. p. 151.)

The Jesuits

Sometime in March 1554, the Jesuit, Diego de Cetina, came as a confessor to Teresa. Although she tried to smuggle him in, to avoid gossip and suspicion among the nuns, she was not too successful. Rumors flew and suspicions spread. Yet, this humble Jesuit of poor health, who was only twenty years old, underesteemed and never appreciative of whom his superiors had written—"He preaches indifferently, hears confessions, no use for anything else"—was a man of prayer and understood the spirit of Teresa. With a spirit of deep compassion for her, he encouraged her to return to mental prayer and to meditate on the passion. She must foster devotion to the Sacred Humanity, and practice penance. Teresa could once again walk the road of prayer in love and freedom. Her health improved, her virtues grew, and prayer became deeper and better.

St. Francis Borgia

The Lord sent a saint to Avila. He was another Jesuit, Francis Borgia, now the Commissary of the Society of Spain. He visited the College of St. Iles, Avila, 1554 and was at once introduced to Teresa. This future General of the Society of Jesus had an interesting history.

Francis was the son of the third Duke of Gandia, and soldiered in the army of Charles V, who created him Marquis of

Lombey, 1530, and appointed him Viceroy of Catalonia, 1539. He succeeded his father as fourth Duke of Gandia in 1543. The turning point in his life came when he was given the honor of identifying the corpse of the great and beautiful Empress Isabella, the mother of Philip II, the glorious Portugese princess, Empress of Germany, and wife of the mighty and magnificent Catholic King, Charles V. The sight and smell from the putrifying body nauseated his sense and spirit as he swore never again to serve a master that was mortal. He exchanged his royal robes for the humble cassock of a Jesuit novice and was ordained priest in 1551. He renounced all property and titles to follow Jesus Christ humbly.

St. Teresa describes her meeting with this Jesuit saint:

> When he had heard my story, he told me that I was being led by the Spirit of God. He thought I should not be doing right to resist Him further. . . . He suggested that I should always begin my prayers with a meditation on one of the incidents of the Passion, and if the Lord should then transport my spirit, I should not resist Him, I should allow His Majesty to have it and make no effort to keep it back. . . . I was greatly comforted. (*Life*, Ch. 24, p. 154.)

Francis Borgia confirmed the diagnosis of Cetina. "It is truly the Spirit of God."

This made Francisco de Salcedo and Gaspar Daza happy and quieted the gossips of Avila.

One sad footnote to the episode—her confessor was transferred elsewhere. "My soul was as if in a desert." (Ibid. p. 154.)

Fr. Baltasar Álvarez was another Jesuit who helped Teresa immensely. Younger men seemed to understand her, for Alvarez was only twenty-six years old, and for six years proved to be a pillar of strength to our saint. The work of purification went ahead under his firm, yet friendly, guidance, as he gently detached the heart of Teresa from certain unhealthy friendships. He persuaded her to pray over the matter and recite the "Veni Creator," to the Holy Spirit. She spent most of one day in prayer, and received the grace of her first rapture.

First Rapture

> There came to me a transport so sudden that it almost carried me away; I could make no mistake about this, so clear was it. This was the first time that the Lord had granted me the favour of any kind of rapture. I heard these words, "I will have thee converse now, not with men, but with angels." This simply amazed me, for my soul was greatly moved, and the words were spoken to me in the depths of the spirit. For this reason they made me afraid, though on the other hand they brought me a great deal of comfort, which remained with me after the fear caused by the strangeness of the experience had vanished. (*Life*, Ch. 24, p. 155.)

The rapture with its agony and ecstasy carried its own grace with it. Although she was to continue to love and love deeply and passionately, her heart had attained a new depth and capacity for friendship. Sinful, selfish, utilitarian, and merely human love was out. "Never since then have I been able to maintain firm friendships save with people I believe love God and try to serve Him, nor have I derived any comfort from any others or cherished any private affection for them." (*Life*, Ch. 24, p. 155.)

Henceforth, her friends had to be people of prayer and lovers of God. The Lord had done in a moment what Teresa had failed to do over the course of many years. She herself had used violence on her heart and body, and her confessors were no less gentle and discreet. It was all to no avail until the moment of the Spirit had arrived, God's charis time, the charismatic moment of catharsis. We are spiritualized by the Spirit of God; Goddified by God Himself; Christophied by the Christ and deified by the grace of the Lord. Teresa saw the light. Her big heart was free, as she loved with a transformed spirit.

More locutions and mystical experiences were to follow while Teresa was still in her mid-forties. She leaves a description,

> The words are not heard with the bodily ear, yet they are understood more clearly than if they were so heard, and however determined one's resistance, it is impossible to fail to hear them. When on the natural plane, we do not wish to hear, we can close our ears, or attend to something else, with the result, that although we may hear, we do not understand. But when God talks in this way to the soul, there is no such remedy. I have to listen

> whether I like it or not, and my understanding has to devote itself so completely to what God wishes me to understand that whether I want to listen or not makes no difference. For, as He is who is all powerful wills us to understand, we have to do what He wills: and He reveals Himself as our true Lord. (*Life*, Ch. 24, p. 157.)

Later on in the book, when discussing mystical phenomena, we will study in greater depth these experiences. As life went on, Teresa's teaching became clearer. Just now she was worried. She knew deception was possible, and she could not discern what came from God, what came from the devil, and what came from her own subconscious. Her spiritual advisors were not so discreet, and although Fr. Alvarez stood by her, the news got out that she was having these experiences. People began to talk about her. Rumors spread through the streets of Avila, and human assurances could not calm her fears at a time when fear was warranted. She was not sure of herself for months, until the Lord spoke, "Be not afraid, daughter, for it is I and I will not forsake thee: fear not." (*Life*, Ch.25, p. 164.)

There is nothing to fear but fear itself, and fear is Satan's greatest tool. Fear based so often on a lie is an illusion and illusionary—a deception perpetrated by Lucifer the father of lies who loves to work in the shadows of projection and doubt.

The heavenly words restored her calm and courage. She was filled once more with conviction and peace. This peace of mind, after the storm, was the sign of the presence and the hand of God. Teresa might have lost a few battles in the darkness of the night; but once the dawn had broken, she was determined to win the war against these dark, subtle, demonic forces that masqueraded as angels of light and false humility.

> I found I was another person and I was not afraid to wrestle with devils, for with the aid of the cross I believed I could easily vanquish them all. Come on, now, all of you, I said; I am a servant of the Lord and I want to see what you can do to me. . . . I had frightened all these devils, for I became quite calm and had no more fear of them. . . . Indeed, they seem to be afraid of me. I have acquired an authority over them, . . . They seem to be such cowards . . . understand that one venial sin can do us greater harm than all the forces of hell combined. (*Life*, Ch. 25, pp. 164–165.)

Teresa knew that the devil is helpless against the innocent, and he controls us only because we are controlled within by our lusts for vanities, honors, pleasures, powers, and cravings.

In an outburst of real freedom and courage, Teresa cries:

> Not a fig shall I care for all the devil's in hell. It is they who will fear me. I do not understand these fears. "Oh, the devil, the devil," we say, when we might be saying, "God, God," and making the devil tremble, . . . I am more afraid of people who are themselves terrified of the devil than I am of the devil himself. He cannot harm me in the least, whereas confessors can upset people a great deal, and for several years they were such a trial to me. (*Life*, Ch. 25, pp. 165–166.)

An innocent, fearful confessor is worse than the devil himself, but Teresa trusted a learned spiritual director more than she trusted angels.

In 1559, there were humans walking about who were more dangerous than the devil and doing more harm. The Grand Inquisitor of Spain, Don Fernándo de Valdes, placed several religious books written in the vernacular on the index of prohibited books. Teresa did not understand Latin very well, and one of the great sources of spiritual consolation and instruction was now taken from her.

The Lord spoke these consoling words:

> Be not distressed, for I will give thee a living book. . . . A few days afterwards I came to understand this very well, for what I saw before me gave me so much to think about and so much opportunity for recollection, and the Lord showed me so much love and taught me by so many methods that I have had very little need of books—His Majesty Himself has been to me a Book in which I have seen what is true. Blessed be such a Book, which leaves impressed upon us what we are to read and do in a way that is unforgettable. (*Life*, Ch. 26, p. 168.)

First Vision

On June 29, 1560, the Feast of St. Peter, Teresa enjoyed the experience of her first "intellectual" vision of Christ.

> I saw Christ at my side—or, to put it better, I was conscious of Him, for neither with the eyes of the body nor with those of the soul did I see anything. I thought He was quite close to me . . . speaking to me. Being completely ignorant that visions of this kind could occur, I was at first very much afraid, and did nothing but weep. As soon as He addressed a single word to me to reassure me, I became quiet again. I was quite happy again and free from fear. All the time Jesus Christ seemed to be beside me, but as this was not an imaginary vision, I could not discern in what form. I felt very clearly that He was at my right hand, and a witness of everything that I was doing. Whenever I became slightly recollected or was greatly distracted, I could not be aware of His nearness to me."

Troubled and confused, Teresa consulted her confessor, who asked her how and what she had been. The paradox of the mystical experience was: "I told him that I had not seen Him at all."

The confessor asked, "How do you know it is Christ?"

> "I told him that I did not know how, but that I could not help realizing that He was beside me and that I saw and felt this clearly. When in the Prayer of Quiet, my soul was much more deeply and continuously recollected. The effects of my prayer were more different from those which I had previously been accustomed to experience; and that the thing was quite clear to me." (*Life,* Ch. 27, p. 170.)

As in the case of Abraham, Moses, and Our Blessed Lady herself, Teresa was perplexed by this new and sudden approach of the supernatural. The God of peace reassured her. Wherever He walks, there is paradise. Teresa became more and more aware of His gentle and loving presence. The most sacred humanity of Jesus Christ became her constant companion. The devil could not feign this favor. Satan may counterfeit imaginary or corporeal visions, but he has little power, when it comes to intellectual visions. The angel of darkness cannot produce the deep peace, the certainty or "the knowledge that is brighter than the sun."

This vision is different from the consciousness granted in the Prayer of Quiet.

"In a vision, the soul distinctly sees that Jesus Christ, the Son of the Virgin, is present." (Ibid. p. 171.)

The Lord may also speak to the soul in a celestial language.

The Celestial Language

> God teaches the soul, and addresses it without using words. This is so celestial a language that it is difficult to explain it to mortals, unless the Lord teaches it to us by experience. The Lord introduces into the inmost part of the soul what He wishes that soul to understand, and presents it, not by means of images or forms of words, but after the manner of this vision aforementioned. God causes the soul to understand what He wills, and also great truths and mysteries. (Ibid. p. 172.)

Since these experiences take place in the depth of the spirit, far deeper than sense, image, or intellect, the devil cannot interfere, and we ourselves cannot by conscious effort or subconscious intrigue produce them.

> I believe that we ourselves do nothing and accomplish nothing. The whole thing seems to be the work of the Lord. It is as if food had been introduced into the stomach without our having eaten it or knowing how it got there. . . . In this experience, I do know who put it there, but not how He did so, for my soul saw nothing and cannot understand how the operation took place. (Ibid. p. 172.)

With the help of this new kind of light our saint grew in the knowledge and love of God. She was inwardly enlightened in the greatest mystery of our faith, the Blessed Trinity.

> The soul suddenly finds itself learned, and the mystery of the most Holy Trinity, together with other lofty things, is so clearly explained to it that there is no theologian with whom it would not have the boldness to contend in defense of the truth of these marvels. . . . One of these favours suffices to change it altogether and make it love nothing save Him, who, without any labour, in its part, renders it capable of receiving such great blessings, and communicates secrets to it and treat it with such friendship. (Ibid. p. 173.)

Prayer is now a matter of stop, look, and listen, be still, receive, and speak by silence.

St. Peter Alacantara

At this time in the agony and the ecstasy of the life of Teresa, the Lord sent another saint along to enlighten and encourage her. St. Peter of Alacantara came to Avila in 1560, as the commissary general of the reformed Conventual Franciscans. A man of sixty, he had the same dreams and ideals as Teresa herself. When her old friend Doña Guiomar de Ulloa heard of his presence, she at once got permission from the Carmelite Provincial to have Teresa stay at her house. The ascetical Franciscan and the mystical Carmelite met in the luxurious surroundings of Doña Guiomar's home.

Teresa admired this extraordinary man, and she has left us an inspiring picture of the ascetic. He walked the roads of Spain, hail, rain, snow, or heat, discalced and unshod. He lived a life of awesome penance for some forty-seven years, keeping alive on an hours' sleep every night. He ate once every three days, and at times would go for a month without food.

Peter's poverty was extreme and his curiosity and awareness more so. He lived in a Franciscan house for three years, and did not recognize a single friar there, except through the sound of his voice. I wonder how he would fare nowadays with all the insistence on dialogue, meetings, sensitivity sessions, affirmation, and confrontation.

Teresa remarks that Peter never looked at women. Can you imagine him in the presence of Teresa? Words can make up for looks, and she confesses that he told her he loved her. That warmed the heart of our saint, as Peter was to prove by deed and courage that he meant what he said. Teresa could soften the heart of a hard ascetic like Peter, and there was no resisting this woman, once she turned on the charm. She also knew that if she had Peter of Alacantara and Francis Borgia and a few Jesuits behind her, all the tongues of Avila could wag and she would still be safe. Teresa was a holy diplomat. This was all the more true, because even in death and after, Peter of Alacantara would appear to guide her.

His life ended in glory and "He is a much greater comfort to me now than when he was on earth." (*Life*, Ch. 27, p. 178.)

Visions

So many people envy the mystical phenomena, the visions, the locutions, the raptures, that blessed the life of Teresa of

Jesus, and yet historically, these very graces caused her the greatest suffering. They confused herself and baffled her confessors. We must not blame the confessors, for they knew no better, and the fear of the mystical, and the abuse of psuedo-mystics blinded them to the reality of the supernatural. We must also thank Teresa herself and St. John of the Cross for sharing their experiences and clarifying the issue for us.

On the feast of St. Paul, January 25, 1561, Teresa enjoyed a vision of the Sacred Humanity, to which she was to have such devotion. When the majestic visions of the Trinity and the Godhead abound, it is an easy temptation to underestimate the place of the Sacred Humanity.

> When I was at Mass, I saw a complete representation of this most Sacred Humanity. Just as in a picture of His resurrection body, in a very great beauty and majesty. . . . I will only say that, if there were nothing else in heaven to delight the eye but the extreme beauty of the glorified bodies there, that alone would be the greatest bliss. A most special bliss, then, will be, when we see the Humanity of Jesus Christ . . . this vision is imaginary. I did not see it with the eyes of the body, but only with the eyes of the soul. (*Life*, Ch. 28. p. 179.)

St. Teresa was gifted with the three kinds of visions: corporeal, imaginative, and intellectual, as she saw the divine truth through the eyes of the body, the eye of the imagination, or the eye of the soul. The intellectual vision was always the safest and most certain. The imaginary vision confused her, and here, she adds, "No sooner had the vision faded—the very moment after it had gone—I began to think I had imagined it." (Ibid.)

She was worried, lest these visions were produced by the devil, that she invented them herself in the depth of the subconscious.

Teresa now illumines us with an enlightening passage that shows the difference between a natural and a supernatural vision. Natural images depend on our will as regard beginning, duration, content, clarity, and effect. The human will cannot decide when and where and how long a supernatural vision will come and last. The clarity and content cannot be invented by the human mind, and the peaceful effects cannot be produced by any psychological trick or power.

> It is not a radiance which dazzles, but a soft whiteness and an infused radiance, which without wearying the eyes, causes them the greatest delight. They are not wearied by the brightness which they see in seeing this Divine Beauty. So different from any earthly light is the brightness and light now revealed to the eyes, that by comparison with it, the brightness of the sun seems quite dim. It is as if we were to look at a very clear stream, in a bed of crystal, reflecting the sun's rays, and then to see a very muddy stream, in an earthy bed and overshadowed by clouds. Not that the sun, or any other such light enters the visions, on the contrary, it is like a natural light and all other kinds of light seem artificial. It is a light which never gives place to night, and being always light is disturbed by nothing. No one however, powerful his intellect, could in the whole course of his life imagine it as it is. And so quickly does God reveal it to us that, even if we needed to open our eyes in order to see it, there would not be time for us to do so. It is all the same whether they are open or closed. If the Lord is pleased for us to see it, we shall do so, even against our will. There is nothing powerful enough to divert our attention from it, and we can neither resist it nor attain to it by any diligence or care of our own. This I have conclusively proved by experience. (*Life*, Ch. 28, p. 180.)

The above is a very important instructive passage to enable directors to discern the nature, the origin, and the value of a vision.

With gift after gift, the loving Christ made his presence felt and seen by Teresa. The Resurrected Christ appeared to her both as man and as God, and she experienced this presence in a very special way after Communion, when He was living and loving within the inn of her soul. Faith came alive.

Our mystical writer now warns us of the counterfeit visions of Lucifer. He is an angel of light and will "go so far as to give false visions of our Lord, to lead us astray and cast aspersions on the authentic."

> He takes the form of flesh, but he cannot counterfeit the glory which the vision has when it comes from God. He makes these attempts in order to destroy the effects of the genuine vision that the soul has experienced. The soul of its own accord resists them. It then becomes troubled, despondent and restless, loses devotion and joy it had before and is unable to pray. . . . The thing is very easy to recognize, unless a soul wants to be deceived. I do not think the devil will deceive it if it walks in humility and simplicity.

> Anyone who has had a genuine vision from God will recognize the devil's work almost at once. . . . There is no suggestion in them of pure and chaste love. In my view, where a soul has had experience, the devil will be unable to do it any harm. (*Life,* Ch. 28, p. 183.)

Although Teresa herself was learning in the bitter school of experience, as her spirit was being hammered out on the anvil of suffering, her confessors, who were far less enlightened and far less audacious, did not understand. They grew afraid of this woman and her visions, and she found it hard to persuade one to hear her confessions. They gossiped among themselves, and damaging reports were circulated. Religious people do not usually speak kindly of their saintly contemporaries. As the Lord leads them one way, they cannot conceive how He may lead another by a different path. There are many quays into the great Pacific Ocean of God's merciful love. The narrow-minded do not carry the map.

And so the religious contemporaries of Teresa were to torment her with their doubts, believing that no woman with a wicked past like Teresa's could have a gifted present or a glorious future. History would have forgotten their names had they not met this wonderful woman.

> I had troubles enough to deprive me of my reason. . . . Though the opposition of good people to a weak and wicked woman like myself, and a timid one at that, seems nothing when described in this way. It was one of the worst trials that I have ever known in my life. And I have suffered some very severe ones. (*Life,* Ch. 28, p. 186.)

Her confessor during these turbulent years was Father Baltasar Alvarez, a discreet and humble Jesuit. A man of prayer and learning himself, he courageously stood beside Teresa, but when it came to guiding her in the world of mystical phenomena, he, like the others, added to her pain. He did not trust his own judgment, and as the visions became more numerous, he definitely concluded that his penitent was being deceived by the devil. He asked Teresa to do one of the most embarrassing things of her life.

> They commanded me to make the sign of the Cross, when-

> ever I had a vision and to snap my fingers at it so as to convince myself that it came from the devil, and it would not come again. . . . To snap my fingers at a vision in which I saw the Lord caused me the sorest distress. For, when I saw Him before me, I could not believe that the vision had come from the devil even if the alternative were my being cut to pieces. . . . This reminded me of the ways the Jews had insulted Him, and I would beseech Him to forgive me. . . . He told me not to worry about it and said I was quite right to obey, but He would see that my confessor learned the truth. (*Life,* Ch. 29, p. 189.)

Her spiritual friends went so far wrong as to tell her to give up prayer altogether. That was a bit too much for His Majesty. "He seemed to me to have become angry, and He told me to tell them that this was tyranny." (Ibid. p. 189)

The Lord now gave Teresa more assured signs of His presence and filled her with a strong supernatural love. Her vehement desires grew, as she prayed even in her sleep, and unbearable impulses welled up within her to see God. "I want to see God." The arrow of love was driven deep into her heart and set her on fire. Wounded by love, she lived between bliss and distress.

It was in the midst of such circumstances that she received, sometime in 1562, the extraordinary gift of the transverberation of her heart.

> I would see beside me on my left hand, an angel in bodily form. . . . He was not tall but short and very beautiful, his face so aflame that he appeared to be one of the highest types of angels who seem to be all fire. They must be those called Cherubim. . . . In his hands I saw a lovely golden spear and at the end of the iron tip I seemed to see a point of fire. With this he seemed to pierce my heart several times, so that it penetrated to my entrails. When he drew it out, I thought that he was drawing them out with it and he left me completely afire with a great love for God. The pain was so sharp that it made me utter several moans, and so excessive was the sweetness caused me by intense pain that one can never wish to lose it, nor will one soul be content with anything less than God. It is not bodily pain, but spiritual, though the body has a share in it. Sweet are the colloquies of love that pass between the soul and God. . . . During the days that followed, I went about as if in a stupor. I had no wish to see or speak with anyone, but only to hug the pain which

> caused me greater bliss than any that can come from the whole of creation. I was like this on several occasions, when the Lord was pleased to send me these raptures, and so deep were they that even when I was with other people, I could not resist. (*Life*, Ch. 29, pp. 192, 193.)

When these moments of grace and glory passed, there were long days of fear and distress ahead. One friend who understood her was Doña Guiomar de Ulloa, who now invited Teresa to her luxurious home to meet Peter of Alacantara. They enjoyed several talks together and the great Carmelite mystic opened the entire book of her life before the eyes of this ascetic and saintly son of St. Francis. Can you imagine the depth of prayer, love, and spiritual communion between those two magnificent Spanish saints? Peter had walked the rocky road of experience as he understood Teresa. His verdict was once again that her visions came from God. Not only did Peter enlighten her, but he offered her the luxury of compassion and he sympathized with her when she was persecuted by good people. Moreover, he spoke to Francisco de Salcedo and her other timid spiritual friends and persuaded them to withdraw their negative diagnosis. She writes, "Fray Peter comforted and calmed me."

Fra Pedro came and Fra Pedro went, but the trials of Teresa continued. Now in her forties, it seemed at times as if she had never experienced the favors she just described. Her understanding seemed stupid and she was confused to a thousand doubts and suspicions. The gates of hell were opened against her, as Satan released his worst forces and wiles, and even appeared to her. Holy water was her secret weapon. "From long experience I have learned that there is nothing like holy water to put devils to flight and prevent them from coming back again." (*Life*, Ch. 31, p. 205.)

Visions of the Demonic World

Teresa was at this time given visions of the devil and the demonic world.

> Once when I was in an oratory, he appeared on my left hand in an abominable form. As he spoke to me, I paid particular

attention to his mouth which was horrible. Out of his body there seemed to be coming a great flame, which was intensely bright and cast no shadow. He told me in a horrible way that I had indeed escaped out of his hands, but he would get hold of me still. I was very much afraid and made the sign of the cross as well as I could. Whereupon he disappeared, but immediately returned again. . . . There was some holy water there, so I flung some in the direction of the apparition, and it never came back. On another occasion the devil was with me for five hours torturing me with such terrible pain and both inward and outward disquiet that I do not believe I could have endured them any longer. The sisters who were with me were frightened to death. (*Life*, Ch. 31. p. 204.)

After such experiences and many more, Teresa was very much aware of the presence and power of the evil one, who literally beat her, tormented her, nauseated her with foul odors and language and tempted her to fear and despair in every possible manner. She was tempted to leave the convent and go elsewhere.

Living in community was a torment. Her sisters knew that Teresa was specially graced by God and was trying to walk the narrow path to perfection, and so they could not tolerate any weakness in her.

Our saint laments:

> When the world sees anyone setting out on that road it expects him to be perfect all at once and detects a fault in him from a thousand leagues' distance; yet in that particular person the fault may be a virtue, and his critic in whom it is a vice may be judging him by himself. They will not allow him to eat or sleep. . . . They forget that he still is in the body. . . . He needs great courage. His poor soul has not yet begun to walk, and men expect it to fly. (*Life*, Ch. 31, p. 211.)

The world is hard on its saints. To be free we must not be attached to fame or reputation. To follow Christ, we must face insult and criticism. Sinners of the world cast their own shadows over the faces of saints.

> I was at prayer one day when suddenly without knowing how I found myself, as I thought, plunged right into hell. I realized that it was the Lord's will that I should see the place the

devils had prepared for me there and which I had merited for my sins. This happened in the briefest space of time, but even if I were to live for many years, I believe it would be impossible for me to forget it.

The entrance, I thought, resembled a very long, narrow passage, like a furnace; very low, dark, and closely confined. The ground seemed to be full of water which looked like filthy, evil-smelling mud, and in it were many wicked-looking reptiles. At the end there was a hollow place scooped out of a well, like a cupboard and it was here that I found myself in close confinement. But the sight of all this was pleasant by comparison with what I felt there. . . .

My feelings could not possibly be exaggerated, nor can anyone understand them. I felt a fire within my soul. . . . My bodily sufferings were so intolerable . . . to say nothing of the knowledge that they would be endless and never-ceasing. These are nothing by comparison with the agony of my soul, an oppression, a suffocation and an affliction so deeply felt and accompanied by such hopeless and distressing misery, that I cannot too forcibly describe it. . . . The interior fire and despair is greater than the most grievous tortures and pains. . . . The interior fire and despair are the worst things of all. In that pestilential spot, it was impossible to sit or lie. I had been put in this place which looked like a hole in the wall, and these very walls, so terrible to the sight, bore down upon me and completely stifled me. There was no light and everything was in the blackest darkness. I do not understand how this can be, but, although there was no light, it was possible to see everything that can cause affliction. (*Life*, Ch. 32, pp. 215, 216.)

Teresa had other and more frightening visions of hell itself that utterly terrified her, as she saw how demons treated the people who were sinful enough to end there.

Although frightful in themselves, these visions had a sobering effect on Teresa because she lost all fear of little pains and aches and disappointments of daily life. The Lord was preparing her for greater trials, and testings when she began the reform of the Order. These visions also filled her heart with deep compassion for sinners and for the Lutherans. She felt they were lost to God on account of heresy. She would undergo any suffering to save one soul. The zeal of the apostle burned within her.

Strange as it may seem, this vision of hell played a leading role in her decision to reform Carmel and open a new convent.

The Lord had prepared this extraordinary woman in an extraordinary manner for an extraordinary mission that would affect the lives of millions not only in Carmel but inside and outside the entire Catholic church for centuries. Her influence today spreads far beyond the cloisters of the Catholic world.

Teresa was not just a reformer of an Order, she was a pioneer in the world of inner space. Thanks to her sufferings, her experiences, and her pains, we have a far clearer map of the spiritual universe that lies far outside the ken of our physical senses and intellect than is really there. The mystic of Avila travelled there and back, a Columbus in the ocean of the spirit. God chose her to teach us, to raise us up, to heighten our awareness and let us know that we are not slaves of the subconscious, or bound by the walls of the conscious, for we, like eagles, are destined to fly in high places amid the lofty peaks of the superconscious. The eternal was very real to Teresa, and, in her rebirth during her forties, the eyes of the spirit were opened to another and more real world. She walked among the unseen, like her great patron Elijah; saw her visions and dreamed her dreams that have left all of us wiser and safer. John in Patmos was allowed entrance into that mystical world. The pure of heart see God, and a mystic is a seer. During those strange and difficult years, the inner spiritual senses of Teresa opened to the supernatural. She saw visions, heard divine consoling words, smelled the heavenly odors of God's presence, tasted the highest delights, and was raptured and entranced by divine touches of love. Her imagination and intellect were opened to peer into a world very few are destined to see, and her will was empowered to undertake the impossible for God, as she outgrew all fear and went forth in courage and confidence. The powers of hell tried their level best to stop her, the angels of heaven came to her aid, as her few human friends were baffled and blinded by the glorious light of the whole affair. Her enemies could suspect, surmise, and gossip, and threaten the inquisitional fires. But one word from the Beloved calmed the fires, "Don't be afraid, I am with you. I love you."

Such assuring words often lifted Teresa quite literally off the floor, as reliable witnesses testify to the phenomena of levitation:

> One day when she was kneeling in the choir, waiting for the

bell, a nun saw her rise about eighteen inches from the floor. According to Yepes, she once ascended higher than the window through which the Bishop of Avila had just given her Holy Communion. (Walsh, *St. Teresa of Avila:* p. 137.)

With St. Paul, our saint could now exclaim more and more, and she was gradually transformed into Christ. "I have been crucified with Christ, and I live now not with my own life, but with the life of Christ who lives in me." (Gal. 2:19–20). Nothing and nobody could stop her now!

4.
The Reform of an Order

Teresa heard of the immense good being done by the soldiers of Ignatius and other religious reformers for the church during the last days of the Council of Trent. The counter-reformation was on its way, and she wondered what she could do as a human for the church she loved in the sixteenth-century Spain.

While all her brothers were out fighting in the new world to spread the boundaries of the political empire of Philip II, she desired with a fierce passion to achieve something beautiful for Christ at home. The kingdom of God had to be rooted first of all in her own heart. She was now ready. The problem must have tormented her for days and nights on end. Reports were flowing of the spread of Lutheranism, and for Teresa, all Protestants, be they followers of Martin Luther, Calvin, Zwingli, or Henry VIII, were Lutheran.

The terrible Huguenot wars were tearing out the heart of the Church of France, and even though France and Spain were at war, Teresa cried and prayed for the unhappy state of the Church in France. Teresa decided, that she, like Moses, would fight the battle of the church with the weapon of prayer. Her Carmelite Sisters would pray and do penance for the real soldiers of Christ, the priests, the preachers, and the learned men. She would not hate; she would not sit down and criticize. She would live, and she would prove that contemplation is the most powerful lever for action.

Teresa was ready by 1562: She had the courage to tackle the

corrupt external world outside and confidence monitoring the powers of the inner cathedral. Her allies were alert and friendly, convinced of her calling and special mission—Pedro Ibañez, Domingo Bañez, Gonzalo de Aranda, Gaspar Daza, Francisco de Salcedo, Baltasar Álvarez, the Saints, Peter of Alacantara, Francis Borgia, the faithful widow, Doña Guiomer de Ulloa. Every pioneer needs a solid support group, and Teresa was careful to build one around her. She needed every one of them.

It might be helpful to paint a faint picture of the background where Teresa worked.

On the larger political scale: In October 1556, The Emperor Charles V returned to Spain from the wars in Northern Europe, which rent and split his mighty empire. He was a sick and broken man. His son Philip II succeeded him. Philip was determined to save his state and church from all the heretics in the north. He was a loyal Catholic, and yet the Spanish troops, under the Duke of Alba, sacked Rome. Theologically united the Pope and Emperor were otherwise at loggerheads. Following the theory of balance of power, politically the papacy backed France and Germany.

After defeating the French at the battle of San Quentin, Philip II began the foundation of the great monastic palace and library of the Escorial, where his father was to be buried. By marrying Mary Tudor, he foolishly hoped to bring England back to the Catholic faith. When Mary died a few years later, he cherished the idea for awhile of marrying her sister, Elizabeth, but the English nobles who had grabbed church and monastery lands, saw to it that Elizabeth remained virginal and Protestant. In the South the Mohammadan pirates scourged the coasts of Italy and captured Tripoli from the Knights of St. John in 1558.

The heresy from the north had secretly infiltrated his own beloved country, and Philip was alarmed to discover that Fray Bartolemé Carranza de Miranda, confessor to his wife, and his nominee for archbishop of Toledo, was suspected of being a Lutheran. Heretical veins had entered the Jeronymite Monastery of St. Isadore. Lutherans held meetings at the home of Don Agustin Cazalla, doctor of the University of Salamanca. There were many more instances. Priest, nuns, nobles, scholars, judges, and knights were found guilty.

Heresy was declared treason. The terrible inquisition was revived, and on May 21, 1559, almost a quarter of a million gathered at Valladolid to witness a great *auto-da-fé* and the burning of heretics.

A kind of panic possessed Spain, and a psychotic shadow fell on saint and sinner alike. Teresa fell under the shadow of this cloud, as people compared her to the Alumbrada Magdalena de la Cruz and some other holy nuns who had been burned as heretics. They suspected Teresa of being a Lutheran, and persecuted her friends. The Inquisitors put many books written in the vernacular on the Index, and Teresa's own works were to be sent to be censored and burned.

The world was falling apart, and the Church of Christ was in real trouble, so Teresa of Avila decided that she would do something to reform and revive, to renew and re-unite. She would open a new convent and found a new religious order.

The primitive Rule of Carmel was not followed at the Incarnation. There was little silence, excessive comfort, and freedom for the wealthy, the enclosure a joke, and prayer life a farce. She herself was seldom in the convent, and when she was, she enjoyed a very attractive cell of her own, detached from the main convent, with two rooms, one above the other. There was a little oratory on the ground floor. Visitors were entertained in the cell. Friends and relatives met here. Her younger sister, Juana, had lived here, and now Maria de Ocampo, the grandchild of her uncle Francisco, enjoyed the privilege.

One special day a little group of inspired people met in Teresa's cell. They included Ana and Inés de Tapia, her cousins, Juana Suárez, Leonora and María de Ocampo, Isabel and Inés de Cepeda, her nieces and Doña Guiomar de Ulloa. The inspiration came from the teenager Maria de Ocampo.

Let Teresa describe this event in her own words:

> One day it happened that a person to whom I was talking together with some other sisters, asked me why we should not become Discalced nuns, for it would be quite possible to find a way to establishing a convent. I had desires of this kind myself, so I began to discuss the matter with a companion—the widowed lady, who, as I said before, had the same desire. She began to think out a way to find the money for such a House. (*Life*, Ch. 32, p. 219.)

The meeting ended. They decided to pray about the project

and see what would happen. The Lord was to make His will very clear as we shall see, but meanwhile, Teresa was to hesitate for a very feminine reason. She was so human. "I was most happy in the house where I was, for I was very fond both of the house and of my cell, and this held me back." (*Life*, Ch. 32, p. 219.)

María de Ocampo generously offered to share her inheritance and Doña Guiomar would do all she could. Then the Lord Himself intervened.

> One day after Communion, the Lord gave me the most explicit commands to work for this aim with all my might. He made me a wonderful promise. The convent would not fail to be established; great service would be done to Him in it: that it should be called St. Joseph's: that He would watch over us at one door and Our Lady at the other; that Christ would go with us; that the convent would be a star giving out the most brilliant light. (*Life*, Ch. 32, pp. 219,220.)

The vision had a powerful effect on Teresa, and as she still hesitated, Our Lord appeared again and again.

Teresa went and informed her confessor, Father Álvarez, and the poor man now who had gone through so much already with this *beata*, was completely bewildered. He could not deny the experiences, but he could not see how it was humanly possible to found another convent in the little city of Avila.

Doña Guiomar approached the provincial, Father Gregorio Fernández, and diplomatically won him over to her side, convincing him that sufficient funds were available. Peter of Alacantara was likewise contacted and the good Francis offered full support.

However, Teresa met with lots of human opposition. The news got out that she intended to leave her convent and found one in an already over-convent clustered Avila. Her Provincial was at first well disposed, but under pressure he, too, changed his mind. The vast majority of the nuns in the Incarnation were highly indignant and insulted. They wanted Teresa imprisoned. A merciless persecution broke out. Teresa, a nun, should stay in her convent and Doña Guiomar, a widow, should look after her home and children. Doña Guiomar was refused absolution. They were to learn what the other great saints like Francis and Dominic suffered, when they founded religious orders. Preachers denounced them from pulpits, and once while Teresa and her sister Doña Juana were listening to a Sermon at St. Thomas, the good priest inveighed against "nuns who left their convents to go and found new orders." Posterity has kindly hidden the name of the preacher and the Dominicans disclaim responsibility.

Another Dominican, Pedro Ibañez, stood by her all during the early days of the Reform, until he died in 1565. Teresa's fear had by now lessened, and she acted from an inner center of personal conviction and responsibility.

> I never for a moment lost my confidence that the foundation would be made. My companion had more faith and whatever people might say to her, nothing would persuade her to abandon it. The abandonment of the project seemed to me impossible. I believed the revelation to be true only in the sense that it was not contrary to what is in Holy Scripture or to the laws of the Church. (*Life*, Ch. 32, p. 222.)

Opposition now arose from a very important and powerfully positioned person, her young Jesuit confessor, Baltasar Álvarez. We must remember, too, that Teresa trusted the decision of a confessor more than she trusted the light of a vision. Álvarez wrote her a letter, suggesting that it was all a dream, her visions an illusion. She was a source of scandal, an occasion of sin and deluded by the devil. The threat of the Inquisition was held over her head: "The devil began to contrive that one person after another should hear that I had received some kind of revelation . . . and that I should have to go before the Inquisition." (*Life*, Ch. 33, p. 225.)

Teresa found all this zeal rather humorous, and she could laugh in her self-confidence. She was so free and detached by now from the whole project. Laughter is a sign of deep faith and confidence. She wrote fearlessly.

> I knew quite well that in matters of faith no one would ever find me transgressing even the smallest ceremony of the Church, and that for the Church or for any truth of Holy Scripture, I would undertake to die a thousand deaths. So I told them not to be afraid, for my soul would be in a very bad way if there was anything about it which could make me fear the Inquisition. (*Life*, Ch. 33, p. 226.)

The little ejaculatory prayer, known as the bookmark of St. Terese, might well sum up her petition for inner peace and self-conquest:

Let nothing disturb thee,
nothing affright thee
All things are passing
God never changes
Patience gains all things.
He who has God wants nothing.
Alone, God suffices.

As pressure was laid on by the opposition team, Teresa had to rally her friends. The good Dominican ally, Pedro Ibañez, was there; there too the good Salcedo, P. Daza, and the new Jesuit rector at San Gil, Gaspar de Salazar, had only to meet Teresa to be won over; he encouraged her confessor Baltasar Alvarez to give his penitent every help and support.

With the approval of Ibañez, Doña Guiomar asked Rome for the authorization to found a new convent according to the primitive rule of Carmel, and place it under the jurisdiction of the bishop. Meanwhile, Teresa kept her silence as she prayed, practiced penance, and planned.

The next move was made in August, 1561. Her sister, Doña Juana, and her husband, Don Juan de Ovalle, were returning to Avila from Alba de Tormes. This was the ruse. The Ovalle family would purchase a house, secretly prepare it as a convent, and at the propitious moment hand it over to Teresa. It would have a chapel, thirteen cells for thirteen nuns, and other offices. The building was rather small. Teresa complained to His Majesty:

> My Lord, how is it that you commandest me to do things which seem impossible? If only I were free, woman though I am! But being bound in so many ways, without money or means of procuring it, either for the Brief or for anything else, what can I do, Lord? (*Life,* Ch. 33, p. 229.)

Although she did not have a farthing to pay the workmen, Teresa went ahead with the house repairs. She was encouraged by a vision of St. Joseph, who "promised" her that funds would not fail. This did not prevent her worry, until one day after Communion, the Lord spoke:

> I have already told you to go on as best you can: Oh, the greed of mankind. So you really think there will not be enough ground for you! How often did I sleep all night in the open air because I had not where to lay my head. (*Life,* Ch. 33, p. 229.)

Another apparition of St. Clare encouraged to found her monastery in poverty.

Teresa seemed to have power over life and death. The Ovalles were not long in Avila, when a wall fell on the little five-year-old Gonzálo and left him for dead. The father carried the body of his lifeless son to Teresa. Teresa lowered her veil, crouched with her head over the child, called to God, and kept calling until the child showed signs of life, caressed her and wanted to play with her. The saintly aunt returned the child to a grateful mother. (Cf. Auclair, *St. Teresa of Avila,* p. 123)

Not many days later, Juana gave birth to her second son, Joseph, named after the patron of the house. He was baptized on September 12, with the faithful friends Doña Guiomar de Ulloa and Don Francisco de Salcedo as godparents. Teresa loved her little nephew and would take him and caress him and say, "If you are not to grow up a good man, I pray God, to take you as you are, you little angel, before you offend Him." The prayer was answered. Joseph was only three weeks old when a fatal illness took him, and hosts of angels came to meet him. (Ibid. p. 123.)

Life went on and the remodeling went on for months. Then, on August 15, 1561, Teresa enjoyed one of her most remarkable visions and raptures.

> I was in a Monastery of the Order of the glorious Saint Dominic, thinking of the many sins which in times past, I had confessed. . . . There came upon me a rapture so vehement that it nearly drew me forth out of myself altogether. I sat down and I remember even now that I could neither see the Elevation nor hear what was being said. While in this state I thought I saw myself being clothed in a garment of great whiteness and brightness. At first I could not see who was clothing me, but later I saw Our Lady on my right hand and my father, St. Joseph, on

my left, and it was they who were putting that garment upon me. I was given to understand that I was now cleansed of my sins. When the clothing was ended, and I was experiencing the greatest joy and bliss, I thought that Our Lady suddenly took me by the hands and told me that I was giving her great pleasure by serving the glorious St. Joseph, and that I might be sure that all I was trying to do about the convent would be accomplished and that both the Lord and they would be greatly served in it. I was not to fear that there would be any failure. They would keep us safe, and her Son already promised to go with us: as a sign that that was true, she said, she would give me this jewel.

Then she seemed to throw round my neck a very beautiful gold collar, to which was fastened a most valuable cross. The gold and stones were so different from earthly things of the kind that no comparison between them is possible. . . . The beauty which I saw in Our Lady was wonderful, though I could discern in her no particularly beautiful detail of form: it was her face as a whole that was so lovely and the whiteness and amazing splendor of her vestments, though the light was not dazzling, but quite soft.

The Glorious St. Joseph, I did not see so clearly, though I could see plainly that he was there. Our Lady looked to me quite like a child. . . . They caused me the greatest bliss and happiness. . . . I was left with a vehement impulse to melt away in love for God. (*Life,* Ch. 33, pp. 230, 231.)

One of the inspirations she received from the Lord was to place the jurisdiction of the convent under the bishop and not under the Order.

Doña Luisa de la Cerda

Doña Luisa de la Cerda, daughter of the second Duke of Medinaceli, was the widow of Don Arias Pardo De Saavedra, marshal of Castile and one of the richest men in Spain. He had died in 1560, and left a heartbroken, depressed and unconsolable wife. Even though she had seven children, and friends galore, no one could help her. Fr. García de Toledo, a Dominican friend of Doña Luisa's, heard of Teresa, and hoped that a saint might lift the gloom that haunted the palace in Toledo.

The Carmelite Provincial was duly contacted, and poor Teresa was soon on her way, at the beginning of January, 1562. It must have been a cold, cold journey, but the warm reception gave recompense to any sacrifice. Teresa grew to love Toledo, a city of merchants, weavers, businessmen, and nobles—the imperial city of Spain, where Moorish influence and art appeared on every palace and church.

Before leaving her own cell, Teresa prayed long and fervently, and during matins on Christmas night, she fell into a deep rapture to hear the Lord say, "I must go without fail." (*Life*, Ch. 34, p. 233.)

So off she went, accompanied by her brother-in-law, Juan de Ovalle, and her faithful friend, Juana Suárez.

Doña Luisa had prepared a luxurious apartment for her saintly visitor, and here she was to stay for some six months, surrounded by wealth, sumptuous living, and luxury. For a while Teresa felt like a fish out of water, but very soon acclimatised herself and won over the wealthy widow.

> The Lord was pleased that the lady should be so much comforted that she began at once to grow markedly better. She felt more comforted every day. . . . She conceived a great affection for me, as I also did for her, when I saw how good she was. (*Life*, Ch. 34, p. 233.)

Teresa made friends wherever she went, and this was true also in Toledo, as she needed wealthy ones, if her dreams were to be carried out. It was here, too, that she met a famous lady, who was later to give her lots of trouble, Ana de la Cerda, Princess of Éboli, a niece of Doña Luisa. Ana was now twenty-one, already known for her beauty, which lost nothing from the fact that she had only one eye. The great Teresa was not intimidated by the grand ladies. She took them with the freedom of an equal, as she admits, "They are as subject to passions and weaknesses as I was myself." (*Life*, p. 234.)

She pitied their slavery to etiquette, high society manners, the whims and fancies of their squires, valets, pages, and maids. "God deliver me from this sinful fuss," laughed our saint.

While at Toledo, Teresa made friends with Pedro Domenech, a Jesuit, and the Dominican García de Toledo. It was García de Toledo who just persuaded her to write the story of her life, and we must be eternally grateful to him. A deep bond of spiritual friendship grew between them.

Another Carmelite after the heart of Teresa came to visit her at Toledo, the beata María de Jesus. María was born at Granada in 1522, and was left a widow when young. She took the habit of the Calced Carmelites at Granada, but left before making her profession, with the intention of founding a reformed house of the order. With whatever money she had sewn in a tight-fitting bodice, she set out barefooted for Rome, where she persuaded Pius IV, to give her a Brief for reform in the spirit of the Council of Trent. On her way, she visited the reformed Carmel of Mantua, and there studied the Rules and Constitutions. Maria must have given helpful hints to Teresa on diplomatic and canonical procedure that left her a wiser and more determined woman. Maria was to found a convent at Alcalá de Henares, some eighteen days after the inauguration of St. Joseph's.

One of the problems that haunted Teresa was how to found her convent in poverty, according to the spirit of the primitive Rule. She consulted the wise and the learned, but the wise and the learned would not go along with her. "True, they sometimes convinced me; but when I betook myself to prayer again and looked at Christ, hanging poor and naked upon the Cross, I felt I could not bear to be rich." (*Life*, Ch. 35, p. 243.)

The convent would be founded, and founded in poverty. "The devil seems to be frightening us with scarecrows here." (Ibid. p. 247.)

St. Joseph's Avila: August 24, 1562

Teresa returned to Avila in July. She had left in the cold and returned to the terrible Castilian heat. The Provincial Angel de Salazar ordered her to return from Toledo to be present at the elections of a new Prioress. Believe it or not, Teresa was one of the hot candidates, which shows she was held in high esteem. Politically others felt this would be a good move to keep her at the Incarnation. Teresa wrote:

> I was warned that many of the nuns wanted to lay upon me the responsibility of being their superior. The very thought of this was such a torment to me that though I was resolved and prepared to undergo any martyrdom for God's sake, I could not possibly persuade myself to accept this. . . . I was never fond of such work, and had not wanted to hold office. . . . I wrote to my friends and asked them not to vote for me. (*Life*, Ch. 35, p. 244.)

Teresa braced herself for battle. The Sacred Apostolic Penitentiary granted the permission to erect the new convent of St. Joseph's in Avila. The brief was dated February 7, and awaited Teresa on her arrival at Avila, five months later. The saintly Peter of Alacantara, and the godly gentleman Don Juan Blázquez, father of the Count of Uceda, at whose house he stayed, were there to help.

They had to obtain the permission of the bishop, Don Álvaro de Mendoze, son of Don Hurtado de Mendoza, brother-in-law of Secretary Cobos, one of the most powerful men in Spain. He was opposed to founding a convent without revenue. During the hot summer days, His lordship was resting at his summer house at El Tiembles, but the fearless Franciscan of Alacantara, though sick and weary, was undaunted and met the lion in his secret retreat. Pleading he persuaded the bishop to allow this little convent for thirteen nuns to be founded in evangelical poverty—just as Jesus and His twelve apostles had done at the beginning of the church. The Bishop was completely charmed and consented.

Peter had carried out his mission, and won for himself and his Franciscan Order an immortal niche of gratitude in the hearts of all Carmelites. He had seen Teresa's vision and dreamed her dream. Teresa loved this old man, and when he left her, never to meet again, she felt both grateful and sad.

The work had to go on and in greater secrecy. One of the most providential sicknesses struck her brother-in-law, Don Juan de Ovalle, and he was forced to stay on at the house in Avila. This gave our foundress a good excuse to be with him. With a little group of friends, Teresa worked night and day, scrubbing, sewing, washing, polishing, and preparing a house that would be the Lord's delight.

At long last, the dawn broke on August 24, 1562, the dawn of a new era in religious history. It was the feast of St. Bartholomew. The convent of St. Joseph, Avila was opened and inaugurated, as the people of the sleeping city woke up to the music of a new bell calling them to prayer to a chapel that would become one of the centers and symbols of mystical renewal. Little they knew of what was really going on.

Let Teresa speak for herself:

> When everything had been arranged, the Lord was pleased that some of the sisters should take the habit on St. Bartholomew's day and on that day too, the most Holy Sacrament was placed in the convent. So with the full weight of authority this convent of our most glorious father, St. Joseph, was founded in the year, 1562. (*Life*, Ch. 36, p. 249.)

Her motive is very clear:

> I made the foundation so that I could withdraw more completely from everything and fulfill my profession and vocation with greater perfection and in conditions of stricter enclosure. (Ibid, p. 250.)

Now notice her freedom and detachment. We know how hard she worked and how enthusiastically she planned and prayed, and yet, she adds:

> I desired it only with the proviso that if I found that the Lord would be better served by my abandoning it entirely, I should do so, as I had done on a former occasion, with complete tranquility and peace. (Ibid, p. 250.)

These words, at such an important moment, let us see a woman who is centered, matured, free, and liberated.

The Order of the Discalced Carmelites had begun. It was heaven living there, in the presence of the Blessed Sacrament and under the felt protection of Our Lady and St. Joseph.

Gaspar Daza celebrated the first Mass. Present were Don Juan de Ovalle and his wife, the happy and helpful Julian of Avila, Doña Guiomar de Ulloa, the faithful friend, Francisco de Salcedo, Don Gonzálo de Aranda, and the three Carmelites, Doña Juana Suarez, Doña Ines de Tapia, and her sister, Ana. Four sisters took the habit that day. Peter of Alacántara brought Antonio de Henoa, Doña Guiomar let go María de la Paz, Gaspar Daza recommended Ursula de Revilla, and Julian of Avila surrendered his own beloved sister, María de Avila. It was a glorious moment, when Teresa and her "four orphans" knelt in the little chapel to give thanks to God, never dreaming of what was ahead.

The Persecution

The ceremony was barely over when Teresa was haunted by demonic, negative ideas and feelings that filled her with doubt and suspicion.

> Was what I had done a mistake. . . ? Did I act against obedience in not having a mandate from the Provincial?
> Will the Provincial be displeased at my placing the jurisdiction of the convent in the hands of the Bishop?
> Would the sisters have enough to eat?
> Would they be happy?
> Would I be able to live this kind of life myself, since I was so often indisposed?
> Would I miss my old friends and all the comforts of the old convent?
> The cold blanket of doubt blinded her completely, and the memory of every vision, locution, virtue and faith was obliterated from her mind.
> I certainly think this was one of the worst times that I have ever spent in my life. (*Life*, Ch. 36, p. 252.)

She prayed, called up all her forces of courage, as she determined to carry the cross and forge ahead. Courage and determination she needed: "After this conflict I was sorely fatigued, but I laughed at the devil, for I saw clearly it was his doing." (Ibid., p. 252.)

Superiors, although they be agents of God, can be more troublesome than the devil himself. Doña Maria Cimbrón, the newly elected Prioress at the Incarnation, and a relative of Teresa's summoned her delinquent subject before her. Teresa left the convent at once, and appointed Ursula de los Santos superior. The little was flock once more orphaned.

The fury at the convent was understandable, as Teresa was accused of being disloyal and disobedient. Who did she think she was? Incapable of following the religious regime at the Incarnation, how could she ever obey the rigid ordinances of the primitive Rule? She deserved punishment and even imprisonment. Some irate sisters would have humiliated her, but the Mother Prioress, somewhat placated by the humble explanation of Teresa, who proved she had not committed any offence against God, Bishops, Order or Rule, (unless trying to strengthen the order for which she would have died were an offence), modified her position; instead of incarcerating her relative, she made her sit down and eat a good meal. She probably needed it.

The Provincial, Ángel de Salazar, was called in. Teresa prepared her spirit for this ordeal:

> "I remembered the trial of Christ, and realized that this, by comparison, was nothing at all.
> "The Provincial gave me a severe rebuke. . . . I would not excuse myself, for I had already resolved not to do so, but begged him to forgive me, to punish me, and not to be annoyed with me any longer." (*Life,* Ch. 36, pp. 253, 254.)

This was the most disarming and best diplomatic approach. It worked, because objectively, she could now speak out, and let her superiors know that she was following a direct command of the Lord, the support of her confessor, the encouragement of the Jesuits, Dominicans, the Bishop, Peter of Alacantara, Pedro Ibañez—and she was armed with a Brief from Rome. The Provincial was faced with formidable opposition and a more formidable woman and he knew it. When the audience had gone he softened.

> Afterwards, when I was alone with him, I spoke to him more plainly, and he was quite satisfied and promised me, if my foundation succeeded, to give me permission to go there, as soon as the city was quiet—for there had been a very great commotion in the city. (*Life,* Ch. 36, p. 254.)

Having won this round of the fight with the Provincial, our heroine had now to face the wrath of the city officials. The powers of church and state came tumbling down upon her. On the morning of August 25, the day after the foundation the Corregidor of Avila, Señor García Suárez Carnajal, after consulting the Procurador General Quinones, the Majordomo Flores, and the notary public Pedro de Villaquiran banged on the door of the little convent of San Jose and demanded that the door be opened or he would break it down. The brave sisters barricaded themselves, and one replied, "We will leave only by command of the one who put us here."

The people of Avila were furious—stones were thrown,

people hammered on the door, and they threatened to destroy the buildings. The four first Carmelites courageously manned the barricades. The pressure was on. The commotion was the talk of the town.

The next move was to hold a solemn meeting of the Junta of Avila. The heads of church and state were there, an imposing assembly to decide on the fate of five poor, prayerful women.

> There were city officials in brilliant costumes braided with gold. There was the Licentiate Brizuela, acting as the provisor for the Bishop. The Chapter of the Cathedral was represented by Canons Perez and Soria and the Archdeacon Sedano. The Dominican convent of St. Thomas sent several delegates, including the Prior, Father Pedro Serrano, and the young theologian, Father Domingo Bañez. For the Franciscans there were the Guardian Father, Martin de Aquirre, and Fr. Hernando de Valderrabano; for the Premonstratensians, the Abbot Father Francisco Blanco, and a preacher. For the Benedictines, the Abbot, Don Pedro de Antoyano, and one of the monks, for the Jesuit College of San Gil, Father Baltasar Alvarez and Jeronimo Ripalda. There were also Maestro Daza and other learned priests and several lay gentlemen from the best families of Avila. (Walsh, *St. Teresa of Avila*, p. 231).

The Licentiate Brizuela defended the bishop who had been accused of irregularity and going beyond his powers. He presented the Brief of Pope Pius IV. As the trial went on, accusation after accusation was made against Teresa, as her so-called friends discreetly kept their silence. The only man among them was the young Dominican, Presentado, or teacher of theology at the Monastery of Saint Thomas, the brave and learned Domingo Bañez. This same Bañez was to fight many other battles in the course of his illustrious career, as he took on Molina and Suarez on the ever-undecided controversy of the freedom of the will. He was now thirty-four years old, and was to remain a staunch supporter of Teresa and her nuns. He helped her revise her *Life, Way of Perfection, Foundations* and *Conceptions of the Love of God*. But this was his moment of heroic glory and bravery. He let the illustrious meeting know that the Bishop and only the Bishop could disestablish the convent. The Bishop stood by Teresa.

Teresa herself boasts, "The fact was that the convent had been destined to be founded, for its foundations was the Lord's will and against that the whole body of them were powerless." (*Life,* Ch. 36, p. 254.)

Pressure and persecution, threat and diplomacy were used against Teresa and her convent. The leaders of the opposition decided to go higher and they sent Alonso de Robledo to Madrid to complain to the Royal Council. Diego de Villena was paid to study the legal aspects of the case in Madrid for fifty days. Father Gonzálo de Aranda went to Madrid to defend Teresa before the Royal Council. All this time we must remember that she was a prisoner at the Incarnation, so her friends on the outside, Julian of Avila, Francisco de Salcedo, and Doña Guiomar rallied round her and raised the necessary funds. Litigation is costly and the enemy intended to "smash" them.

Weary of the battle, Teresa complained to the Lord: "Lord, this house is not mine . . . it has been founded for Thee . . . and now there will be no one to carry on the negotiations, so Thy Majesty must do so."

The Lord replied, "Knowest thou not how powerful I am? What dost thou fear." (*Life,* Ch. 36, p. 255.)

He assured her the foundation would not be dissolved.

By September a compromise was worked out. The City Council would permit the foundation, provided it was enclosed. Her friends succumbed and the Holy Mother was tempted. "I was so wearied, more by all the trouble my helpers were having than by my own, that I thought it would not be a bad idea to accept some money until the storm subsided, and then to give it up. . . . In the end I agreed to this arrangement." (*Life,* Ch. 36, p. 256.)

Then the Lord appeared. "The Lord told me that I must not agree to such a thing."

Neither had they allowed for the power of Peter of Alacantara, now that he was at home in another world. Peter had been contacted shortly before his death by Salcedo, and had written to Teresa. He died on October 18, 1562, and appeared to her.

> His appearance caused me no fear—indeed, it made me very happy, for he always appeared as a glorified body, full of bliss, and it gave me the greatest joy to see him . . . all he said was that I was on no account to accept any endowment and asked why I would not take his advice. (*Life,* Ch. 36, p. 257.)

Teresa was now decisive. The lawsuit might continue, but the endowment would not be accepted. When she informed Salcedo of the appearance of Peter of Alacantara, he agreed with Madre Teresa. Then Father Peter Ibañez was appointed prior of the Dominican monastery of St. Thomas. In 1560, he had written to Rome for the bill of approval, and now he put all his power and prestige behind Teresa. Within a few months all opposition died down.

> He managed to get our Father Provincial to give me leave to go and live in the new house and to take some other nuns with me so that we might say the office and instruct the sisters who were there. (Ibid., p. 258.)

The long war and waiting was over, and so sometime in March, 1563, Teresa returned to St. Joseph's, taking with her four nuns, Ana de los Angeles, María Isabel, her cousin Isabel de San Pablo, and Ana de San Juan.

She adds, "It was the happiest of days for me when we went in." (Ibid.)

Before entering the convent she visited the little church, and fell into a rapture.

> I saw Christ, who seemed to be receiving me with great love, placing a crown on my head and thanking me for what I had done for His mother. . . .
> On another occasion, after Compline when we were all praying in the choir, I saw Our Lady in the greatest glory, clad in a white mantle, beneath which she seemed to be sheltering us all. From this I learned what a high degree of glory would be given to the nuns in this house. (*Life*, Ch. 36, p. 258.)

All's well that ends well. The people not only accepted the nuns, they supported them and came to love them. Today Teresa is the pride of Avila, La Santa Madre.

> Often His Majesty says to me, as a sign of His great love: "Now thou are mine and I am thine." (*Life*, Ch. 39, p. 287.)
> I often say to Him with my whole will: "To die, Lord, or to suffer: I ask nothing else of Thee for myself but this." (*Life*, Ch. 40, p. 297.)

If you ever doubt that prayer is answered, pray the above prayer and see what happens.

5.
The Foundress

Teresa was on fire with divine love for God and Church, and this fire could not be contained within the four walls of St. Joseph's Avila. Goodness diffuses itself. In spite of opposition and in the face of what appeared insurmountable obstacles she would extend her reform and her dream all over Spain.

> As time went on, my desires to do something for the good of some soul grew greater and greater, and I often felt like one who has a large amount of treasure in her charge and would like everyone to enjoy it, but whose hands are tied so that she cannot distribute it. (*Foundations*, Ch. 1, p. 3.)

The Lord often uses external events and persons to wake our consciousness. A Franciscan friar, Fra Alonso Maldonado, who had been commissary general to the West Indies, had returned home, and was invited to address the entire community at St. Joseph's. The picture he painted stirred the heart and spirit of Teresa. Millions were perishing, because there was no one to preach or to pray. She tells us what happened:

> I went to one of the hermitages, weeping sorely, and called upon Our Lord, beseeching Him to find me a means of gaining some soul for His service, when so many were being carried away by the devil. (*Foundations*, Ch. 1, p. 3.)

Her prayer and pain were answered. One night Our Lord appeared to her and said very lovingly, "Wait a little, daughter, and thou shalt see great things." (Ibid, p. 4)

Teresa was never to forget these words. Some six months later events played into her hands. Fra Giovanni Battista Rossi (latinised as Rubeo) visited Spain in response to an invitation by Philip II. Rubeo was born at Ravenna, 1507, entered the Carmelite Order at seventeen, studied at Siena and Padua, and became a professor at the University of Rome. He was elected General of the Order in 1564.

The General was received by Philip II in June 1566, travelled all over Spain, leaving a name behind him as a strong and ruthless reformer. Coming to Avila in April 11, 1567, he stayed a month, held a Provincial Chapter, at which Alonso González was elected Provincial of Castile, and Angel de Salazar Prior of the monastery at Avila.

It was with some trepidation that Teresa awaited the visit of her General.

> I was troubled, because as already has been said . . . St. Joseph's was not subject to the friars. I was afraid of two things: first that the General might be angry with me, and if he did not know how these things had happened, his anger would be justified; secondly, that he might make me go back to the Convent of the Incarnation. (*Foundations*, Ch. 2, p. 4.)

In fact, her fear was to be unfounded. Once Rubeo looked into those deep, loving, sincere eyes, he knew he was in the presence of a saintly woman. They understood each other, and she opened up her soul to him. He reassured her, and encouraged her work. He gave her patents, authorizing her to found more houses. The first was dated, in Avila, April 27, 1567, placing the new foundations under the jurisdiction of the Order, and stipulating that no more than twenty-five nuns live in the same house. The second patent, dated in Madrid, May 16, 1567, limited the foundations to new and old Castile. This was to cause Teresa much trouble later. With genuine affection towards her superior, Teresa writes:

> I was sorry when I saw my Father General returning to Rome. I had conceived a great love for him, and felt very much deserted when he left. He showed me very real and genuine kindness . . . he was one to whom the Lord must have granted great favors. (*Foundations*, Ch. 2, p. 6.)

Teresa had another dream and request granted. She knew how important it was to have some friars following the same Rule as the nuns. She prayed a lot about this. The General listened to her request and sent patents for the foundation of two reformed monasteries for the friars. The patent is dated August 14, 1567, from Barcelona. Teresa had the patent and the permission, but she did not have a friar in the province to put them into effect. She writes humorously, "Here was a poor Discalced nun, without help from anywhere, except from the Lord, loaded with patents and good wishes, but devoid of all possibility of making them effective." (*Foundations*, Ch. 2, p. 7.)

Medina del Campo

Medina del Campo, some seventy-five miles from Avila, was chosen by Teresa as the place for her second foundation. Medina was a prosperous city, and Teresa had friends there. Baltasar Álvarez was rector of the Jesuit College, and Antonio Heredia was the Carmelite prior. She knew she could trust these men.

Julian of Avila went ahead to find a suitable house and obtain permission. Eventually he rented a house near the Augustinian Monastery.

Teresa, with borrowed money, six professed nuns, Julian of Avila as Chaplain, and all her necessities in a wagon, left Avila on August 12, 1567, on her first missionary journey. She did not receive a warm send off from the Avilans. "Some said I was mad, others, that this folly would soon come to an end. The bishop thought it the height of folly." (*Foundations*, Ch. 3, p. 9.)

Nonplussed by these uncharitable sentiments, Teresa set out with her convent on wheels, Christ's restless gadabout. In her covered wagon, the little community of six carried out their prayer life, times for silence, and Mass every morning. They had just reached the outskirts of Arevalo when the cleric, Alonso Esteban, came riding toward them with bad news. Alonso Alvarez, from whom Julian of Avila rented the house, had withdrawn his consent, under pressure from the Augustinians, who did not want another convent too close to them. Disappointed, but undaunted, Teresa decided to forge ahead, trusting on divine providence. To her great delight, Fr. Bañez, O.P., was in Arevalo, and he thought it would be possible to settle the difficulties with the Augustinians. Next morning the Carmelite Prior, Antonio de Heredia, who had ridden some thirty-five miles that night, arrived at Arevalo to suggest that they take the house he had agreed to buy from Doña Maria Suárez. It was a tumble-down shack, but it had to do. At midnight, August 14, 1567, Teresa and her little band arrived at Medina. They knocked on the doors of the Carmelite monastery, and Fra Antonio welcomed them. Then, with three friars guiding them, this motley group of Carmelite nuns and monks made their way through the streets of Medina during the early hours of the morning. Julian observed, "We looked like gypsies who had been robbing some church." Preparations were already under way for the great fiesta next day in honor of Our Lady, and our weary pilgrims ran into a flock of spirited bulls and their drivers on the street. We need little imagination to reconstruct the comment.

Let's recount Teresa's first impressions of her new convent:

> The walls seemed to me in a very tumble-down condition, and by day they appeared worse still. The Lord must have been pleased that the blessed Father should have become blind or he would have seen that it was not fitting to put the Most Holy Sacrament in such a place . . . there were holes in the roof, and the walls were not plastered. . . . We did not know what to do for nails, so we started to look round the walls, and at last after some trouble we collected a sufficient number. Then the the banging was begun, while we nuns set to work to clean the floor. We all worked so quickly that by daybreak the altar was set up and the bell hung in the gallery, so that Mass was said immediately. We had the Most Holy Sacrament reserved.

And she adds, as mission was accomplished for the feast of the Assumption, 1567: "I was very pleased, for it gives me the greatest joy, when I see one more church, in which there is reservation of the Most Holy Sacrament." (*Foundations*, Ch. 3, pp.11–12.)

Her joy was of short duration. After Mass, she looked out a window, only to see that the walls had collapsed. Fear gripped her heart. Her enemies had reason to criticize her, and she dreaded the desecration of the Blessed Sacrament by the Lutherans. A terrible depression set in, and she felt she had been deluded about the entire project. She contemplated abandoning the whole foundation. Some men were found to guard the Blessed Sacrament night and day, and she herself would get up at night to make sure they did not sleep.

At the end of a week a merchant named Beas de Medina offered the Carmelites the upper part of his own home. It had a very large gilded hall, which could be used as a church. Doña Elena de Quiroga, a niece of the great Cardinal, helped them. Doña Elena herself took the Carmelite habit on October 14, 1581, at Medina del Campo, where her daughter, Jerónima de la Encarnación, was already a nun. Her money and her influence were now appreciated by Teresa, who could repair Doña Maria's house and make it a fit place for the Blessed Sacrament and her nuns. Teresa could now enjoy peace of mind, as she rested, before beginning her next project.

Reform of the Friars

Teresa was continually preoccupied about monasteries for the friars. She prayed about it, and then one day opened up her heart to Antonio de Heredia, the Prior of the Carmelite monastery at Medina del Campo. Antonio was delighted and promised that he himself would be the first to join.

> I took that for a joke and told him so, for although besides being a learned man, he was a good friar, given to recollection, very studious and fond of his cell, he did not seem to me to be at all the man for the beginning of an enterprise of this kind; he had not sufficient spirituality, nor could he have endured the necessary privations, being delicate in health and not accustomed to them. (*Foundations,* Ch. 3, p. 14.)

Antonio felt the Lord calling him to a more strict form of life, and he even contemplated joining the Carthusians who would have accepted him, but Mother Teresa was not fully satisfied as yet and made him wait a year, a year during which he was to be persecuted and suffer a great deal. It was a year of probation. The Lord tests founders.

It was here at Medina that the first meetings took place between the two great Carmelite reformers, Teresa of Jesus and

John of the Cross. The young friar was then known as John of St. Matthias and had been ordained a few days previously at the Carmelite monastery of Santa Ana. John was twenty-five years of age, and Teresa was fifty-two—old enough to be his mother.

Juan de Yepes was born in 1542 at Fontiveros, near Avila. His father, Gonzálo de Yepes, came from a good Toledan family, and his mother, Catalina Alvarez, was a silk and wool weaver. Poverty came over them, and shortly after the birth of Juan, Gonzálo died, leaving his widow with three young children, Francisco, Luis, and John. Life was hard and young John knew hunger.

One day he fell into deep water and was rescued by Our Lady, the Lady of whom he was to sing years later, whose Order he would reform and whose habit he would wear.

When he was nine, his mother moved to Arevalo to work for a weaver. Later the family moved to Medina del Campo, and there John worked in a hospital, collecting money and caring for the victims of smallpox. He studied at the Jesuit college. In 1563 he became a Carmelite and took the name of John of St. Matthias. The Carmelites sent him to the *studium generale* at Salamanca, the Athens of Spain, and there he enjoyed a good scholastic education.

Let us read Mother Teresa's account of her first meeting with this extraordinary saint and mystic.

> Shortly afterwards there happened to arrive a young father who was studying in Salamanca. With him was a companion who told me great things about the life which that Father was leading. His name is Fray Juan de la Cruz. I praised Our Lord, and when I spoke to the friar, I liked him very much. He told me that he too was preparing to go to the Carthusians. I described to him what I had in view and begged him earnestly to wait until the Lord gave us a monastery, pointing out what a great blessing it would be, if he were destined for a higher life, that he should lead it within his own Order, and how much better service he would render to Our Lord. He gave me his word to do this provided there were no long delay. When I saw that I had two friars to make a beginning with, the thing seemed to me settled, although I was still not satisfied with the Prior. (*Foundations*, Ch. 3, pp.14–15.)

It is said that Teresa burst into the community room, exclaiming "Blessed be God, for I have a friar and a half for the foundation of my monastery." John was a few inches above five feet tall.

Malagón

Doña Luisa de la Cerda asked Teresa to make a foundation at Malagon. She was very fond of our saint. Malagón was a small place, and Teresa felt it would never support a community. But Doña Luisa promised to endow the house. On Palm Sunday, 1568, the nuns opened another convent at Malagón in honor of St. Joseph. The house proved to be too noisy and unsuitable for contemplation, and the good Doña Luisa allowed them another and better house in a quieter part of the city the next year.

Valladolid

Don Bernardino de Mendoza, brother of the bishop of Avila, had visited Teresa and offered her a house with a big garden and vineyard a short distance from the city of Valladolid. It was too good a gift to refuse. Some two months later, Don Bernardino, who had not lived a holy life, fell sick and died, unable to confess his sins, and the Lord let Teresa know how He had compassion on him for his generosity by giving a house for a convent in honor of His Mother, and he would not be freed from purgatory until the first Mass had been celebrated there. This worried Teresa, and she hastened to found the convent. Arriving at Valladolid on the feast of St. Lawrence, 1568, she inspected the new property, and found that, although beautiful, it was dangerously near the river and needed repairing. Sick herself and somewhat discouraged, she worked away. The first Mass was offered, and Teresa had a vision of Don Bernardino being released from purgatory. "I saw a vision of the young man, with a happy and resplendent countenance, standing beside the priest with his hands joined together, and thanking me for what I had done to enable his soul to be freed from purgatory and go to heaven. (*Foundations*, Ch. 10, p. 48.) (Note that Don Bernardino's liberation is to be seen in one of Ruben's paintings in Antwerp.)

Teresa and her little community took possession of the convent of the Conception of Our Lady of Carmel on the feast of the Assumption, August 15, 1568. They were not there long when sickness broke out and Don Bernardino's sister, Doña Maria de Mendoza, widow of Don Francisco de los Cabos, who had been Mayor of Leon and Secretary to Charles V, kindly offered them a foundation in a more healthy location and nearer the city. They took possession on February 3, 1569. Among the treasures of this convent is the Valladolid autograph of "The Way of Perfection."

Duruelo

Rafael Mejia Velázquez a relative, offered Teresa a farmhouse at Duruelo and some eight leagues from Avila. Duruelo was a little village with some twenty families and this poor place was to be immortalized as the first place to have a monastery of Discalced Carmelite Friars under the leadership of John of the Cross and Antonio.

Sometime in June 1568, Teresa, Julian of Avila and Sr. Antonia de Espiritu Santo, visited the farmhouse. She wrote:

> I always remember the fatigue of that roundabout journey. We arrived only a little before nightfall. When we entered the house, we found it in such a condition that we dared not spend the night there, so dirty was it and so numerous were the harvesters who were about. It had a fair sized porch, a room divided into two, with a loft above it, and a little kitchen. That is all there was of the building which was to be our monastery. . . . My companion, though a much better person than I am, and a great lover of penance, could not bear the thought of my founding a monastery there, "Mother, she said, "I am certain that no one however good and spiritual could endure this. You must not consider it." (*Foundations*, Ch. 13, p. 62.)

Teresa thought differently. The reform of the friars could begin quietly in this poor Bethlehem and the powers that be would offer no resistance, while they might well object to a great big house. She spoke to Fra Antonio at Medina. The noble Prior answered, "He would be willing to live, not only there, but in a pigsty if Fra John of the Cross agreed with him." (*Foundations*, Ch. 13, p. 63.) Teresa admired the courage of her two sons.

The foundress stayed at Medina as negotiations went ahead. The Carmelite Provincial, Fra Angel de Salazar, was not very enthusiastic over Duruelo, but Antonio went ahead collecting necessary items. Meanwhile, the Holy Mother took John of the Cross with her to make the Valladolid foundation and instructed him about the Rule and way of life. Her humble comment, "He was so good a man that I, at least, could have learned much more from him than he from me." (*Foundations*, Ch. 13, p. 64). This was a charismatic moment in the lives of our saints.

The nuns at Medina made a habit for John, and he was the first friar to receive it from Mother Teresa herself. He took off his shoes and the first Discalced Carmelite friar was clothed and unshod to walk his way into the history of the order and the church.

John of the Cross celebrated the first Mass at Duruelo on November 28, 1568. Teresa herself visited John and Antonio during the Lent of 1569. This is what happened:

> Fra Antonio de Jesus was sweeping out the church porch with that happy expression which never leaves him. 'How is this Father?' I said to him. 'Whatever has become of your dignity?' He answered, 'I curse the time when I had any!' Then I went to the little church and was amazed to see what spirituality the Lord had inspired there. And I was not alone in this, for two merchants, who were friends of mine, and had come as far as this with me from Medina, did nothing but weep. There were so many crosses about and so many skulls! (*Foundations*, Ch. 14, p. 66.)

The choir was in the loft. They had converted the two corners next to the church into hermitages, which were filled with hay to keep out the cold. Since the roof was low, they had to sit or lie. The hermitages had two little windows overlooking the altar. After finishing midnight matins, the friars would remain here in prayer until Prime. So earnestly did they pray that sometimes their habits were white with snow without their noticing it.

During the day they went out barefooted to preach and hear confessions. In gratitude and appreciation, the local people supplied ample food. Mother Teresa was highly edified, but she left Duruelo with a word of advice: "Being weak and wicked myself, not to practice such severity in matters of penance, I was afraid that the devil might be trying to bring their work to an end before my hopes could be fulfilled." (*Foundations,* Ch. 14, p. 69.) She left happy.

John and Antonio did not remain at Duruelo very long, for an admirer, Don Luis de Toledo, lord of the five towns, offered them a church and place at Mancera some four miles away. Here Don Luis had built a church for a picture of Our Lady. The Carmelites took it over and continued their prayer life here.

Toledo, the City of Merchants

Martín Ramírez was a wealthy Toledo merchant, who decided to found a church but not until after his death. When the Jesuit, Pablo Hernández, to whom Teresa at an earlier date confessed her sins, heard of this, he persuaded Martín to found a monastery instead of a church. The honorable old gentleman consented, but before the final deeds were signed he died, leaving his brother Alonso Alvarez Ramírez in charge.

Teresa herself reached Toledo, on March 24, 1509, and was received with great joy by her old friend Doña Luisa. Her companions were Isabel de San Pablo and Isabel de Santo Domingo. The faithful Julian of Avila was sick, and Gonzálo de Aranda took his place.

The long negotiation began, and Teresa found Alonso Alvarez and Diego Ortiz, a theologian, not very amenable to reason. He stipulated so many conditions that he almost drove Mother Teresa out of her mind. Moreover, she could not find a suitable house.

Authorization was slow. The good will of the other religious orders was lacking, and authority from the archbishop and town was slow in coming. The archbishop, Bartolomé Carranza, was a prisoner of the Inquisition, suspected of Lutheranism, and Don Gómez Tello Giron was now the Ecclesiastical Governor of the diocese. Teresa spent two months searching and haggling. Eventually, she decided on a more direct and personal approach.

> I determined to approach the Governor (Giron) and going to a church near his house, sent to beg him to be good enough to come and speak to me. . . . When I saw him, I told him that it was hard that there should be women anxious to live in such austerity and perfection, and strictly enclosed, while those who

> had never done such things themselves, but were living a comfortable life, should try to hinder work which was of such service to Our Lord. I told him all this and a good deal more, speaking with a resoluteness with which I was inspired by Our Lord. This touched his heart and before I left him he gave me the license. (*Foundations*, Ch. 15, p. 71.)

Teresa left happy, and with her three or four ducats and bought two paintings to hang behind the altar, two mattresses and a blanket. Teresa and three ducats nothing ... Teresa, God and three ducats, anything.

Negotiations between Teresa and Diego Ortiz broke down, and there she was in Toledo without friends, money, or patrons. Even her friend Doña Luisa played cool and distant. When human effort had failed her, Teresa turned to prayer and help came from an unexpected quarter. A holy Franciscan, Martín de la Cruz, sent a young student named Andrada to the rescue. Andrada came to her one morning while she was attending Mass, a most unlikely kind of real-estate agent. Teresa introduced Andrada to the nuns.

> They had a good laugh at me and told me not to rely on a person like that or the result would be that our project would come to everybody's knowledge. But I would not listen to them, for as he had been sent by that servant of God, I was confident that there must be something he could do and there was some mystery about it. (*Foundations*, Ch. 15, p. 72.)

Teresa sent her young envoy off, bound to strictest secrecy, and next day he returned with the keys to a house. The house was suitable, and the nuns stayed there a year. "The ways of God amaze me," exclaimed Teresa. The rich could not help her, and a poor student came to the rescue. It's good to know that his young man later married and had a large family.

Teresa took possession of the house on May 1569, and Andrada must have been astounded when he noticed that her only possessions were two mattresses and a blanket. Teresa and the two Isabels got to work, found a few workmen, and the Carmelite Fathers provided the liturgical furnishing.

But the trouble was not over yet. When the owner of the house heard that it had been made into a church, she raised hell. Teresa quieted her down with the promise of a good price.

Members of the council were enraged, not knowing that she had received a license from the governor. They were astounded by the audacity of this woman, and tried to prohibit the Carmelites from having Mass. Once again Don Pedro Manrique came to their rescue.

For some days the nuns tasted poverty. They were cold. "We had not so much as a scrap of brushwood to broil a sardine on." (*Foundations,* Ch. 15, p. 74.) They were grateful, when some kindhearted soul left a bundle of wood in the church. It seemed incredible that Doña Luisa should have allowed them to live in such poverty, but the rich have a way of forgetting. Some friends rallied to their side. The convent grew and prospered. Soon the nuns looked sad. "We do not seem to be poor any longer." (*Foundations,* Ch. 15, p. 75.)

The Ramírez family eventually handed over the money to buy some houses, providing Teresa undertook to build a chapel in which Don Martín and his family would be buried. The chapel was dedicated to St. Joseph.

By Pentecost, May 28, 1569, the convent in Toledo was fully founded, and Teresa looked forward to some time for peace, prayer, and contemplation. This luxury was not granted her, for a messenger came from Ana de Mendoza y la Cerda, Princess of Eboli, demanding a foundation at Pastrana.

Pastrana

Ana de Mendoza y de la Cerda was the wife of the second most powerful man in Spain, and Teresa was diplomatic enough not to hurt her feelings, for this great lady was as capricious and whimsical as she was powerful and noble. At the age of sixteen she married Roy Gomez de Silva, a Portuguese, who had come to Spain as a child with Doña Leonar de Mascareñas to be a page in the court of Charles V. There he became the special companion of Philip II, who later took him wherever he went, and made him his adviser. The Princess Ana was now thirty years old, the mother of nine children, but still as beautiful and vivacious as a teenager. An accident earlier in life had left her with one eye, the black patch which covered the other rather enhanced her beauty and the mystery of her personality. Hence, history knows her as the blind Princess of Eboli.

The whim of the Princess was law, and when she wanted something, she got it. Now she wanted a Carmelite monastery at Pastrana. The invitation worried Mother Teresa, and she went to the Lord in prayer. "A message came to me from Our Lord. telling me to go without fail, for there was far more afoot than that foundation, and to take with me the Rule and Constitutions." (*Foundations*, Ch. 17, p. 80.)

This heavenly message was not sufficient in itself to convince Teresa. Deep down she had the intuition of trouble ahead, and so consulted her confessor, Vicente Barrón, O.P. The good Dominican told her to go, and so she left Toledo the day after Pentecost, May 30, 1569, travelling in style this time in the magnificent coach of the princess. Isabel de Santo Domingo and the Carmelite, Fra Pedro Muriel, went with her. They passed through Madrid and stayed a few days at the Franciscan convent founded by Doña Leonor de Mascareñas. It was here she met extraordinary men, one an engineer, the other a portrait painter, who were living as hermits near Pastrana.

Ambrosio Mariano Azaro was a Neapolitan doctor of noble birth, and a skilled mathematician and engineer. As theologian he attended the Council of Trent. He had served in the court of Queen Catherine of Austria, wife of Sigismund II, King of Poland. He became a Knight of the Order of St. John of Jersualem. Later he left the Polish court to join the forces of Philip II in the low countries, and fought at the battle of St. Quentin. Subsequently, he was unjustly accused of murder and spent two years in jail. He went to Spain, where Philip II engaged him in the canalization of the Tagus and the Guadalquiver. Then he met the hermit, P. Mateo de la Fuente, and decided to become a hermit. In 1568, Philip II summoned him to irrigate the country around Aranjuez with water from the Tagus. On his way back to the hermitage he met Teresa.

The other soldier of fortune was also from Naples, John Narduch, who had come on a pilgrimage to Compostela only to remain in Spain as a hermit. He studied painting and was later to draw a portrait of Mother Teresa. When the picture was finished, she said, "God forgive you, Fra Juan. To think that after all I have suffered at your hands you should paint me so bleary eyed and ugly." (Walsh, p. 367) This portrait of Juan de la Miseria has come down as the best and most faithful that we have of St. Teresa, and it does not flatter her, and does show her as bleary-eyed.

The Council of Trent decreed that hermits should join an Order, and when Teresa showed her Rule to Mariano and John, they were won over. Roy Gómez had given him a good hermitage, and he would give this over to the Order. The provincial and bishop cooperated, and Teresa had founded her second monastery of friars, at Pastrana. Mariano and John joined as lay-brothers. Mariano was ordained priest in 1574, on the order of the general, and was to play a historic role in the reform during the following years.

Meanwhile, trouble brewed at the palace. Teresa arrived only to find that the building was not ready. The princess haggled and haggled over endowments and insisted that an Augustinian nun, Catalina Machuca, become a Carmelite at Pastrana. Teresa did not want her, and Catalina was to avenge herself later, by letting the princess know all about the *Life* of Teresa. Ana demanded the copy of the *Life*, and even though she promised secrecy, before long the household was reading this most personal and sacred document. Teresa felt insulted and betrayed.

The convent of nuns was eventually opened on June 28, 1569, with pealing of bells and solemn processions. Ana de Mendoza y la Cerda, Princess of Éboli, did things in style. She also dispatched Mother Teresa in style back to Toledo in her own luxurious coach. When a mad priest saw the holy mother getting out of it, in front of the convent, he insulted her in the parlor. "So, you're the Saint who is deceiving everybody and going about in a carriage." Teresa's humble answer was, "You are the only one courageous enough to point out my faults." (Auclair p. 211) From that day on, Teresa travelled in much poorer carts.

Salamanca

The Rector of the Jesuits at Salamanca, Martin Gutiérrez, invited Mother Teresa to Salamanca. Although the city was poor, she consented at once, and obtained the license from the bishop. On her way she passed through Avila, where Anne of St. Bartholomew had become the first lay sister, and the beautiful Ana de Lobera was now named Anne of Jesus.

Teresa took María del Sacramento along with her, a tried

veteran. They arrived at the house in Salamanca, on All Saints Eve, 1570. The house had been rented to university students who left reluctantly, leaving the place in a mess. Teresa describes the night of All Saints in that big lonely house.

> The house was very large and roomy, with a great many attics and my companion could not get the students out of her mind. She thought that one of them might still be hiding there. We shut ourselves up in a room where the straw was, for this was the first thing I got in for the foundation, as if we had some straw we should not be without a bed. That night we slept on the straw with two or three blankets which had been lent us. . . . The devil must have helped in putting thoughts of danger into her mind in order to upset me, for with my weak heart, very little is enough to do this. "What are you looking for?" I asked her. "Nobody can possibly get in here." "Mother," she replied, "I am wondering what you would do all alone if I were to die here. . . ." I said to her, "Well, sister, I shall consider what is to be done if the occasion arises, now let me go to sleep." (*Foundations*, Ch. 19, p. 94.)

A good example of the pragmatic Teresa.

As they had two bad nights, sleep soon drove all fear away. More nuns arrived the next day, and the good mother saw to it that the place was clean and proper. "In this respect, God has shown me great favor, for I have always liked to be in the forefront of work, and I would provide even the smallest things for the comfort and convenience of the nuns, just as if I had to live in that house all my life." (*Foundations*, Ch. 19, p. 94.) The foundress was a compassionate, thoughtful mother.

The community of St. Joseph's, Salamanca, grew and was blessed while the holy mother spent some ten weeks with them, but the old house was always cold and damp, and three years later they transferred to another more suitable convent. They took possession Michaelmas Eve, August, 1573. Teresa did all in her power to make sure her nuns were healthy, happy, and joyful. Above all, she wanted them to cultivate the virtue of joy, which to her was greater than penance.

Alba de Tormes

Francisco Velazquez, contabador of the Duke of Alba, and his wife Teresa de Layz, offered Teresa a house at Alba de

Tormes. This Teresa had an extraordinary story. Born of noble parents, of pure Christian blood, she was the fifth daughter. Her parents were so disappointed that they did not have a son that they reluctantly baptized her after birth and then left her alone unwanted. The woman who looked after her found her the night of the third day, thought she was dead, took the little thing in her arms and exclaimed "Why, my poor little child, anyone would think you were not a Christian." The child raised its head and said, "I am." Teresa married a man she had never seen, a rich graduate of the university of Salamanca, who became its treasurer. In 1566 the Duke of Alba employed him as his treasurer and although wealthy and successful, he felt poor, because he had no children. Teresa prayed and the only consolation given her was a vision: near a well, she beheld a beautiful flowery meadow, and St. Andrew spoke to her, "These are different children from those thou desirest." (*Foundations*, Ch. 20, p. 100.)

She knew she must found a convent, and a Franciscan told her about the Discalced Carmelites. Teresa went to Alba de Tormes. She knew the nuns could not live there without an endowment, and Father Bañez, who was now teaching at the university of Salamanca, persuaded her to accept. She wrote, "I have no belief in the foundation of a house with an endowment that is inadequate. I think it better that it should not be founded at all." (*Foundations*, Ch. 20, p. 103.) The foundation was made there on January 25, 1571.

It was here at Alba de Tormes that Our Lord addressed these words to Teresa, "Thou art continually desiring trials, yet when I send them thou refusest them. I order things according to what I know to be thy will and not according to thy sensuality and weakness. Strive, for thou seest how I am helping thee. I have wised thee to gain this crown. In thy time thou shalt see the Order of the Virgin make great progress." (*Spiritual Relations* XIV, vol. I, p. 340.)

From Alba Teresa returned in March, through Salamanca to Avila, where she met Anne of St. Bartholomew, the first lay sister, her future great and loyal friend and companion. Ana García came from a poor peasant family. As a child she was favored by Our Lord. She grew up beautiful and intelligent, but spurned the many suitors who wanted her as wife. At the age of twenty she was given a vision of a convent, where silence and poverty reigned, and later under the guidance of her parish priest, she identified it as St. Joseph's in Avila. There Ana entered and St. Teresa loved this simple lay sister who was so full of her favorite virtues—common sense and humor. Ana was beside Teresa all during her last hours on earth, when she died at Alba de Tormes.

Years later she accompanied Anne of Jesus to found the Reformed Carmel in France.

6.
Light and Darkness

During those early years of the seventies, Teresa enjoyed many mystical favors. We may read an account in her *Spiritual Relations*. (XIII, vol. I. pp. 339, 341, 342, 343.)

One day, when I was greatly concerned about the relief of the order, the Lord said to me, Do what lies in thee and leave me alone and trouble thyself about nothing. Rejoice in the blessing which has been given thee, and which is very great. My Father delights in thee and the Holy Spirit loves thee. . . .

One day after communicating, I had the clearest vision of Our Lord. He said to me: Thou seest me here, daughter, It is I. Show me thy hands! And He seemed to take them and put them to His side. He said, See my wounds. Thou art not without me. Life is short and soon passes. From some of the things He said to me I learned that, since ascending into the heavens, He had never come down to earth again to communicate Himself to anyone, except in the Most Holy Sacrament. He told me that, after His resurrection, He had visited Our Lady, because she had been in great need. . . .

My soul began to kindle with fire and I seemed to have the clearest realization of the presence of the Most Holy Trinity in an intellectual vision, through which in a sort of picture, or figure of the truth, my soul learned how God is Three and One. It seemed to me all Three Persons were speaking and were distinctly present within my soul. They told me that from that day onward I should find myself better in three respects, for each of the Three Persons was granting me a favour.

One would give me charity;

One, joy in suffering;
One, a consciousness of that charity, with an enkindled soul. I now realized the meaning of these words spoken by the Lord—that the Three Divine Persons will be with the soul that is in grace—for I experienced their presence within me. . . .

Today while I was thinking about this, the Lord told me that I was wrong to think of things of the soul in the same terms as those of the body. I must realize that the two are very different, and that the soul has a capacity for great fruition. This seemed to be shown me by the illustration of a sponge which takes up and absorbs water. Just so my soul was filled with the Godhead and in a certain sense it had within itself the fruition and possession of the Three Persons. I also heard these words: Labour not to hold me enclosed within myself, but to enclose thyself within me. It seemed to me that these Three Persons were present within my soul and that I saw Them there, and that They communicated Themselves to all created things, and never either failed to do this or ceased to be with me.

Prioress of the Incarnation

The Lord with these special favors was preparing His bride for the loftiest graces, but He had more work and crosses in store for her. Teresa was needed at her old convent of the Incarnation. Much against her will, the apostolic visitator, Pedro Fernández, asked her to be Prioress there and restore law and order to her old alma mater. Only a vision from the Lord could move her. He appeared. "Oh, daughter, daughter, these nuns of the Incarnation are sisters of mine and thou holdest back from helping them. Take courage then—See, I will it so, and it is not as difficult as it seems to thee; thou thinkest that by thy going there, these other houses will lose, whereas in reality both will gain. Resist not, for great is my power." (*Spiritual Relations*, XV, p. 344.)

Teresa did not resist, and ruled as Prioress at the Incarnation for three years. One hundred and thirty rather disgruntled nuns awaited her arrival with very mixed emotions. Some resented the imposition of this woman upon them: their right to vote had been suppressed, as they surmised that their lives of laxity, visits, and dissipation would soon come to an end.

Teresa took the good and gentle little Anne of St. Bartholomew along with her. She needed human solace, and Anne served as ointment to the frayed nerves and tempers of the sisters, as Teresa took up office in October 1571. The provincial, Angel de Salazar, was there to induct her. He read the patent amid jeers and blows. Hell broke loose in the choir. Sides were taken and war waged among those "devils." Finally, a constable restored peace. Teresa had once written, "I fear a discontented nun more than I fear many devils." She must have been very fearful that day. However, she remained calm and master of the situation.

Our diplomatic Prioress made one master move. Leaving choir for a few minutes, she returned with the statue of Our Lady and placed it in the stall of the Prioress. Sitting down at Our Lady's feet, she exclaimed, "Sisters, here is your Prioress, Our Lady of Mercy." She placed a statue of St. Joseph in the stall of the Sub-Prioress. She told them not to fear her, for she, too, had her weaknesses, and she was there to serve and love them. Gradually the community was won over. Isabel de la Cruz was appointed her Sub-Prioress, and together, gently but firmly, these two women reformed the Incarnation. She also called in the help of John of the Cross. Teresa built a little hut for him nearby, and her "little Seneca" guided the spirits of these poor sisters along the way of perfection. I wonder if these nuns realized that they were being blessed by two of the greatest mystical saints that ever lived. John was joined by Fray Guzmán de San Matias, and these two Discalced friars took the place of the more liberal Calced priests at the convent. Prayer, discipline, and the business acumen of Teresa restored religious life and order.

Many of Teresa's letters date from these years, and they portray a motherly prioress seeking the material welfare of her daughters, knowing that she had to feed them before she could reform them, and so we find her begging money, vegetables and turkeys from benefactors like Francisco de Salcedo, her sister Juana, and the Duchess of Alba. These letters really reveal our saint as a down-to-earth human woman. For Lent she abolished all visits, but when one gentleman would not take "no" for an answer, the Mother Prioress faced the bravado in the parlor; and when she threatened to call the king and have his head cut off, the blusterer soon left her alone. Teresa could be gracious and charming, but she was also very strong and determined.

Mystical Marriage

Teresa of Jesus was the bride of Christ and the loving daughter of Mary, the Mother of God. Heaven was very close to our mystic. On January 19, 1572, Teresa had this mystical experience.

> At the beginning of the Salve, I saw the Mother of God with a great multitude of angels, descend to the Prioress's stall, where Our Lady is enthroned and seat herself there. I do not believe I saw the image then, but only this Lady. . . . Our Lady remained there during the whole of the Salve, and said to me, "Thou has done well to place me here; I will be here when praises are offered to my Son and will present them to Him." After that I remained in the state of prayer which I experience when my soul is in the company of the Most Holy Trinity. I thought that the person of the Father drew me to Himself and spoke words that were most comfortable. Among them were these, which showed me the love He had for me: "I give thee my Son and the Holy Spirit and this Virgin. What canst thou give me?" (*Spiritual Relations*, XXV, p. 346.)

On Palm Sunday, Teresa was seized by a rapture, and when she recovered her mouth was full of the blood of Christ.

> On Palm Sunday, after communion, my faculties were completely suspended, so that I was not able even to swallow the Sacred Form, and finding it in my mouth, when I had come around a little, I really thought that my mouth was full of blood. I also thought that my face and my whole body were covered with it, as though the Lord had just shed it. It seemed warm to me and made me feel excessively tender. The Lord said to me: "Daughter, it is my will that my Blood shall profit thee; be not afraid that my mercy will fail thee. To shed this blood cost me great pain, and, as thou seest, thou hast the fruition of it with great joy. I am rewarding thee well for the welcome thou hast given me this day. (*Spiritual Relations*, XXVI, p. 346.)

St. John of the Cross was rather cautious when it came to mystical phenomena, and he often mortified Teresa, by withholding what he considered earthly pleasures. He knew that his spiritual mother liked large hosts, and one morning during Mass, he gave her half a host. Teresa may have been somewhat upset, but her heavenly Bridegroom gave her one of her greatest spiritual experiences which was to seal the mystical marriage between them, in mid-November, 1572.

> On the octave-day of St. Martin, I was making my communion, and the Father, Fray John of the Cross, who was giving me the Most Holy Sacrament, divided the Host between another sister and myself. I thought he was doing this, not for lack of Hosts, but because he wanted to mortify me, for I had told him that I was very pleased when the Hosts were large ones, though I knew I should be receiving the Lord, whole and entire, if I took only the smallest particle. "Have no fear, daughter,' His Majesty said to me, "that anyone will be able to part thee from me." Then He revealed Himself to me in an imaginary vision, most interiorly, and gave me His right hand, saying to me, "Behold this nail. It is a sign that from today onward thou shalt be my BRIDE. Until now, thou hast not merited this, but henceforth thou shalt regard my honour not only as that of thy Creator and King and God, but as that of My very BRIDE. My honour is thine, and thine, Mine." (*Spiritual Relations*, XXXV, pp. 351-352)

For a whole day Teresa of Jesus, the mystical bride of the Lord, remained in mystical absorption. A new phase in her inner life had begun. Teresa enjoyed her Thabor, but it was to lead her to Calvary.

Meanwhile, she continued to have her visions and ecstasies. On the feast of the Blessed Trinity, John of the Cross visited Teresa at the grill in the parlor of the Incarnation. The topic of conversation must have been the mystery of the Blessed Trinity, because for months Teresa had received new lights and insights on this august mystery. They both fell into deep ecstasy, and when Beatriz de Ocampo came in, she beheld an awesome sight: John of the Cross, under the power of the Spirit, was raised upwards and was touching the ceiling.

In August, 1573, Teresa was in Salamanca, transferring her nuns to a new House. Julian of Avila has left us an account of the journey:

> To avoid the terrible heat, the little band left late at night, and in the darkness, first Antonio of Jesus and later a servant girl, fell from their mounts. Then the donkey carrying the money was lost, and spent a long time in search. Next night they lost Mother Teresa herself. Search parties were sent out, but eventually the astute woman bribed a local peasant to guide her back. After those adventures they needed a restful inn.

> We stumbled upon an inn so overcrowded with muleteers that they were even sleeping on the ground, and it was impossible to take one step without treading on harness or on sleeping men. At last, we found a small space for our holy Mother and sisters, although there were but six feet of empty space. To fit in at all, they were obliged to stand up. Such inns had one good point about them: we impatiently awaited the hour of our departure. (Auclair, p. 245.)

Segovia

On March 19, 1574, Teresa, together with John of the Cross, founded the Monastery of St. Joseph at Segovia. Julian of Avila and a generous layman, called Antonio de Gaytán, went with her. A widowed lady, Doña Ana de Jimena, offered the property. Teresa had a verbal agreement with the bishop, who happened to be absent in March, and his vicar-general refused to allow Mass there. He even threatened to imprison John of the Cross. Teresa had taken possession, and nobody would frighten or move her. She held her ground, although they did remove the Blessed Sacrament. Teresa spent some six months in Segovia, haggling with Mercedarians, Franciscans, and chancery officials. "It seemed no foundation could be made without our having trouble of some kind, and during the six months that I was there I was ill the whole time." (*Foundations*, Ch. 21, p. 105.)

Severe fever of body and dark aridity of soul kept Teresa in deep pain. Her three years in office as Prioress of the Incarnation was coming to a close, and Teresa left Segovia for Avila on September 30, 1574.

The Princess of Eboli Becomes a Carmelite

Ruy Gómez, Prince of Éboli, died at Madrid, July 29, 1573. Two Discalced Carmelite priests were present, Baltasar of Jesus and Ambrosio Mariano. His wife the princess, the extraordinary Ana de Mendoza y la Cerda, was not resigned to his death, nor to a life in the world without the man she loved. He had left her with ten children, but these could not assuage her mad grief. In a scene that might be taken out of the pages of a classic opera, while her husband lay in state in his Madrid palace, she took the Carmelite habit from Fray Mariano, draped it about her own beautiful body, and declared that she was renouncing the world to become a Carmelite cloistered nun at Pastrana. Without consulting anybody, without getting permission from Teresa, prioress, or bishop, she set off for the convent, with her mother, servants, and entourage. When Mother Isabel, the prioress at Pastrana, saw this she exclaimed, "What, the Princess a nun, it will be the end of this convent." And it was the princess who took the lovely name of Anna of the Mother of God, but that was all that was lovely about her. Peace flew out the windows of the cloister, as the willful and moody princess took over. She was above all rules, constitutions, and traditions. Pastrana was her convent, and she could do what she wanted. To add to the comedy she was five months pregnant. After a few months of religious life, she returned to her palace, where she was more at home, but from here, she continued her persecution of the the Carmelites. She refused them food and revenue.

When Mother Teresa heard of the sad predicament at Pastrana, she acted firm and fast. She decided to smuggle the nuns from Pastrana and bring them to the new convent at Segovia. Julian of Avila and Antonio Gaytán scaled the cloister walls at night and secretly led the fourteen nuns out of the cloister through the village to a few carts that were waiting on the outskirts. On the way to Segovia, they were almost drowned crossing the river, but Julian eventually landed them safe and sound into the arms of Teresa at their new convent.

Beas

Beas is on the border of Castile and Andalusia, and it was here Teresa founded her next convent on the feast of St. Matthias, February 25, 1575. The donors were the two daughters of a local gentleman, Sancho Rodriguez de Sandoval, and Doña Catalina Godinez. Maria and Catalina became Carmelites there. Teresa had to enter many of her foundations during the darkness of the night. She entered Beas in sunlight and triumph, with a tremendous welcome from priests and people.

Gracian

At Beas, Teresa met the man who was to play the leading role in her life over the next seven years. This was Fray Jerónimo de la Madre de Dios, better known as Gracian. She was now sixty years old, but she loved and admired this man who was only half her age. She nicknamed him "Paul" because, like the great apostle, he was either on the mountain tops of joy or in the depths of the sea of despair. At other times she nicknamed him "Eliseus" because he had a large bald head.

Gracian was born at Valladolid in 1545, studied at the University of Alcalá, was ordained priest in 1570, and joined the Discalced Carmelites at Pastrana, April 25, 1572. This gifted, eloquent, and able priest was made novice master while still a novice, and a few months after his profession was appointed Apostolic Visitor to the Calced Carmelites in Andalusia, on August 4, 1573.

Teresa described "this angel."

> He was a man of great learning, understanding and modesty. It seemed Our Lady had chosen him for the welfare of this primitive Order, when he was in Alcala. Our Lord saw well how necessary such a person was for this work. . . . He would organize everything for our Order. . . . The Virgin, Our Lady, to whom he is extremely devoted, was anxious to reward him, by bestowing her habit upon him. . . . When the Virgin brought him to Pastrana, he came under a misconception, for he thought he was there to obtain the habit for a nun, whereas God's purpose in bringing him was to give him the habit for himself. (*Foundations*, Ch. 7, pp. 119–201.)

Teresa was fascinated by the charm and personality of this young priest. They could share deeply, and she could reveal all the secrets of her soul to him. She trusted Gracian more than John of the Cross in practical matters and she felt that he would be the savior of the Order. "The monasteries had in them the germs of rapid decay; since having no province of their own, they were governed by the Calced Fathers . . . Our Lady had chosen him to be the salvation of her Order." (*Foundations*, Ch. 23, p. 121.)

Teresa's letters speak glowingly of her relationship with Gracian. "I shall never spend happier days, than these I lived with my Paul." She felt lonely when he was absent, and looked forward like a loving mother to his visits. She followed him with solicitous admonitions, "not to fall off his donkey," and she would write, "May God keep you near me, for I like you very much." (Letter 140.) To the end of her days the Holy Mother remained so human and so loving. There was never so human a saint.

On August 4, 1573, Gracian was appointed Apostolic Visitor to the Calced Carmelites of Andalusia. This appointment was bitterly resented, and the Calced Carmelites complained to the General. The General persuaded Gregory XIII to revoke these faculties later, leaving the foundress with the solid conviction that there would never be peace and progress until there were two separate provinces, judicially, autonomus, Calced, and Discalced. Teresa felt Gracian was the captain to lead her team into the future. The Nuncio sent for Gracian, and Teresa was thrilled when he was given power to rule the Discalced friars and nuns of Castile.

"When I saw him, the Lord seemed to show me all the good that was to come to us through him, and during these days I was extremely comforted and happy." (*Foundations*, Ch. 24, p. 122.)

Marcelle Auclair has an interesting comment:

> Mother Teresa bent Gracian to her will by the means all women employ, be they saints or sinners, geniuses or fools, to bring men under their domination. She vowed obedience to him, promised to do only what he commanded all her life long, unless it should be anything against God or the ecclesiastical superiors to whom she had duties. She likewise undertook to hide from him nothing of her interior life, or her sins—in short, she put him, both interiorly and exteriorly, in the place of God. After this it only remained for Gracian to submit.   (p. 262.)

Seville

Gracian now commanded the Mother Foundress to open a convent in Seville in Andalusia. They discussed the matter at Beas, and although Andalusia frightened her, Teresa fell for the persuasive charm of Gracian. "When I began to talk to him, I was happier still, for he pleased me so much that it seemed to me as if those who had praised him to me, hardly knew him at all." (*Foundations*, Ch. 24, p. 122.)

The archbishop, Don Cristóbal de Rojas, had already given his consent; the city was rich and the people well disposed.

Finally a Carmelite house of prayer there would counteract the power of the heretics. Teresa reluctantly obeyed. Deeper instincts warned her.

Teresa and her companions set out on the long eight-day journey to the sunny south on May 18, 1575. Seven nuns and Julian of Avila, Antonia Gaytán, and Gregorio Nacianceno comprised the brave band. The summer sun beat down mercilessly upon the little Carmelite caravan group, and they were forced to take siestas under eucalyptus trees or under bridges. At regular hours the bell rang for prayer, office, and silence. Thirst was a problem, and they had to survive on a starvation diet of bread and cherries. At night, sleep came hard and slow, and they were forced to listen to the shouts of drunken men and the clanging sounds of guitars and clicking castanets.

Fever burned up the already frail and sickly body of Teresa. She was dumped on a bed, which she describes: "It was so full of ups and downs that I would rather have lain on the floor, it seemed to be full of sharp stones. I preferred to endure the sun in the open than in that little room." (*Foundations*, Ch. 24, p. 124.)

More painful adventure lay ahead. When they reached the banks of the Guadalquiver river and tried to cross, the ferryboat ropes broke and the current carried boat and carriages with it. The dumbfounded spectators began to shout and pray, as the boatman's little son, in terror, watched his father being swept away by the rapid current. His Majesty had compassion on them, and the boat ramped into a sandbank. They were saved from the water only to go astray in the dark that same night.

Pentecost Sunday found our little band tramping the crowded streets of Cordova. They were stopped at the bridge, because they did not have the proper license. Teresa next made her way to the church of the Holy Spirit to attend Mass on the great feast of the Holy Spirit, to whom she was so devoted. A great procession to the church was in progress, and when the people spied the Carmelite nuns and their weird looking habit, they were more than curious.

> When the people saw us in the white frieze mantels, and our hemp-soled shoes, it was enough to cause a commotion, and a commotion there was. This was a great shock for me, and for all of us, and it must have taken away my fever altogher. (*Foundations*, Ch. 24, p. 126.)

At another place the sisters had to witness a sword battle between groups of devilish individuals. Seville was reached on May 26, 1575, and our writer could add, "None of our foundations were made without my enduring great sufferings." (*Foundations* Ch. 24, p. 127.)

Mariano had gone ahead to make the final arrangements, and the Foundress had hoped that everything would be ready, only to be disappointed once more. Mariano was rather reticent and silent. He was afraid to tell her the full story, for the fact was there was no license, no endowment, no benefactor, no friends, and not a farthing left after the journey. Teresa had to go and borrow money in rich Seville. She was so disturbed that she even contemplated abandoning the entire project and return to Beas. The Calced Fathers did not help, and Gracian was really worried. Eventually, the archbishop came to visit them and fell captive before the charm of the Castilian Carmelite. "He told me to do just what I liked, and as I liked." (*Foundations*, Ch. 24, p. 129.)

Teresa, the Castilian, did not like Seville and the Andalusians. Many of her comments were sarcastic. We can understand her disappointment. This city was wealthy and did not come to her rescue. Eventually her brother Lorenzo, recently returned from Lima, where he made lots of money, helped her financially, and so the house could be bought and paid for, Mass celebrated, and the Blessed Sacrament reserved. A great procession was organized, people thronged, rockets were fired, and salvos of artillery shot. Seville turned on the fireworks, but in the midst of the jubilation tragedy struck. Some powder exploded.

> A huge flame leapt up to the top of the cloister, the arches of which were covered with silk hangings . . . the stone wall of the arches was blackened with smoke, and yet the hangings were not touched . . . the devil must have been angry at the solemnity. . . . May His Majesty be blessed forever and ever, Amen. (*Foundations*, Ch. 24, pp. 133–134.)

Sufferings and trials were to follow. "I do not think any foundation has caused me so many trials—most of them interior ones." (*Foundations*, Ch. 26, p. 134.)

Teresa remained in Seville for a little more than a year. The first novice, Beatrice of the Mother of God, to whom she devotes an entire chapter in her *Foundations*, gave her great joy; but another beata, renowned for her sanctity in the city, was to cause endless trouble. This novice, whom history in its kindness leaves nameless, was not able to live the austere life of the cloister, and when she left, humbled and disgruntled, she decided to take revenge. To the Holy Office of the Inquisition she betook herself to make all kinds of false accusations against the saintly Foundress that would embarrass her and cast the dark shadow of the Alumbrados over her and the convent. The Carmelites were denounced as heretics, and the officers of the Inquisition descended upon the little foundation. Mother Teresa met them serene and confident, knowing she was innocent and that the accusations brought against her were unfounded. The sisters went to confession to her; they were flogged, and they were heretics.

Misunderstanding Among Superiors

The misunderstandings among her superiors caused endless trouble to Teresa at this time. Gracian had been appointed Apostolic Visitor by the King and Nuncio Ormaneto, while his own General Rubeo did not approve. The general had not given any permission to the Reformed Carmel to make foundations in Andalusia, and here was Gracian using his power contrary to the wish of the general. Rubeo felt that Gracian and Teresa had gone too far. Letters went astray and communication between Rome and Spain was erratic. The General Rubeo and the provincial, Angel de Salazar, fulminated against her and Gracian. Much of the misunderstanding may have been due to the indiscretion of Gracian, and we have a letter from Teresa warning her beloved son to be more prudent, less stubborn, more obedient and gentle.

When the Provincial ordered Gracian back to Spain, he refused to go. His excuse, was he had to obey the king and Nuncio. Gracian was surely in a dilemma, but he did not handle the situation very diplomatically.

The General Chapter held from May to June, 1575, dealt severely with the unrepresented Discalced Carmelites. All the monasteries founded without the permission of Rubeo were ordered suppressed. Teresa was forbidden to make any new foundations, and she was to return to Castile, never again to leave the convent of her choice. The mighty foundress was to be a prisoner. The provincial declared her apostate and excommunicated, and her Discalced sons and daughters were branded as rebellious, disobedient, and contumacious.

To make matters worse, an ugly slander campaign was set afoot by the Calced, to taint the beautiful relationship that existed between Teresa and Gracian. Gracian pens his wounded heart in his book, *Peregrinacion.*

> You must know that she loved me very tenderly, and I her, more than any creature on earth, after my own mother, who also loved me with a more particular love than any other of her sons. But this great love that I bore Madre Terese of Jesus, and she for me, is a very different kind from what is usually had in the world, for that love is dangerous, vexatious, and causes thoughts and temptations that offend and slacken the spirit, disturb sensuality. But this love that I had for Madre Teresa, and she for me, produced in me purity, the spirit and love of God, and in her consolation and relief for her trials. I should not want even my mother to love me more than she did. . . . Malicious people judged from the great communication and familiarity that we two had that it was not a holy love, and even if she had not been as holy as she was, and if I had been the most evil man in the world, wickedness should not have been suspected of a woman sixty years old, and so cloistered and modest. With all that, we had to conceal this very intimate friendship, so that we should not be maligned. (Walsh, p. 464.)

Maligned they were, as for more malicious people cast their own shadows on this saintly nun and heroic priest.

Caravaca

On January 1, 1576, Teresa founded her convent at Caravaca. Doña Catalina de Otalora, a wealthy widow, was the benefactress. She had taken three well-to-do ladies into her house, and determined not to leave, until a convent was founded there. Julian of Avila and Antonio Gaytán inspected and prepared the foundation. When the Commandery of Santiago demanded that the convent be placed under their jurisdiction, Teresa wrote to the king, and obtained a free license. The convent was dedicated to St. Joseph. Two of the young ladies received the Carmelite habit, and the other was sent home because of her melancholic temperament. This was one foundation Teresa could not make in person. She gives some advice on admitting poor girls.

> Never refuse to receive those who come to you and want to be nuns on the grounds that they have no worldly possessions, provided that they have virtues, that you are satisfied with their desires and abilities, and that they come not merely to find a home for themselves, but to serve God in greater perfection. . . . I have never failed to receive anyone because she lacked means. . . . It has given me less pleasure to receive those who brought a great deal with them than those I took for God's sake alone. Indeed I had misgivings about the former, whereas those that were poor comforted my spirit and made me so happy that I would weep for joy. (*Foundations*, Ch. 27, p. 144.)

7.
The Storm Breaks

Teresa begins Chapter 28 of her *Foundations*, with these sad words:

> After the Seville convent had been founded, my foundations came to an end for more than four years. The reason for this was the very sudden beginning of the great persecutions which both friars and nuns of the Discalced Reform had to endure; though they had had many already, none of them were so severe as these last, which almost brought the Reform to an end. It became clear how angry the devil was at this excellent beginning, which Our Lord had made, and which, as it prospered so greatly, was clearly His work. The Discalced friars, and more especially their leaders, suffered greatly from the gross calumnies and opposition which came from nearly all the Fathers of the mitigation. They made the Father General very displeased with me, and this was the greatest trial that I have had to bear while making these foundations (*Foundations*, Ch. 28 p. 149.)

The friendly papal Nuncio, Niccolò Ormaneto, died in Madrid on June 18, 1577, and was succeeded by a more prejudiced Filippo Sega. In obedience to the decree of the General Chapter, Teresa had shut herself up in the convent of Toledo since the end of June 1576. There she was a virtual prisoner, so she had to continue the war through her pen. We have many of her most revealing letters from Toledo. Here, too, she began her greatest work on prayer, *The Interior Castle*. While war waged outside, there was an amazing creative fountain of peace springing up within the soul of our writer.

In March, 1576, the man who was to cause most pain and turmoil arrived in Spain. He was a Calced Carmelite, Portugese by birth, who had served as prior in Barcelona, provincial in Catalonia, worked for the general in Italy, and was now sent by the general as his personal representative to carry out the decrees of the Piacenza Chapter that ordered the suppression of the Discalced foundations. Tostado was his name. Conflict was inevitable. Tostado represented the General. Gracian as apostolic visitor, derived his power through Vargas from the pope. The king favored Gracian. So with a certain amount of evidence and defiance, Gracian called a General Chapter of the Discalced Carmelites at Almodóvar on September 8, 1576. There they voted to set up a separate province. They would obey the general of the order or a Discalced father delegated by him. Two men were to be sent to Rome to explain the whole situation to the pope.

Gracian may have exceeded his powers here, since only a General Chapter could establish a new province, and we have letters from Teresa begging her favorite son to be more prudent and never lose the gracious good will of the General Rubeo. The channels of communication had broken down between Rubeo and Teresa, and the mind of the general was colored by people who wanted the Discalced Carmelites crushed.

Election at the Incarnation

In the midst of all this trouble, events took a strange turn at the convent of the Incarnation in Avila. The nuns, who six years previously refused to have anything to do with Teresa, now wanted her back as prioress. Fifty-five nuns voted for her; forty-four against. Tostado was furious and sent the Calced provincial, Juan Gutierrez, along to annual the election. We are fortunate to possess a letter of Teresa describing the historic event.

> I assure your Reverence that I believe such a thing as has happened at the Incarnation has never been seen before. By order of Tostado, the Provincial of the Calced, went there a fortnight ago to preside over the election of the Prioress. He threatened with severe censures and excommunication any sister who gave her vote to me. However, they took no more notice of it than if he had not spoken. Fifty-five of the nuns voted for me. As each

of them gave him her vote, he excommunicated and anathematized her, ground the voting papers with his fist, struck them repeatedly, and finally burned them. These religious have been excommunicated for the last fortnight. He has forbidden them to hear Mass or to enter the choir even when the Divine Office is not being recited, and no one, not even their confessors or relations, is allowed to speak to them. The wonderful part of it is that the day after this election of thumps, the Father Provincial sent for the nuns who had voted for me and told them to make their election. They replied that there was no election to make, for they had made it. Whereupon he again excommunicated them and summoning the remaining forty-four nuns, chose a Prioress from among them, and sent to Tostado to confirm the choice. This has been done, but the rest of the sisters are determined and declare that they will only obey her as Vice-Prioress. Everyone is astonished and shocked at such doings. I should willingly forgive my supporters if they would only leave me in peace, for I do not want to live in the Babylon again, especially with my bad health which grows worse in that house. May God direct all as serves him best and deliver me from these nuns. (Letter 148. vol. II. p. 317.)

Philip II later insisted that the fifty-five nuns be released from all censures, and Tostado reluctantly agreed. The next victim of the persecution was John of the Cross. On the night of December 4, 1577, assisted by the police, the prior of the Calced Carmelites, P. Maldonado, broke into the huts of John of the Cross and German of San Matias. They had been directors to the nuns at the Incarnation. John escaped their clutches the next morning, ran back to his cottage, tore up some letters from Mother Teresa; the ones he could not destroy, he swallowed, lest they be used in evidence against her. The kidnappers imprisoned John at Toledo, and Teresa was very worried because she did not know where her greatest son was. She stormed heaven and earth and wrote a letter of appeal to the king.

> For the love of Our Lord, I implore your majesty to command that the confessors should be set free at once and that the sufferings inflicted on the poor Discalced by these of the cloth should be stopped. The Discalced do nothing but endure in silence, gaining great merit, but scandal is given, as the same kind of thing takes place in other towns. At Toledo, this spring, Fray Antonio, a holy old man, who was the first to embrace the Reform was

seized and imprisoned for no reason. The Mitigated say the Discalced must be abolished by order of Tostado. God have mercy on us. Unless your majesty commands that matters should be remedied, I do not know what will happen for we have no other earthly aid. May Our Lord spare you to us for many years. (Letter, 20, vol. III, pp. 5–6.)

Philip sent for Mother Teresa, and the brave woman set out in the middle of December from Avila to Madrid. The Duke of Alba was her friend in court, and we can well imagine this holy old lady in her patched Carmelite habit, her heart breaking with sorrow, prayerfully making her way through the gardens and statues of the Escorial, oblivious to all its worldly wealth, intrigue, and grandeur, concentrated on one mission, the protection and release of her saintly son. We have a part of her letter written to Doña Inés Nieto describing the historic meeting between these two great Spaniards who were to shape the fate of history.

> Imagine, Doña Inés, what this insignificant woman must have felt in the presence of so great a King. I was too confused to speak, for his penetrating gaze—one of those that probe the soul itself was fixed on me and seemed to pierce me through and through. I cast down my eyes and stated my cause as briefly as possible. After explaining matters, I looked at him again, and his expression had changed, being kinder and more mild. He inquired whether that was all I wanted. I answered that I had asked a great deal. "Then," he replied, "you may be at peace, for all shall be done as you wish." I knelt to thank him for his extreme kindness. He bade me rise, and making this wretched nun, his unworthy servant, the most courteous bow I ever saw, he gave me his hand to kiss. I went away in jubilation, praising God in my soul for the help this Caesar had promised me. (Letters 105, vol. III. pp.16–17.)

Teresa returned to St. Joseph's in Avila. There was no immediate help from the king, and to add to her tribulations, she fell and broke her arm on Christmas Eve, as she made her way to pray compline, lighting her way with a little oil lamp that she carried. Even though a *curandera* was called, the left arm never healed—and she could never dress or undress again without help.

Even the Jesuits seem to have turned against Mother Teresa,

when one of them, Gasper de Salazar, was rumored as joining the Carmelites. Painful letters passed between the Jesuit Provincial and Teresa, and the friendly cooperation that had existed between these two young orders cooled a little.

In late August, Teresa had learned of the fate of John of the Cross, who had been locked up in a cell six-feet wide and ten-feet long. A small window let in some light. In the refectory, where he ate his meal of bread and water, he was scourged by the community, until the blood ran down his little body. The tunic on his back stuck to the wounds, and he had to wear it without change for nine months. But all the suffering in the world could not break his indomitable spirit or lessen his loyalty to Mother Teresa and her reform. From his broken heart was to come forth the loftiest and most sublime poetry and mystical song ever penned by human hand.

On the vigil of the Assumption, August 14, 1578, Our Lady appeared to him in a vision, showing him how to escape. He made a rope out of his bedcovers and slipped down over the wall to nine feet down to the river bed. He made his way to the Convent of the Discalced Carmelite nuns, who hid him from his pursuers in the infirmary. When the coast was clear, he escaped to Almodovar to attend the General Chapter called by Gracian.

Gracian made one of his worst mistakes in calling this chapter at this time with the purpose of setting up a separate province. Teresa had warned him not to proceed without permission from the Pope and the General. John of the Cross did his best to prevent the move. All was to no avail. Teresa and Gracian quarreled. Here is her letter.

> Jesus be with your paternity, you who are both my Father and my superior as you say, which caused me no little laughter and pleasure. In fact, whenever I recall your words I am amused at the solemn manner in which you declared that I must not judge my superior. O my Father! how little need there was for you to swear, even like a saint, much less like a muleteer, for I thoroughly realize that fact. (*Letters*, 225, vol. III., p. 82.)

Events moved fast. On September 4, General Rubeo died, and with his death hopes for a reconciliation grew dimmer. He appreciated the work of Teresa, and, even though in his latter years he had, through lack of communication, grown disenchanted with the Reform, Teresa never lost her affection and gratitude for the man who understood her dream and vision, when no other did. She grieved at his passing.

On October 16, Sega annuled the decisions of the Almodóvar Chapter, excommunicated and then imprisoned its members. He dissolved the new province, and placed the Discalced under the jurisdiction of the Calced.

The name of Teresa was mud to the Nuncio Sega. When Juan de Jesús Roca tried to defend her, Sega exclaimed, "Do not mention her name! She is a restless gadabout, disobedient, contumacious woman who promulgates pernicious doctrine under the pretense of devotion. She leaves her cloister against the orders of her superiors and the decrees of the Council of Trent. She is ambitious and teaches theology as though she were a doctor of the church in spite of St. Paul's prohibition." (*Letters*, vol. III pp. 157–158.)

It is amusing to read how the highest representative of the Church in Spain judged this great Doctor of the Church in 1578. When the king heard of all this, he was enraged and urged the Discalced friars and nuns not to obey Sega. Gracian was imprisoned at Alcalá. Rumors were spreading that he was softening and meditated leaving the Reform. His brave Polish mother, who had given life to twenty children, ordered him never to leave Our Lady's Order because of cowardice, or she would never write to him again. The Count de Tendilla threatened to stab him if he deserted Teresa. When Teresa heard the rumor, she wrote:

> God give your strength to be steadfast in the right amid such great peril. Blessed are such trials, however grave, when they do not turn us from the right path. I am not astonished that those who love your paternity endeavour to free you from them and seek for the means, though it would not be well to forsake the Virgin in a time of such distress. I venture to declare that Doña Juana (his Mother) would not advise it, nor would she consent to such a change. God preserve us from it. (Letters, 252, vol. III. p. 166.)

The world seemed to collapse around Teresa. Foul charges were still being circulated againt Gracian and her nuns. To crown the agony of the year 1578, on Christmas Eve, she received a sad letter from Gracian that made her cry, "God give me patience. Now, Lord Thou art granting my desires for suffering."

She refused all food and shut herself up in her cell in prayer. Anne of St. Bartholomew persuaded her to come to the refectory that night, where the good laysister saw Our Lord take some bread, bless it, put it to the saint's mouth, saying, "Eat this for love of me." (Letters, 225, vol. III. pp171.)

She expected to be sent away to a Calced convent to be jailed there like John of the Cross. Excommunication was also possible. "I wondered whether excommunication was to be fulminated against me today, as a small document came with the large one. I do not merit the grace of sufferings as Fray John's." (Letters, 255, vol. III, p. 174.)

Imagine the woman who lived and served the church so loyally being excommunicated by the same church, on account of ecclesiastical politics and intrigue.

1579: Light at the End of the Tunnel

Early in 1579 events looked brighter for Teresa and her reform. Nicolás Doria had taken over, while Gracian was silenced and shut up. This shrewd Genovese banker had friends at court, and his voice could reach the ears of Philip II. Inside the court, the Duke of Alba was already working for the Discalced, and the Court of Tendilla was still fulminating on behalf of Teresa. As a matter of fact, an angry outburst by the Court against Sega led the Nuncio to complain to Philip. Although he rebuked the overzealous count, he also manifested his wrath to the representative of the Pope. He let the Nuncio know of the hostility and persecution of the Discalced by the Mitigated friars, and bade him favor virtue. Philip appointed four men to study the entire affair and then report to the Nuncio—Don Luis Manrique, Canon Villavicencio, the two Dominicans, Pedro Hernández and Hernándo del Castillo. They favored setting up a separate province for the Discalced, and when Sega heard all the facts, he was less prejudiced against the reform. Both King and Nuncio agreed to appeal to the Pope. This request had to be granted.

The prisoners were released. The gentle Angel de Salazar was appointed Vicar General of the Discalced. Angel ordered Teresa to visit and inspect her convents, while he appointed Gracian as his representative in Andalusia. John of the Cross became rector of the college at Baeza.

By June, Teresa, "an old crone," as she called herself (see Letter 283), was once more on the roads, visiting Medina, Valladolid, Alba, and Salamanca. In early November, she was back in Avila, but almost at once set out for Toledo. She was at Malagon, on November 25, saw the community move into a new house on December 8, and remained with them for two months. In every house, she boosted the morale, took care of economic problems, and prepared the superiors to take leadership. We have a wonderful letter from her to Maria Bautista at Valladolid on the wisdom of Christian government.

> You know, I no longer govern in the way I used to. Love does everything now. I am not sure if that is because no one gives me cause to reprove her, or because I have discovered that things go better in that way. (Letter 276.)

Villanueva de la Jara

On February 21, 1580, Mother Teresa founded her thirteenth monastery at Villanueva de la Jara. Nine noble ladies of rank under Doña Catalina de Cardona had been living there as beatas leading a life of penance and prayer. Doña Catalina wore the habit of the friars in Madrid once she caused some scandal and shock, when it was reported that a Carmelite priest was travelling around in a carriage with some ladies. Summoned by the Nuncio, this bold, liberated woman simply gave him her blessing, as she would any simple rustic on the street. Catalina died in 1577, and her community now wanted to become Carmelite. Teresa arrived there, the first Sunday of Lent, February 21, 1580, and received a warm, tumultuous welcome from clergy and people. The fame of Mother Teresa was now spreading, and crowds came out to greet her wherever she went.

Holy Week found Teresa at Toledo. "Ever since Maundy Thursday, I have suffered from one of the most violent attacks of paralysis and heart affliction that I have had in all my life." (*Letters,* vol. IV, p. 15.)

By June 15, this sick woman was in Segovia. There she learned the sad news of the death of her beloved brother, Lorenzo. She wrote humorously, "I am four years older than my brother, yet I never manage to die." (*Letters,* 333, vol. IV, p. 49.)

She was sixty-five. While at Segovia, she revised her *Interior Castle*. By August, Teresa was on the road again, visiting Avila and Medina, and on to Valladolid. Her letters depicted a very busy woman looking after her brother Lorenzo's affairs and family, consulted on marriages, supervising monasteries, counselling Gracian, consoling widows, and giving spiritual advice. High fever made her a very sick woman, and the sisters feared she would die.

Palencia

Still undaunted by health, old age, cold weather, or fatigue, Teresa was at Palencia on December 29 to make her fourteenth foundation. Don Álvaro de Mendoza, who had helped the first convent, was now bishop of Palencia and wanted a Carmelite foundation in his diocese. Teresa was enthusiastic, but adds, "It is a trial to be ill and suffer great pains. I am distressed to see how the poor soul has to share in the frailty of body." (*Foundations*, Ch. 29, p. 166.)

The Mother Foundress was also working on a new convent in Burgos, and felt bewildered at times, when the Lord spoke to her, "What dost thou fear? When have I ever failed thee? I am the same now as I have always been. Do not give up either of these foundations." (*Foundations*, Ch. 29, p. 167.) Courage returned. She had Canon Reinoso rent a house. Six months later her little community of five founded the monastery of Saint Joseph of Our Lady of the Street, June 1, 1581.

Our Saint has words of highest praise for Palencia, its bishop and people. "The people as a whole are the best and noblest I have ever seen, and every day I rejoice more and more that I made the foundation there." (*Foundations*, Ch. 29, p. 169.)

Separate Provinces

June 22, 1580, is a date to be remembered in Carmelite history, because on that day Gregory XIII issued a Bull recognizing the Discalced reform as a separate province. Teresa was at Palencia when the separation took place. She credits Philip II for drawing the whole sordid story to a happy conclusion. On

March 3, 1581, the Discalced Carmelites held their chapter at Alcalá. The Dominican, Juan de las Cuevas, was moderator. Gracian, to the delight of Mother Teresa, was elected the first provincial. The king bore the cost of it all, and commanded the university to cooperate. After twenty-five years of persecution and trouble, this was one of the happiest days in her life.

> Now, Calced and Discalced alike, we are all at peace, and no one hinders us in Our Lord's service. Therefore, my brothers and sisters, make haste to serve His Majesty . . . let it be said of us, as is said of some other Orders, that they do nothing but laud their beginnings. Fix your eyes always on the soil from which we have sprung—the soil of those holy prophets. How many Saints we have in heaven who wore this habit! Let us with a holy boldness, and with the help of God, dare to be like them. (*Foundations*, Ch. 29, pp. 176–177.)

There is fire in this old woman.

Soria

On June 3, 1581, Teresa opened her monastery in honor of the Blessed Trinity at Soria. Bishop Alonso Velazquez suggested this foundation, and a wealthy lady, Doña Beatriz de Meamonte y Navarra, supplied the house and means. Soria was a happy foundation.

Prioress of St. Joseph's

On August 16, Teresa left Soria to return to St. Joseph's Avila. The first convent needed her badly. She travelled in terrible heat, and the young driver did not know the way at Segovia. At times they had to make the journey on foot, "The carriage went along steep precipices till it almost hung in the air." (*Foundations* Ch. 30 p. 183). When she arrived at Avila, Teresa was elected Prioress there. She protested in vain to Gracian, the Provincial. He simply told her, "Kiss the floor, accept the office," as he intoned the *Te Deum*. Writing to Maria de San Jose, she says:

> They made me Prioress from sheer hunger. Considering my age and work, you can imagine how fit I am for it. I do not know what will become of the sisters laden with debt as they are. Pray for them and for me too, for nature is wearied by this office of Prioress. I am sorry you resemble me in any way, for everything about me is bad—very bad, especially my health. The pills have done me much good and have no unpleasant effects; be sure to try them. (*Letters*, 404, vol. IV, p. 234.)

Teresa was by now a sick old woman of sixty-six, disillusioned by the spiritual and economic setbacks at St. Joseph's. As we see in her letters to Gracian, Julian of Avila—in his old age, in his capacity as confessor to the community—was the cause of a great deal of the trouble. Teresa calls him "an annoyed Father Julian." (*Letter* 402, vol. IV. p. 228.) He was too lax and complacent. The Mother Foundress worked hard to restore peace and harmony, prayer, discipline, and economic stability to her little flock.

In November, John of the Cross visited her at Avila. She had not seen her saintly son since his arrest some four years before, and this was to be their last meeting on earth. We can only imagine the love, the insights, the experiences, the mystical wisdom, and the prayer shared by these two great souls when they talked.

Burgos

Burgos was to be the last of the foundations, and it involved six long months of suffering. Teresa had not anticipated so many difficulties. The archbishop, Don Cristobal Vela, was a relative, and the saintly widow, Catalina de Tolosa, was a reliable benefactress. Her two sons and five daughters entered the order, and she herself joined at Palencia in 1587. Teresa left Avila for Burgos on January 2, 1582, full of warm hopes, although the weather was cold, wet, and wintry. The journey turned out to be an ordeal and a nightmare. Although the roads were flooded, Teresa carried on. Once she had the awful experience of seeing the first carriage balance precariously over the flooded bank of the river and almost topple in, but Teresa volunteered to stand in the gap of danger and go first.

> We could not cover our day's mileage on account of the bad roads, for it was quite usual for the carriages to sink into the mud and the animals would have to be taken out of one of the carriages to drag out another. . . . I was suffering from a troublesome sore throat, and eating caused me the greatest pain. (*Foundations*, Ch. 31, pp. 190–191.)

Tired, sick, cold, and weary, the little group of eight, under the leadership of Teresa and Gracian, reached Burgos on January 26. She expected that everything would be plain sailing from then on, only to be disappointed, for the archbishop's mood and good will had changed. There was no written license and the archbishop vacillated and negotiated until he almost drove provincial Gracian to despair.

With no house, no sureties, no permission for Mass, no friends around, the little group of Carmelites faced a dilemma. Gracian, although staying in the house of an old friend and college mate, Dr. Pedro Manso, grew impatient. He had to be free for his Lenten preaching.

The Lord spoke once more. "Now, Teresa, hold fast." (*Foundations*, Ch. 31, p. 194.)

Hold fast Teresa did. The jealous confessors of Doña Catalina threatened to refuse her absolution if she did not drive Teresa and company out of her house. It seemed she had promised the property to these "fathers." Doctor Manso found temporary quarters for the Carmelites in the haunted rooms of the hospital of the Conception. The devil of Burgos was around. They were able to have Mass there, and Teresa warmed the wards with her love and compassion. They prayed St. Joseph to find them a home, and on March 18, the eve of his feast, a suitable place was located. The price was high, but the Lord whispered to Teresa, "Art thou hesitating on account of money?" (*Ibid*, p. 198.) She hesitated no longer. The property was purchased, and on April 19, Dr. Manso celebrated the first Mass in the monastery of St. Joseph of St. Anne in the city of Burgos.

In January, Anne of Jesus had made a foundation at Granada. So Burgos was the seventeenth convent founded by Teresa.

8.
Death and Glory

Toward the end of July, Teresa departed from Burgos, tired of travelling. "I shall not have to go travelling about anymore, for I am very old and tired." (See Letter 422) She spent three weeks in her beloved Palencia, and by August 20, she was at Valladolid. There she was troubled and tormented by family problems. Teresa was the only saint in her clan, and after her brother Lorenzo's death, the solution to all the squabbling over property fell on her old and tired shoulders. Her letters at this time were full of heartaches and headaches. Her nephew Fancisco laid greedy eyes on the money his father Lorenzo had willed to the Carmelites at Avila. Teresa took her own niece Teresita, who was now fifteen, with her wherever she went, lest she be influenced by family intrigue. Teresita was only nine years old when she returned with her father from Ecuador. She stayed with her aunt for some years at St. Joseph's Avila. Her relatives wanted her to return to the world more interested in her dowry than in her salvation.

Her cousin, the businesslike and thrifty Marie Bautista, was prioress at Valladolid, and she did not treat Teresa with hospitality. In fact, she sided with the family against the old foundress, and prejudiced Teresita against her saintly aunt. Her other niece, Beatriz de Ovalle, was the victim of scandalous gossip. A jealous wife accused her of an affair with her husband. The girl's life was in danger. Teresa came to rescue. Sometime later, when the fiery wife died, the gentleman proposed marriage, but Beatriz turned down the offer and decided to become a Carmelite instead.

Teresa felt alone and lonely. Her friends had deserted her. Against her wishes her beloved Gracian had gone to Andalusia. She wrote a pathetic letter on September 1:

> Your frequent letters to me do not suffice to alleviate my distress. So keenly did I feel your being away at such a time that I lost the desire to write to you . . . I have had a dreadful time here with Don Francisco's mother-in-law. She is a strange woman. Do not meditate turning yourself into an Andalusian. . . . For the love of God think very carefully what you are doing. Do not pay too much attention to what the nuns say, for I can assure you, if they want to do a thing, they will give you a thousand arguments in its favour. . . . My kind regards to Fray John of the Cross. (Letter 434)

Teresa left Valladolid with a heavy heart, and as she accompanied her venerable guest to the door, the rather arrogant Prioress Marie Bautista said, "Goodbye, and don't come back here again." (Note to letter, 462.)

Cold Medina

On September 17, Teresa arrived at Medina. The Prioress Alberta Bautista, another austere Prioress, gave our saint a very cool reception. Over the years Teresa had reason to correct and soften this rather severe woman, and Alberta Bautista, did not take the correction too kindly. Now she was superior and Teresa a guest. Teresa came to Medina with pains in her head, throat, and everyone of her bones. She looked forward to a good rest, before she set out for Avila.

Without giving her saintly visitor a welcome, time to rest or food to eat, Alberta ordered her to go at once to the parlor, where the vicar-provincial, Antonio de Jesus, awaited her. Antonio was now seventy-two years old. For years Teresa tried to keep the lines of communication open between them, but he never answered her letters. Antonio never liked women, and he harbored some grievances against Teresa, as he knew she wanted Gracian and not this bad-tempered man as Provincial. In a letter to Graician, Teresa writes:

> Enclosed is a letter written to me by Fray Antonio de Jesus.

I am astonished at him but as he is now my friend again (to tell the truth I thought he always was), and we are corresponding with one another, all will be well. (Letter 458.)

When this dying woman met at the parlor grille the man to whom she owed obedience, all was not well. He commanded her to leave the next day for Alba de Tormes, where the Duchess of Alba needed her during the last days of the confinement of her daughter-in-law. Our saint obeyed. She entered her garden of Gethsemene. The prioress did not bother to invite her guest to supper. Teresa slept her last night at Medina, hungry, broken-hearted, and in pain.

She set off the next morning a disappointed woman, deserted by friends, handed the Judas kiss by Antonio, hurt deeply by Alberta Bautista, snubbed by her cousin, María Bautista, and far away from her favorites Gracian and John of the Cross. Now she was on her last journey and pilgrimage performing like Our Blessed Lady an heroic act of charity at the birth of a little baby. Her one consolation was the presence of her faithful companion, the little laysister, Anne of St. Bartholomew. The powerful ones of her Order were far away. Her young niece, Teresita, was also there.

The brave little band travelled in the carriage of the duchess, but they had no food. Anne failed to buy two eggs with her four *reales*. That night was sheer agony spent in a miserable inn. Next morning news came that the baby was born and they no longer needed the saint.

Alba

On September 21, Teresa came to Alba to die. She had hoped to return to Avila, but the Lord willed otherwise. The gentle Juana del Espiritu Santo welcomed her. Next morning she was at Mass and Communion. There were still some business matters to take care of and Teresa courageously did her duty to the last.

Anne stayed with her day and night. Heavenly lights were seen in the convent windows. When the elegant Duchess of Alba came to vist her dying friend, Teresa feared she would be nauseated by the smell of medicine, but when she entered the holy presence, the whole room was scented by a celestial fragrance.

On October 2, Teresa knew she was dying. She asked Fray Antonio to hear her confession, give her absolution for her sins, and bring her the Viaticum, the food for her journey home.

The old man came and knelt humbly by her bed. There, in the face of the reality of death, old grievances were forgotten and there was nothing but love. Teresa's great heart could now flood with divine love. It would break of love.

The nuns gathered around her to listen to her last counsels:

> For the love of God, I beg that you will take great care with the keeping of the Rule and Constitutions, and pay no attention to bad example that this wicked nun has given you, and pardon me for it. (Walsh, p. 578.)

Teresa was humble to the end. She was heard often to repeat, "Lord, I am a daughter of the Church."

When the priest brought her Holy Communion, she raised her body on the bed without any help. This temple of the Holy Spirit was aglow with light, as her Divine Spouse approached for the last embrace. Her joyful soul broke into song.

> O, My Lord and my Spouse, now the desired hour is come.
> Now it is time for us to go. Now is the time to set forth,
> may it be very soon, and may your most holy will be accomplished.
> Now the hour has come for me to leave this exile, and my soul
> rejoices at one with You for what I have so desired.
> (Ibid, p. 579.)

She spoke of forgiveness for sin and prayed Psalm 51:

My sacrifice, a contrite spirit,
A humbled, contrite heart you will
not spurn.
A pure heart create for me, O God
Put a steadfast spirit within me.

At nine o'clock Teresa asked to be anointed. She joined in the prayers. When Fray Antonio asked her whether she wanted to be buried in Avila or Alba, she humbly replied, "Do I have to have anything of my own? Won't they give me a bit of earth here?"

All day long she lay quietly and deeply in prayer. And at nine o'clock she gently breathed her last, her spirit carried off on a stream of ecstatic love.

Her body exuded a heavenly fragrance and her countenance shone with the beauty of a radiant sun. The inner light shone diaphonously through her body. Blessed Anne of St. Bartholomew saw Our Lord and myriads of angels at the front of her bed.

The Duchess of Alba had her body covered with cloth of gold. Teresa was buried the next day. Alba wanted the body of the saint so desperately that the ceremony was carried out in haste, lest Avila clamor for the sacred remains. Anne of St. Bartholomew relates that the body was not embalmed. They poured quicklime upon the corpse and piled stones and bricks on top of the coffin to make sure the body would soon be consumed and the remains never removed. Finally two carloads of earth were piled upon the grave.

The heavenly fragrance continued to come from the tomb. The sisters were curious, and when Gracian visited them some nine months later, they persuaded him to open the grave. We have Ribera's account:

> They began to remove the stones very secretly. There were so many that it took him and his companion four days. . . . The coffin was opened on July 4, 1583, nine months after internment: They found the coffin lid smashed, half rotten and full of mildew, the smell of damp was very pungent. . . . The clothes had also fallen to pieces. . . . The whole body was covered with the earth which had penetrated into the coffin and so was all damp too, but as fresh and whole as if it had been only buried the day before. (Auclair, p. 430.)

Gracian adds:

> She was in such a perfect state of preservation that my companion, P. Cristobal de San Alberto, and I retired while they undressed her: they called me back again when they had covered

> her with a sheet; uncovering her breasts, I was surprised to see how full and firm they were. (Ibid.)

The sacred body was clothed in a new habit and placed in the coffin. Before closing the coffin, the Provincial cut off her left hand.

> I took the hand away and wrapped it in a coif and in an outer wrapping of paper; oil came from it. . . . I left it at Avila in a sealed casket. . . . When I severed a little finger which I carry about on my person. . . . When I was captured, the Turks took it from me, but I bought it back for some twenty reales and some gold rings. (Ibid., p. 431.)

Avila never surrendered its claim to the body of the Holy Mother, and at a meeting of the Discalced fathers at Pastrana, on November 24, 1585, it was decided that the body of Teresa should be stolen secretly from Alba. Fathers Gracian and Gregory were chosen as agents. They were joined by Julian of Avila and Canon Don Juan Carrillo, chancellor of the cathedral at Avila.

On Sunday night, November 25, the two friars went to the convent. The body was exhumed. The nuns asked to see it. They were filled with joy to see their holy mother still beautiful and fresh. The community retired to recite the Divine Office in Choir, and then the two friars got down to the real business. They notified the Prioress and sub-prioress about the chapter letter decreeing that the body should be returned to Avila. Gregorio amputated the left arm to be left in Alba as a relic. This is Ribera's account of the operation.

> With extreme repugnance—he has since told me that it was the greatest sacrifice he ever made for Our Lord—in fulfillment of his vow of obedience, he drew a knife he was carrying in his belt . . . and inserted it under the left arm which was the one from which the hand was missing, and which had been dislocated when the devil threw the holy mother downstairs. Wonderful to relate, without using any more effort than in cutting a melon or a little fresh cheese, as he said, he severed the arm at the joints as easily as if he had spent some time before hand trying to ascertain their exact position, and the body remained on one side, and the arm on the other. (Auclair, p. 432.)

The little band arrived at Avila with our Saint's body on Monday, November 26, 1585, three years after her death. The nuns received her with awe and reverence. The bishop and the dignitaries of Avila came to pay their respects. A wonderful odor still emanated from the incorrupt body.

So Teresa was home at last. Life's fitful fever was over and she could rest in the first convent she founded. But not for long. The powerful Duke of Alba was very angry, when he heard the precious body had been taken from his city. He used all his political power to persuade the Nuncio Speciano to have Teresa returned to Alba. The following August the body was exhumed once more, transported secretly back to Alba de Tormes, where it has remained ever since.

However, that sacred body was dismembered and desecrated to satisfy the whims of many people. Even in death, Teresa was at the service of others.

The incorrupt body remains at Alba. Her right arm and her transverberated heart are to be seen in reliquaries there also. The right foot is in Rome. The left hand lies in Lisbon. The right hand and part of the flesh are sheltered in relics all over Spain and the wide world. She has given herself to the whole church.

Honored after Death

Within a year of her death, some of her writings were printed. In 1586, the Madrid Definitory authorized the publication of her writings. Luis de Leon edited the first collection of her works, including the *Foundations* at Salamanca two years later.

In 1590, Francisco de Ribera published the first biography of the saint, at Salamanca.

In 1591, the informative process for beatification was taken up at Salamanca.

On April 24, 1641, she was beatified by Paul V. On March 12, 1622, Gregory XV declared Teresa of Jesus a saint together with St. Isidore, Ignatius of Loyola, Francis Xavier, and Philip Neri. What illustrious company!

Other honors were to follow:

> 1627—She was declared patroness of the Kingdom of Castille.

1644—Teresa was declared the second patroness of Naples.
1922—The University of Salamanca declared her a doctor.
1965—September 10, Paul VI declared Teresa the principal patron of the Catholic writers of Spain.
1970—September 27, Paul VI declared Teresa of Jesus the first woman doctor of the church.

The whole world loves her.

Part Three
Prayer Life Within

9.

The Castle Within

I always admire the greatness of St. Teresa. As I contemplate her face, her frame, her eyes, her hands, and her handwriting, the feeling of magnanimity, power, space, and vastness stirs me. This feeling comes from a mere external superficial glance, but when I study her loftiest writings, especially, *The Interior Castle,* I seem to get lost in a vast ocean of depth, dignity, mystery, variety, and beauty. The world mapped by Teresa is the interior world, the cosmos of the spirit, where the human and the heavenly caress and unite.

The inner spirit of man has oftentimes been depicted and symbolized as a small cup, filled with mud, darkness, sin, and selfishness, a cup which must first be emptied of the negative and evil through a process of detachment, death, and mortification, before it can be filled with the light, life, love, and joy of God. St. Teresa's symbol reminds me more of the Pacific Ocean. It is easier to plumb the depths of the Pacific than to reach the confines, scan the mysteries, or penetrate the life, the variety, the splendor, and the capacity of the human soul. We are not merely human: We are partly divine. Human beings are created to the image and likeness of God. There is a rich world within us of which we little suspect and less enjoy. The Pacific Ocean could, I suppose, in time and centuries be drained dry, but the potentiality and capacity of the human spirit for life, love, truth, and joy is infinite and without limit. We are precious in the eyes of God.

> Think of the love that the Father has lavished on us by letting us be called God's children and that is what we are. —John 3:1.

No pen has chartered the mysterious world of inner space better than the pen of Teresa of Jesus. Her chosen symbol is the Castle. One good symbol is better than a library of ideas. Meditation deals with concepts. Mysticism relishes symbols.

Diego de Yepes testifies that Teresa told him how she received divine illumination before writing the book:

> This holy mother had been desirous of obtaining some insight into the beauty of a soul in grace. Just at that time, she was commanded to write a treatise on prayer, about which she knew a great deal from experience. On the eve of the festival of the most Holy Trinity she was thinking what subject she should choose for this treatise, when God, who disposes all things in due form and order, granted this desire of hers, and gave her a subject. He showed her a most beautiful crystal globe made in the shape of a castle, and containing seven mansions. In the seventh and innermost was the King of Glory in the greatest splendour, illuminating and beautifying them all. The nearer one got to the centre, the stronger was the light: outside the palace limits everything was foul, dark and infested with toads, vipers and other venomous creatures.
>
> While she was wondering at this beauty, which by God's grace can dwell in the human soul, the light suddenly vanished. Although the King of Glory did not leave the mansions, the crystal globe was plunged into darkness, became as black as coal and emitted an insufferable odour, and the venomous creatures outside the palace boundaries were permitted to enter the castle. (*The Interior Castle,* Introduction, pp. 187–188.)

This book on prayer is the fruit of many years of personal experience, human ingenuity and divine inspiration. Let us listen to our great saint as she leads us into the world of inner space:

> I began to think of the soul, as if it were a castle made of a single diamond or of very clear crystal, in which there are many mansions. The soul of the righteous man is nothing but a paradise, in which, as God tells us, He takes His delight. . . . I can find nothing with which to compare the great beauty of a soul and its great capacity. In fact, however acute our intellects may be, they will no more be able to attain to a comprehension of this

> than to an understanding of God. As He Himself says, He created us in His image and likeness. From the very fact that His Majesty says it is made in His image means that we can hardly form any conception of the soul's great dignity and beauty. (*Interior Castle*, I, 2, p. 201.)

Teresa laments that we do not know ourselves. We do not appreciate ourselves. We do not love ourselves. We are not aware of our dignity, goodness, and destiny by being God's children and sharing the divine nature. Heaven is within us, the garden of paradise is within us, the illuminated crystal palace of the Trinity shines within. We are transparent and translucent, and the divine may shine diaphanously through us. It is important as we begin our jouney into prayer and the cosmos within to start with a proper Teresian symbol. It grieves the heart of Teresa that so few Christians are authentically interested in the inner world. They are too materialistic, pragmatic, and utilitarian. They do not live by faith.

> As to what good qualities there may be in our souls, or who dwells within them, or how precious they are—these are things which we seldom consider and so we trouble little about carefully preserving the soul's beauty. All our interest is centred in the rough setting of the diamond, and in the outer well of the castle—that is to say, in these bodies of ours. (*Interior Castle*, I, 1, p. 202.)

The castle is a mystical castle, and we must not be overlogical in analyzing the symbol. The walls are not cement. They are made of glittering transparent crystal, so that we can see through and see deep into the spiritual word of infinity.

> Let us now imagine that this castle contains many mansions, some above, others below, others at each side; and in the centre and midst of them all is the chiefest mansion where the most secret things pass between God and the soul. (Ibid, p. 202.)

The first thing the good reader must realize is that there are not just seven mansions or rooms. The inner world is spacious and irregular, full of freedom.

> With regard to these first mansions I can give some very useful information out of my own experience. I must tell you to

> think of them as comprising not just a few rooms, but a very large number, literally millions. (Ibid., p. 210.)

Teresa is not so much interested in the rooms, as she is in the innermost room, the Holy of Holies within the sanctuary of the spirit where the Lord lives, loves, and communicates with the human bride.

> You must not imagine these mansions as arranged in a row, one behind another. Fix your attention on the centre, the room or palace occupied by the King. Think of a palmito, which has many outer rinds surrounding the savoury part within, all of which must be taken away before the centre can be eaten. Just so around the central room are many more, and they are also above it. In speaking of the soul, we must always think of it as spacious, lofty and ample. This can be done without the least exaggeration, for the soul's capacity is much greater than we can realize. The sun, which is in the palace, reaches every part of it. (*The Interior Castle* I, 2, p. 208.)

Teresa is centered and singleminded. The pure of heart see God. It is so easy for the rest of us to lose the essential and get lost in the psychological labyrinth of the mind. We are united to the Lord through our spiritual powers of faith, hope, love, and gifts of the spirit. I have seen so many people mistake the psychological for the spiritual, and become more interested in psychological phenomena rather than on spiritual reality. The truth sets us free.

God is at the center of Teresa's cathedral, and she wants us to have a truthful and biblical image of God. The imagination plays an important role in prayer. Here we must have an image of God, as good, great, merciful, compassionate. We tend to make God to our own image and likeness and so project our own weaknesses and shadows onto the Almighty.

We must contemplate the goodness of a God who comes to dwell within us. This is the world of love.

> If anyone loves me he will keep my word, and my Father will love him, and we shall come to him and make our home with him.

—John 14:23

The Lord loves the generous, joyful soul, and we can't have this joy unless we contemplate the goodness of God in Himself, in others, in nature, and in ourselves.

> It does us no harm to think of the things laid up for us in Heaven, and of the joys of the blessed, but rather makes us rejoice and strive to attain them just so it will do us no harm to find that it is possible in this our exile for so great a God to commune with such malodorous worms, and to love Him for His great goodness and boundless mercy. I am sure that anyone who finds it harmful to realize that it is possible for God to grant such favors during this our exile must be greatly lacking in humility and in love of his neighbour. (*The Interior Castle* I, 1, p. 202.)

Teresa adds that these divine favors are gratuitous and free. God bestows them on us not because we are holier than others, but to manifest His power and the glory of His grace. Yet, these graces are reserved for the noble and the great. The Lord enters the soul that is fortified by the virtues of magnanimity, magnificence, and munificence. We must dream the impossible dream.

Now that we know of the existence and beauty of the Interior Castle, how do we enter it? Prayer is the door. Without prayer, we are paralyzed, deafened, and dumb. We must also burn with an ardent, passionate desire. Detachment is also necessary.

> I was told by a learned man that souls without prayer are like people whose bodies or limbs are paralysed. They possess feet and hands but they cannot control them. In the same way, there are souls so infirm and so accustomed to busying themselves with outside affairs that nothing can be done for them. It seems they are incapable of entering within themselves. (Ibid, p. 203.)

We must admit that certain people are so materialistic that they have no time or interest in the higher realms of the spirit. Nothing can be done for them. We become what we love. These people, like Lot's wife, become pillars of salt, instead of glorious living cathedrals of God. Given the power and grace to converse with God, they refuse and become miserable. Prayer brings such joy.

Ours is an era of psychology, when scholars study the psychic world and the mysterious workings of the mind. It is very timely that the church puts Teresa de Ahumada before the eyes of the world once more, to guide us and inspire us at a time when writers push drugs and young people seek mystical experiences and search for relevant religion in esoteric religious practices, rush to gurus and blind masters to answer their questions and satisfy their starving spirits. As the searchlights of psychology and psychiatry are focussed on the interior life of man's mind, more and more people study the great mystics.

Teresa de Jesus is the greatest woman mystic, and women are naturally more mystical than men, more attuned to the real and the inner womb of the spirit. Teresa has so much to feed the querying mind in her *Interior Castle*. Let us hope that the young women of today who in college campuses the world over seek relief from the nostaglia and ennui of life in hash, L.S.D., marijuana, and alcohol, may find in the pages of St. Teresa new lights and hopes to realize something about the wonderful world of grace that is possible to the woman who prays. We get our power from within. We don't have to turn to dope to turn us on or light us up. Life is worth living and living well. It is so sad to see so many young lives destroyed in suicide, and so many others bored to death by existential neurosis.

The human soul as seen by Teresa is rich, brilliant, with many rooms and several mansions. It is the Father's house and in the Father's house there are many mansions,

> Do not let your hearts be troubled. Trust in God still and trust in me. There are many rooms in my Father's house.
>
> John 14:1

Teresa describes the soul as "Beautiful and resplendent, this Orient pearl, this tree of life, planted in the living waters of life, namely in God." (*The Interior Castle*, 1, 2, p. 205.)

The water of life is the Holy Spirit who lavishes His graces and gifts upon us and converts our inner sanctuary into the garden of paradise. Paradise is not behind us, but within us. Heaven is within, a banquet of consciousness: Prayer is a growth in consciousness.

This inner life is possible to all. Every Christian is called to contemplation, that deeper, more enlightened loving knowledge and enjoyment of God and His creation. Nobody is excluded. It is open to the married, the child, the teenager, the busy professional as it is to the cloistered Carmelite nun.

Teresa puts an ideal before us that entices, and she does this in a way that is practical, simple, unenigmatic, and clear. She bids us to have courage. It is striking to notice that the cardinal virtue Teresa stresses most in the context of prayer is fortitude, and the filial virtues of perseverance, patience and determination. We need the guts to begin and the guts to continue. Teresa abhors souls that are small, spirits that are soft, natures that are sensitive, and people who are afraid. Men and women of prayer who wish to climb the summit of Mount Carmel are not meant for safe havens. They must be ready to fly like eagles and not grow dizzy on the craggy and sublime heights of the divine. They must have the spirit of the Castillian conquistadores, the hearts of the troubadours, the imagination of poets, the searching mind of the explorer, and faith and live great enough to move mountains of selfishness and pettiness. Carmel is the land of the noble and the brave, the home of the wild and the free. It is a land of light and joy, a land of love, peace, and mysticism.

Too often in the past Carmel has been presented in terms and images of darkness, aridity, death, and desert. The desert is there. The desert is arid, but the desert is beautiful and mysterious. The great mystic and founding father, the trusted friend and faithful ally of Teresa, John of the Cross, has been depicted as a doctor of negation, and gloom, whereas his teaching is beautiful, positive, and inspiring. Even his poem, "The Ascent of Mount Carmel," which frightens away so many would-be admirers, is full of symbols and images of light and joy. It is a poem on romantic happiness.

A cursory glance through the poem proves this. The mystical doctor sings of a "happy chance," "kindled in love," "restful house," "yearning love," "burning light," "night more lovely than the dawn," "union of lover and beloved," "transforming love," "flowery heart," "sleep, caresses, gentle breezes, gentle touches ecstasy," "leaving my cares forgotten among the lilies."

His "Spiritual Canticle," and "Living Flame of Love" celebrate the freedom and ecstatic joy of a soul in union. And so these two mighty Carmelite mystics are of one mind, as they describe the inner life of the human spirit, and its capacity through prayer for love and glory.

When God made man, He meant him for joy and greatness.

> What is man that you should keep him in mind, mortal man that you care for him? Yet you have made him little less than a god; with glory and honour you have crowned him,
> gave him power over the works of your hand,
> put all things under his feet.

> Psalm 8.

The ultimate purpose is always *"as laudem gloriae Dei,"* the praise and glory of God, and the person who renders greatest praise and glory to God is the person who is most alive. He lives life to the fullest and develops all his powers, faculties, and gifts. It is sad to know that at best most of us develop only 10 percent of our powers, when at the end of time, God will ask us, "Why didn't you become you?"

> O Kind of glory and Lord of all Kings, Thy Kingdom is not fenced in by trifles, but is infinite. (*Life,* Ch. 37, p. 264.)

God's Life Within the Castle

As Teresa writes in *The Interior Castle,* her mind is haunted with the truth of God's presence in the depth of our soul. The Lord of all life, love, and light dwells in the center of the spirit. In Him, we live, move, and have our being, and He floods our soul with the light of his loving presence. Teresa gently leads us into the depths and shows us how to communicate with the Father, Son, and Holy Spirit. We are shrines of His presence; we are temples of the Holy Spirit.

> Didn't you realise that you were God's temple and that the Spirit of God was living among you? If anybody should destroy the temple of God, God will destroy him, because the temple of God is sacred, and you are the temple.

> —1 Cor. 4:16

> Anyone who is joined to the Lord is one spirit with him. . . . Your body, you know, is the temple of the Holy Spirit. He is in you, since you received him from God. You are not your own property. You have been bought and paid for. That is why you should use your body for the glory of God.
>
> —1 Cor. 6:17, 18–20

Teresa made of her body a shrine of His presence. God so loves us, too, that He makes His home within us, and here at the core of our being, we may communicate with the Three Persons of the Blessed Trinity. Here we live life at its best, as the Divine Spirit touches our spirit and inundates us with life and light and love. Only the mystic knows how to live life to the fullest.

Most people live a life that is dull, superficial, and external, a life centered around the material world and the body with its needs, senses, desires, and emotions. They are wasted lives of quiet desperation. The scholar and the scientist may make abundant use of the intellect and will, as they study the laws of nature, but the mystic penetrates the depth of the Spirit, alone with God, and His Eternal law in the celestial castle.

> We have a wisdom to offer those who have reached maturity: not a philosophy of our age . . . we teach what scripture calls: the things that no eye has seen and no ear has heard, things beyond the mind of man, all that God has prepared for those who love him.
> The Spirit reaches the depths of everything, even the depths of God. . . . The depths of God can only be known by the Spirit of God. We have received the Spirit that comes from God to teach us to understand the gifts that he has given us. Therefore we teach, not in the way in which philosophy is taught, but in the way that the Spirit teaches us. We teach spiritual things spiritually. An unspiritual person is one who does not accept anything of the Spirit of God: he sees it all as nonsense: It is beyond his understanding, because it can only be understood by means of the Spirit. . . . We are those who have the mind of Christ.
>
> 1 Cor. 2:6–8, 10–15,16

Teresa had the mind of Christ, she was attuned to the Spirit, understood spiritual things spiritually and reached the depths of God. She was blessed with the gift of wisdom.

"God is love." This is the magnificent revelation of the New Testament. He says to each one of us.

> I am who I am
> I am here, now, in you, with you and within you.
> Don't be afraid
> I Love you.

St. John revealed this truth to us,

> God is love
> Anyone who lives in love lives in God
> And God lives in him.
>
> —1 John 16

> "As long as we love one another
> God will live in us
> And his love will be complete in us."—1 John 4:16

> "If anyone acknowledges that Jesus
> is the Son of God, God lives in him,
> and he is God."—1 John 4:15

God's tremendous and merciful love that draws Him so close and intimate to us is the basis of our life of prayer and contemplation. The lover enters the beloved. The beloved enters the world of the lover. Because God is love and He loves us, He gives us a gift. This gift is nothing less than the gift of the Three Persons of the Blessed Trinity. At Baptism our bodies are consecrated as temples of the living God, who shares His nature with us, and the Father, Son, and Holy Spirit come to live, love, and dwell within our souls. This is a supernatural gift—the gift of increated grace. We are divinized by God Himself.

Unfortunately our faith is often too weak to be aware of the divine life going on within. God is within, but we are living outside. We will never find God until we learn to find Him within ourselves in that gentle, inward movement, the glance of faith, love, and hope.

Teresa writes of the people who have the courage to take the first step into the castle of prayer.

> They are very much absorbed in wordly affairs: but their

desires are good. Sometimes, though infrequently, they commend themselves to Our Lord. They think about the state of their souls, though not very carefully. Full of a thousand preoccupations, they pray only a few times a month, and as a rule they are thinking all the time of their preoccupations, for they are very much attached to them. Where their treasure is there is the heart also. . . . Eventually they enter the first rooms on the lowest floor, but so many reptiles get in with them that they are unable to appreciate the beauty of the castle or find any peace within it. Still, they have done a good deal by entering at all. (*The Interior Castle* I, 1, p. 204.)

Prayer is listening to the Spirit, and we cannot listen to the Spirit unless we first learn to listen to ourselves. The whisper of the Spirit is heard in silence and solitude.

The doctrine of the Indwelling Trinity, so well founded in Sacred Scripture, gave tremendous light and consolation to Teresa. She knew by experience that God lived within her, but some of her unlearned directors cast aspersions and doubt on her experience. St. Augustine came to her rescue. In *The Way of Perfection* she writes:

"If you know that God is everywhere, and this is a great truth, for of course wherever the King is, or so they say, the court is too, that is to say, wherever God is, there is Heaven. No doubt you can believe that, in any place where His Majesty is, there is fullness of glory.

"Remember how St. Augustine tells us about his seeking God in many places and eventually finding Him within Himself . . . we need no wings to go in search of Him, we have only to find a place where we can be alone and look upon Him present within us . . . Remember how important it is for you to have understood this truth—that the Lord is within us and that we should be there with Him." (*The Way of Perfection* 28, pp. 114–115.)

I will give here just a few passages from Sacred Scripture on which we may well meditate to help us appreciate the biblical foundation of Teresa's teachings. Our saint was very careful to base all her teaching on the Word of God and the orthodox doctrine of the church.

At the Last Supper, Our Lord said, "If anyone loves me, he will keep my word, and my Father will love him and we shall come to him and make our home with him." (John 14:23)

The above is the favorite passage of all the mystics, and these few golden words are a mine of contemplative insight. They are sufficient fuel and food in themselves for a lifetime of prayer.

> Anybody who loves me will be loved by my Father and I shall love him and *show* myself to him.
>
> —John 14:21

Love is the revelatory power. The Word together with the Father and the Spirit live in any soul that loves, and there amid the flames of charity they manifest themselves as living, loving, compassionate, and uniting friends. The greatest mystics like Teresa and John of the Cross sing of this wonderful manifestation of divine condescension.

This prayerful love is all-powerful. Christ adds to it an unbelievable guarantee and apostolic vigor.

> Whatever you ask for in my name I will do, so that the Father may be glorified in the Son. If you ask for anything in my name, I will do it.
>
> —John 14:31–14.

Asking in the name of Jesus is asking in the person of Jesus. With burning love in our hearts for His mystical body we believe that He is the Son of God, and when we pray, He prays in, with, through, and for us. Jesus is the great high priest praying in us, His Temples.

Our Lord once more reminds us of the consoling truth of our union with Him in the image of the vine.
I am the vine
You are the branches.
Whoever remains in me, with me in him
bears fruit in plenty.
Cut off from me you can do nothing.

> —John 15:15.

"Make your home in me, as I make mine in you." (John 15:4.)

This loving union through faith and hope with Christ the true vine is the one condition laid down by the Lord for the efficacy of prayer. Prayer is the greatest power on earth, because when I pray, I pray as a branch in the vine. As the vine is in the branch, and the branch is in the vine, Jesus is in me, and I am in Him. His divine nature, His life, His power, His Father, His Spirit, His sap, His glory, His prayer is in me. He is the one. The life in the vine is the life in the branch. The power in the vine is the power in the branch. The prayer of the vine is the prayer of the branch. And at the same time the prayer of the branch is the prayer of the vine, the fruit on the branch is the fruit of the vine, the beauty of the branch is the beauty of the vine. We are all one and Jesus needs us. This union is awakened in prayer. The prayer that ascends to God from a heart full of love and goodness gives greater glory to God and brings down more graces on the world than all books written and sermons preached, or wars waged. Saints save the world and live life fully. Our beloved Pope John XXIII quoted the words of Bernanos, "The only sad thing is that we are not all saints." This proves the power and efficacy of the prayer apostolate carried out by Carmelites and contemplatives the world over. St. Therese of Lisieux, the best known daughter of St. Teresa of Avila bears this fact out. She is the greatest saint of our century, and with St. Francis Xavier, is the patroness of the missions. Her secret way direct to the Heart of God was through prayer, penance and her little way of childlike trust on the merciful love of God. It will be sad for the church and the world when this form of life is despised and derogated.

This is a very lofty form of life, beyond the reach of our human powers and capacities. But the Lord has bestowed on us supernatural spiritual powers. We can fly freely into the bright realms of the spirit.

Christ knew this, so He promised and gave us the Holy Spirit of life and the Spirit of Love, the mighty Paraclete and Advocate who would teach, mother, and console us in this earthly exile after His ascension.

I shall ask the Father
and He will give you another Advocate,
to be with you for ever, the Spirit of truth
You know Him . . .

He is with you, He is in You . . .
I will not leave you orphans . . .
You will understand that I am in my Father,
you in me and I in you . . .
He will teach you everything and
remind you of all I said to you.

—John 14:15–17, 19, 20, 26.

To synopsize Romans 8, Paul teaches that we are spiritual:

Since the Spirit of God has made his home in you . . .
You possess the Spirit of Christ . . .
The Spirit makes us cry out, "Abba, Father . . ."
when we cannot choose words in order to pray properly,
the Spirit expresses our plea in a way that
could never be put into words.

—Rom. 8:8–27.

The spirit of Jesus, the spirit of the Son draws us lovingly to the Father so that we can approach and commune with the Father like little children who call Abba, "Daddy." Teresa indeed spoke to the Lord as a friend speaks to a friend, as a daughter speaks to her father. This relationship was not so much a matter of words as of life and being. She was a daughter of God and she lived and knew it. Teresa was a spiritual woman, a woman moved and possessed by the Spirit; a woman whose spirit touched and invoked the Spirit within, a woman who allowed full freedom to the working and inspiration of the Holy Spirit within, a woman redeemed with the grace of the freedom of the children of God, whose supernatural prayer throughout the last twelve years of her life was carried out through the help of the Holy Spirit and His gifts, who expressed within her and through her pleas and prayers to the Father unutterable and inexpressible in human language. Teresa was indeed the living temple of the Holy Spirit, the prayerful shrine of His presence. Wed to the Spirit, she conceived the word and incarnated Him in life and prayer.

With the Holy Spirit acting freely within, the spiritual life of man in the depths of the soul is transformed. The Spirit, spiritualizes, deiforms, and reforms us.

St. John of the Cross teaches the same truth. Purification, transformation, and perfection are ultimately carried out through love. We cannot do it by ourselves. Love makes equal and so that we may be made equals with God and raised up, the Spirit transforms us. By baptism, we share in the divine nature, and this sharing comes to full flower in the profoundest prayer of contemplation.

To most of us this awesome mystery lies hidden. God has hidden His face, but He revealed it to the great mystics like Moses, John, Paul, Augustine, Teresa, John of the Cross, and Catherine. We should listen to them as they tell us about this sweet encounter. Christian soul, contemplate your dignity. We can surmise our power, our dignity, and destiny as the mystics sing to us of their experiences.

We are sons in the Son, loving in the Spirit and one with the life of the Father. The Three Persons of the Blessed Trinity live within us, involve us in Their life and each in his own way communicate Himself to us. The mystic is aware of this communication. He consciously shares in God's love and then willingly shares that love with others in good done. It is interesting to note that St. Teresa wrote her greatest book during the six months when she was externally most active and suffering most for the Order she founded.

When the Light Goes Out

The human soul has the capacity and the power to live a life splendid, rich, and exuberant, but it has also the freedom to sink into the mud of wickedness and sin. There is a choice in life. Teresa laments the loss of those who enter the first mansion of the castle and then fall into mortal sin. The tree of life withers in "A pool of pitch-black, evil-smelling water that produces nothing but misery and filth . . . a tree rooted in the devil." (*The Interior Castle*, I, 2, p. 206.)

Perhaps one of the most vivid psychological and symbolic portraits ever painted by a mystic on the state of a soul in sin has been depicted by St. Teresa in Chapter Two of *The Interior Castle*. This is a well-known passage which may help us appreciate the beauty of grace, when contrasted with the fetidness of evil.

> When the soul falls into a mortal sin, no thicker darkness exists and there is nothing dark and black which is not much less so than this. . . . Although the sun Himself, who has given it all its splendour and beauty, is still there in the centre of the soul, it is as if He were not there for any participation which the soul has in Him, though it is capable of enjoying Him as is the crystal of reflecting the Sun.
>
> While in a state like this the soul will find profit in nothing. Being as it is in mortal sin, none of the good works it may do will be of any avail to win it glory. They will not have their origin in that first Principle, which is God, through whom alone our virtue is true virtue. Since the soul has separated itself from Him, it cannot be pleasing in His eyes. After all, the intention of a person who commits a mortal sin is not to please Him but to give pleasure to the devil. As the devil is darkness itself, the poor soul becomes darkness itself likewise. . . . When the soul through its own fault becomes rooted in a pool of pitch-black, evil-smelling water, it produces nothing but misery and filth.
>
> It should be noted that it is not the spring, or the brilliant sun which is in the centre of the soul that loses its splendour and beauty, for they are always within it, and nothing can take away their beauty.
>
> If a thick black cloth be placed over a crystal in the sunshine, although the sun may be shining upon it, the brightness will have no effect upon the crystal. (*The Interior Castle* I, 2, pp. 205–206.)

Saddened by this awful vision Teresa cries:

> O souls redeemed by the blood of Jesus Christ! Learn to understand yourselves and take pity on yourselves . . . what a state the poor rooms of the castle are in! How distracted are the senses which inhabit them! And the faculties which are the governors and butlers and stewards—how blind they are and how ill-controlled! After all, what kind of fruit can one expect to be borne by a tree rooted in the devil. (Ibid, p. 206.)

Without God's help, we are all-powerless. We must be humble. Any good we do does not have its source in ourselves, but in the spring of life.

When we fall into mortal sin, the ocean of life, light, and love turns into a fetid bog where vipers wallow and death smells. The spirit is numbed, paralyzed, dumb, and deaf to the things of God. Moral disintegration is followed by the psychological symptoms of distracted senses, blinded faculties, uncontrolled emotions and a general feeling of fear and frustration. We cannot concentrate. We cannot center. The house of God is turned into a devil's den, and the tree of life roots in stagnant waters.

> May God in His mercy, deliver us from such evil, for there is nothing in the whole of our lives that so thoroughly deserves to be called evil as this, since it brings endless and external evils in its train. (*The Interior Castle*, I. 2, p. 206.)

Aware of the good and the beautiful, the mystic is also conscious of the reality of evil.

The First Steps

At the center of the crystal globe of the soul God dwells. God is real. To attain union with God I have to travel a dangerous, mysterious labyrinthine path through my own psyche. That world of inner space is haunted by good and evil spirits. It is also a complex computer of human powers, of which some are conscious, some unconscious, and others that are superconscious. So we must know ourselves. So many people rush in where angels fear to tread.

> Self-knowledge is so important that, even if you were raised right up to the heavens, I should like you never to relax your cultivation of it. So long as we are on this earth, nothing matters more to us than humility. (*The Interior Castle* I. 2, p. 108.)

True self-knowledge and humility are twins. Without God we can do nothing in prayer. Prayer is a supernaturally infused gift. The journey along the spiritual road consists of a loving knowledge of self in relationship to God. "Lord that I may know myself: Lord that I may know thee," prayed Augustine.

Without knowledge we will go astray. Competent directions are necessary.

> O Lord, do Thou remember how much we have to suffer on this road through lack of knowledge. The worst of it is that, as we do not realize we need to know more, when we think about Thee, we cannot ask those who know . . . we suffer terrible trials

because, we do not understand ourselves. (*The Interior Castle* IV, 1, pp. 233–234.)

> We shall never succeed in knowing ourselves unless we seek to know God. Let us think of His greatness and then come back to our own baseness. By looking at His purity, we shall see our foolishness. By meditating upon His humility, we shall see how far we are from being humble. (*The Interior Castle*, I, 2, p. 209.)

Teresa condemns all forms of pseudohumility that emanates from cowardice, fear, and pusillanimity of spirit. Humility is truth. The humble soul is centered on God, trusts Him completely, does His will, and does not lose time on narcissistic psychological self-analysis or asking foolish questions: "Can anyone as wretched as I engage in so lofty an exercise as prayer." (*The Interior Castle*, I, 2, p. 209.)

Such questionable misgivings come from lack of self-knowledge. We never stop thinking about ourselves:

> We must set our eyes upon Christ our God from whom we shall learn true humility. Our understanding will then be ennobled, and self-knowledge will not make us timorous and fearful. . . . Terrible are the crafts and wiles which the devil uses to prevent souls from learning to know themselves and understanding his ways. (Ibid, pp. 209–210.)

Novices along the spiritual journey oversimplify. They do not know how to diagnose the various powers at work upon them. We are passive to so many hidden forces from the divine, the demonic, the physical, and the psychological realms. Teresa warns us about these demonic forces.

> The devil has many legions of evil spirits in each room to prevent souls from passing from one to another. As we poor souls fail to realize this, we are tricked by all kinds of deceptions. The devil is less successful with those who are nearer the King's dwelling-place. (*The Interior Castle* I, 2, p. 210.)

People who begin prayer are not yet detached, and so they leave themselves wide open to the enticements and temptations that come from the material world outside. Distraction weakens the light.

> Though not in a bad state, the soul is so completely absorbed in the things of the world, and so deeply immersed in possessions or honours or business, that although it would like to gaze at the castle and enjoy its beauty, it is prevented from doing so, and seems quite unable to free itself from all these impediments. (*The Interior Castle*, I, 2, p. 211.)

Psychological and spiritual self-knowledge is so necessary. Teresa opens up to us the rich nature of the human soul, but she also knows that we have been wounded and weakened by original sin. The amazing human computer does not work as it ought. The light of God floods the depths of the spirit, but there can be darkness and war in the various faculties, emotions, and senses. The more interior part of the soul, the still point, the ocean of tranquillity, may be habitually at peace, while the more exterior part of the senses, imagination, emotions, and thoughts are in turbulence.

> It exasperated me to see the faculties of the soul occupied with God and recollected in Him, and the thoughts confused and excited. . . .
>
> Just as we cannot stop the movement of the heavens, revolving as they do with such speed, so we cannot restrain our thoughts. . . . The soul may be wholly united with Him in the mansion very near His presence, while thoughts remain on the outskirts of the castle, suffering the assaults of a thousand wild and venomous creatures. (*The Interior Castle*, IV, pp. 233–234.)

The spiritual knowledge of God keeps us balanced. We know that God is all (*todo*) and we are nothing (*nada*). This truth creates peace that nothing can disturb. Every contemplative spends time on this reality, the abyss that separates the all and the nothing. Teresa enjoyed a vivid awareness of the majesty of God, and the misery of the creature, especially when spoiled by sin. Snakes, vipers, and venomous creatures may invade the castle. There are forces of evil lodged within us. Man, capable of the loftiest, is also open to the heinous. We discover within ourselves the concupiscence of the flesh, the concupiscence of the eyes, and the pride of life. Human nature is disordered and driven by many drives, cravings, lusts, pride, covetousness, anger, gluttonies, envies, and sloth. Environment and heredity affect us, while we have so many diversified temperaments, personal habits, unconscious drives, phobias, fixations, and defense mechanisms. We play so many games in the name of spirituality.

Only the Lord can enlighten and guide us. We shall never succeed in knowing ourselves unless we seek to know God. Then He gives us knowledge.

> When the Spirit of God is at work, there is no need to go looking for ways of inducing humility. The Lord reveals these to us in a very different manner from we can find by means of our puny reflections, which are nothing by comparison with a true humility proceeding from the light given us this way by the Lord. (*Life*, 15, p. 95.)

Understanding motivation is a tricky business. Teresa condemns a false zeal, an envious fervor that masquerades under a cloud of hypocritical care and concern for externals and superficialities that do not matter. Religious can kill one another under the veil of kindness. The devil decieves the hypocritical zealots. A hypocrite is a person who fools himself.

> Beware, my daughters of cares which have nothing to do with you. . . . It is most important that we should not cease to be watchful against the devil's wiles, least he deceive us in the guise of an angel of light. (*The Interior Castle* I, 2, p. 211.)

The devil uses good. It is amazing how many communities of prayer have been split by differences over what is good. Faith, hope, love, a ready will to forgive at once, and a free spirit of spontaneous joy and celebration keep people together. These are the columns of the castle. The devil surreptitiously uses "a noiseless file" to saw away the foundation. The history of the spiritual life is filled with the stories of many fervent religious who ruined their own lives and the lives of others by a false zeal, which was, in fact, nothing more than a raw ambition for power. They spy on others.

> Another sister is inspired with zeal for the greatest possible perfection. This is a very good thing, but the result of it might be that she would think any little fault on the part of the sisters a serious failure, and would always be looking out for such things

and running to the prioress about them. (*The Interior Castle* I, 2, p. 212.)

The devil's aim is to cool charity. How can a sister who has really tried to harm another sister in the name of religion or some lesser law expect the Spirit of love and peace to come to her during prayer. Community prayer in such a case is a legal farce. It is not Christian prayer.

Teresa brings us back to the center:

> Let us realize that true perfection consists in the love of God and of our neighbor, and the more nearly perfect our observance of these two commandments the nearer to perfection we shall be. Our entire Rule and Constitutions are nothing but means which enable us to do this more perfectly. Let us refrain from indiscreet zeal, which may do us great harm. Let each one look to herself. (*The Interior Castle* I, 2, p. 212.)

The longer I live in religious life, the more I appreciate the wisdom of the counsel given by John of the Cross—that each one should live in the monastery, as though he were the only one there. In other words, only people who can mind their own damn business are ready to enter the second mansion.

These fervent zealots who don't have great love in them, then turn to indiscreet asceticism. They burden themselves with the penances of beasts and soon behave accordingly. They are miserable themselves and wallow in the company of others who are foolish enough to listen to them. Thousands have been ruined. In the end she ruins her health and is unable to do what her Rule demands. You see what this apparently good thing has led to. (Ibid, p. 211.)

Mutual love, reverence, and respect are all important virtues to foster in the first mansion of prayer.

The Second Mansion

Courage is needed in prayer, the courage to begin, and the courage to persevere. To face the Almightly as Elijah discovered is an awesome adventure. Many people are interested in prayer, study prayer, attend retreats on prayer, pray for awhile, but they lack perseverance and dedicated commitment. They still have their feet in two worlds, the world of the spirit and the world of business and pleasure. Sin happens easily. Then follows the fear, guilt, worry depression. The Lord like a good friend keeps calling inward.

> They gradually get nearer to the place where His Majesty dwells. He becomes a very good neighbour to them. Such are His mercy and goodness that, even when we are engaged in our wordly pastimes and business and pleasure and keep falling into sins and rising again. . . . He calls us ceaselessly, time after time, to approach Him. (*The Interior Castle* II, 1, pp. 213–214.)

Teresa is aware of the compassionate and ever-merciful heart of God. We are fragile, limited, destined to live most of our lives in the desert and the void. Very often we are going to fall like boats without an oar or a sail out on a vast ocean at midnight, lost in the mist without star or moon to guide us. The dark night of sense and spirit haunts most of our lives, and we must face it. The great lights, the peak experiences are tiny oases in a Sahara Desert for most of us. There is the attraction of the world. We can be very lonely, misunderstood, not knowing our own basic attitudes, craving attention, love, and affection, suffering sexually and often put down by authority figures who have a power complex and don't know it. Keep going. Keep trucking! His Majesty keeps calling to us. He has His chosen instruments. We are not going to hear heavenly voices like Paul.

> His appeals come through the conversations of good people, from sermons, good books. . . . Or they come through sicknesses, and trials, or by means of truths which God teaches us at times when we are engaged in prayer. (*The Interior Castle* II, 1, p. 214.)

What the Lord wants now are good desires. Desire is important. We don't have the courage to burn, to convert the red fire of passion into the white fire of mystical love to lay our lives on the line and die to self. As William McNamara, O.C.D. writes:

> I know what's wrong with me: I am not passionate enough. I am not being aroused and lured into the sheer totality of me which God desires with infinite desire to fashion out of the undreamed of and underdeveloped potentialities of my being. I am

> not completely in tune with the universe, with the universality of being, with Being itself. If I am alienated, frustrated, lonely, it is because I am out of touch with the center of things If I am out of touch with the center of things, with God, it is because I do not take God with unconditional seriousness; that is to say, I do not allow myself to be ruled and governed by one pure passion (*Mystical Passion*, p. 6.)

We need simplicity of vision, purity of heart, and tenacity of will. Teresa cried, "Strive and strive and strive."

We must be patient. God's time is not our time. God's time is called *chairos*, the sacred moment of the Spirit, which is laden with grace and can change the whole course of our life in seconds. The Lord of History is not bound by chronos or clock time.

Once inside the walls of the cathedral of prayer and distanced from the external material obstacles, the devil plays havoc with the imagination. Imagine a young Carmelite nun now in her cloister, removed from the things of the world, disciplined in body and sense and intent on doing her best. She may be in prayer, her senses closed and body stilled, when all of a sudden the storm breaks out in the imagination. The imagination is the door to the inner world and here Satan has placed his best commandoes.

> The devils once more show the soul these vipers—that is, the things of the world. They pretend that earthly pleasure are almost eternal. They remind the soul of the esteem in which it is held in the world, of its friends and relatives, of the way in which its health will be endangered by penances and of impediments of a thousand other kinds. (*The Interior Castle* II, 1, p. 214.)

What tools have we now to counteract the guiles and wiles of Satan? Teresa tells us to use the higher faculties and powers of reason, memory, and faith. The Word has shared His light with us in the light of reason. Clear, radical, good thinking drives away the obfuscated half-truths and lies of Lucifer. The truth makes us free. Clear thinking reveals the truth.

> Then the will shows the soul how this true Lover never leaves it, but goes with it everywhere and gives it light and being. The

> understanding comes forward and makes the soul realize that, for however many years it may live, it can never hope to have a better friend. The world is full of falsehood and these pleasures which the devil pictures are accompanied by trials and cares and annoyances. The understanding tells it to be certain that outside this castle it will find neither security nor peace. (*The Interior Castle* II, 1, p. 215.)

There is no greater weapon than the cross. We must bear suffering patiently. The castle is built on the solid walls of moral character, psychological maturity, physical fitness and love for prayer. It is foolish to try to build the castle on spiritual favors, personal experiences, and psychic consolation.

> All that the beginner in prayer has to do—and you must not forget this—is to labour and be resolute and prepare himself with all possible diligence to bring his will into conformity with the will of God. . . . Often it is the Lord's will that we should be persecuted and afflicted by evil thoughts, which we cannot cast out, and also by aridities. . . . Do not lose heart or cease striving. . . . Even out of your fall God will bring good. . . . Believe me, unless we have peace and strive for peace in our own home, we shall not find it in the homes of others. (*The Interior Castle* II, 1, p. 217.)

People of experience, good resurrection friends are good companions. We must have them. But above all, we must learn how to cut out the outer world, close the senses, quiet the emotions, the imagination, and the mind and enter gently into recollection.

> The door by which we can enter the castle is prayer. It is absurd to think that we can enter heaven without first entering our own souls. We must get to know ourselves, reflect upon the wretchedness of our nature and what we owe to God, and continually imploring His Mercy. (*The Interior Castle* II, 1, p. 218.)

Third Mansion

The steadfast soul enters the third mansion and most people spend their lives ruminating around the rooms. It becomes the mansion of the complacent.

The third mansionites who are afraid to dig deeper and get burned in the fire of divine love waste a lot of time on externals. They are legalistic, pragmatic, and utilitarian. They will not rock the boat. The external props so necessary to beginners may now become a hindrance.

> Nor must you set store by the fact that you are cloistered and lead lives of penitence—nor must you become confident because you are always talking about God and engaging in prayer, withdrawing yourselves from the things of the world. All that is good, but it is not enough to justify us in laying aside our fears. (L.C. III, 1, p. 221)

> What matters is not whether or no we wear a religious habit, it is whether we try to practise the virtues, and make a complete surrender of our wills to God and order our lives, as His Majesty ordains. (*The Interior Castle* III, 2, p. 226.)

There are many rooms in the third mansion and plenty of space to harbour all kinds of people from the lukewarm to the brave. Teresa describes the typically good person:

> There are many such souls in the world. They are most desirous not to offend His Majesty. They avoid committing venial sins. They love doing penance. They spend hours in recollection. They use their time well. They practice works of charity. They are very careful in their speech and dress and in the government of their household if they have one. (*The Interior Castle* III, 2, p. 221.)

What hinders people like this from going farther? They are like the rich young man in the gospel. They keep the commandments, do their duty, but they are not generous enough interiorly to listen to Jesus as He calls.

> If you wish to be perfect, go and sell what you own and give the money to the poor, and you will have treasures in heaven, then come, follow me. —Mt. 19:20–22.

We must detach ourselves ever more from our works and our possessions, our doing and our having and learn to be. The fiery people of the third mansion find it hard to be still, recollected, and quiet.

> Enter in, enter within yourselves. Get away from your trifling good works. . . . Look at the saints who have entered the King's chamber and you will see the difference between them and yourselves. (*The Interior Castle* III, 2, p. 222.)

Aridity in prayer is very common now. These people pray, but they are not willing to let go of the older, well tried, but worn out forms of prayer and enter the still waters of contemplation. The Lord keeps calling. They refuse to follow. They insist on taking control of their lives. They will not surrender themselves with childlike confidence to mercifal love of God, as St. Therese did. They refuse to follow. Many give up prayer and get lost in the turmoil of action. They become more horizontal and less vertical. Because they are so good and do so many good things, they imagine they have a right to higher favors. Like Martha, they worry and fret about so many things. Yes, they welcome the Lord and are busy serving. Yet they somehow draw attention to themselves.

> Lord do you not care that my sister is leaving me to do the serving all by myself? Please tell her to help me. —Luke, 11:40.

They do not yet have the wisdom of Mary to sit at the Lord's feet and listen. Lacking humility, which Teresa calls "the ointment of our wounds," they grow depressive, despondent, and restless. True humility is needed.

> Where there is true humility, even if God never grants favors, He will give it peace and resignation to His will, with which it may be more content than others are with favors. (*The Interior Castle* III, 2, p. 233.)

We are fonder of spiritual sweetness than of crosses. His Majesty gives the favors to the weak. The strong hammer out their salvation on the anvil of suffering and the wood of the cross. It is, when tested by trial, that we get to know ourselves, and humble self-knowledge is required.

It is very disappointing to find souls who have reached this state falter and founder in the face of adversity. When their upright and carefully ordered lives are upset, they reveal their real color. Legalistic in mind, they try to fix life and the Lord into their little boxes of laws and rituals. They may master the world, and still be slaves of their inner emotions. Teresa gives us the picture of what happens, when they are disturbed. They are disturbed because they are not detached and free.

> His Majesty sends them tests which have been by no means exacting, and they become so restless and depressed in spirit that they have exasperated me. I have been made thoroughly afraid of them. It is no use offering them advice for they have been practicing virtue for so long that they think they are capable of teaching others, and have ample justification for feeling as they do. . . . It is useless to argue with them. . . . they brood over their woes . . . they make up their minds they are suffering for God's sake. (*The Interior Castle*, III, 2, p. 224.)

These good, moral Christians still worry too much over their finances, their properties, their name, fame, and reputation. They are extremely sensitive to criticism and correction. They have not obtained mastery over their passions. They meditate on the passion, do their little penances, practice their little charities, but they are too discreet to disturb their carefully ordered lives. They will advance but only at a snail's pace. They are not ready to sail out into the deep, open up the sails and let go.

> When we proceed with all this caution, we find stumbling blocks everywhere. . . . Let us make real effort. Let us leave our reason and our fears in His hands and let us forget the weaknesses of our nature which is apt to cause us so much worry . . . we shall be making a great mistake if we worry over our health. It will not be improved by our anxiety about it—that I well know! (*The Interior Castle*, III, 2, p. 226.)

The journey demands guts and great humility. Without complete self-renunciation and freedom of spirit the journey into the *Interior Castle* becomes long, arid, and difficult.

Teresa has some words of wisdom for people in the third mansion.

> Let us look at our own shortcomings and leave other people's alone. Those who live carefully ordered lives are apt to be shocked at everything. We might well learn very important lessons from the persons who shock us. Our outward comportment and behavior may be better than theirs, but this, though good, is not

the most important thing. There is no reason to expect everyone else to travel by our own road. We should not attempt to point them to the spiritual path when perhaps we do not know what it is, . . . It is better to attempt to do what our Rule tells us—to try to live ever in silence and in hope, and the Lord will take care of His own. (*The Interior Castle* III, 2, p. 229.)

10.
Prayer

Ours is an age of rapid change and revolution. The speed and noise of the urban and industrial world today is deafening. Technology sweeps us along with so much speed and noise coming from jets, jazz bands, television, stereos, and machines, that modern man can scarcely hear the voice from within. With so many movies, magazines, advertisements, and distractions of all kinds, he does not have time or energy to look at himself fully and deeply or scan the mysteries of a world that cannot be seen by the human eye and reason. A pioneer in outer space, he is lost in inner space.

We must all learn to be quiet, to stop, look, and listen to the real. To survive as humans we must learn to pray and contemplate.

There is a prayer center in every human heart, a sacred sanctuary where the Divine is present, sharing His life, light, love, and joy. Prayer flows from our mysterious depths, a welling up of the word of God inside us under the breath of the Holy Spirit. The Father has poured the Spirit of His Son into us "And it makes us cry out, 'Abba, Father.'" (Rm. 8:15)

> The Spirit too comes to help us in our weakness. When we cannot choose words in order to pray properly, the Spirit himself expresses our plea in a way that could never be put into words.
> —Rm 8: 26–27.

Prayer is the highest expression of the Christian spirit.

Christ lives, loves, and prays within us. We share in his priesthood. St. Augustine put this truth beautifully.

> As our priest He prays for us. As our head He prays in us, As our God He is prayed to by us. Let us recognize our voice in His. Let us recognize His voice in us.

The devil uses good. He is an angel of light. He uses our very virtues, so he can do evil. Our apostolic zeal is premature. Let us remember at this stage that there is no one else in the world save God and the soul. Our very distress over the sins and fate of others is nothing but worry and a distraction. I have seen people fall into fits of depression. Good intention does not save us from filling our inner temple with useless images, fearful thoughts, negative emotions, anxiety, worry, and guilt. This does not please God. We must keep our inner world quiet and peaceful to be prayerful within and apostolic without.

> Safety for the soul that practices will consist in ceasing to be anxious about everything and anybody, and in watching itself and pleasing God. This is most important. If I were to describe the mistakes I have seen people make because they trusted in their good intentions. (*Life*, 12, p. 78.)

Intellectuals are negative people, more at home with problems than with virtues, and they find it difficult to take a long, loving look at the good qualities of the people around them. The mind is the villain. It refuses to stop working, judging, analyzing, composing speeches that it mistakenly takes for prayer: analysis—paralysis.

All we have to do is to imagine ourselves in the presence of Christ, spend time with Him, talk to Him, take delight in Him, lay our needs before Him, and stop thinking. So many people believe that the only thing important in prayer are thoughts and words. The whole person prays. A Christian is a prayer.

The director plays an important role in prayer life. Choose him with care. St. Teresa suffered torment on account of directors who were simpletons. The only people the gentle St. John of the Cross sends to hell are directors who spoil the work of the Holy Spirit. They cramp, cripple, and constrain the children of God who are called to freedom. The kingdom of prayer is as vast as the Pacific and there are many ways to that great ocean of God's compassionate love. Some directors discover a narrow, little tortuous byroad of their own and force others to follow them. We must respect the dignity and personality of each person and help him discover his way. Spirituality must be based on truth, learning, experience, and Sacred Scriptures. The Lord deliver us from the foolish devotions of ignorant directors.

Faith is founded on reason, and the more learned the director the better. St. Teresa placed more faith in the wisdom of the learned than in the sentimental sensationalism of the devout.

> Those who walk in the way of prayer have the greater need of learning. The more spiritual they are, the greater is their need. Let us not make the mistake of saying that learned men who do not practice prayer are not suitable directors. . . . I think devils are very much afraid of learned men who are humble and virtuous, knowing that they will find them out and defeat them." (*Life*, Ch. 13, p. 81.)

In prayer we center, concentrate, and recollect our scattered powers on Jesus. He is at the center. Keep our eyes on the Lord. He is the way, the truth. The life.

We enjoy a long, loving, listening look on the Lord. Remain in His presence, the mind hushed in silence.

Prayer is a growth in awareness and consciousness. Through conscious effort, I am freed from the cave of the subconscious to fly free in the realms of the superconscious, where a profound act comes forth through the infused love of the Indwelling Holy Spirit. This act of love may surface in many forms—a sigh, a cry, an adoration, a petition, thanks, praise, apology, a word, a dance, a silent insight, a beautiful liturgy.

Prayer is a descent of the mind into the heart, the very core of my being, where I encounter my Lord and my God, at a depth deeper than words, cliches, emotions, ideas, acts, rites, rules, or rituals. Spirit meets spirit and the feeling is peace. Prayer heals. Prayer is awe. Prayer is wonder.

Prayer is spiritual in the sense of St. Paul. "You are spiritual, since the Spirit of God has made his home in you . . . you possess the Spirit of Christ." (Rm. 8:9, 10.)

The Spirit of God, the breath of God breathes through our inner temple, and as He breathes, He fills the shrine within with life, love, peace, and praise. As the soul of our souls, He informs us, He transforms us, He reforms us, He conforms us to the image of the Risen Jesus, He deifies us, He godifies us, He spiritualizes us, and when we die He will raise us up.

As our Paraclete, He is the one who teaches, guides, inspires, counsels, and defends. The Spirit is our advocate against the lies, the accusations, and the doubts inseminated by the accuser. The Holy Spirit is the living fountain of water, the lake of life, from whom all life and love and inspirations grow. In the warm waters of His grace, He washes, cleanses, comforts, purifies and calms the passionate fires of desire. This divine poet is the one who writes the poem and composes the symphony of praise within me. The Christian marries the Spirit, as Mary did, and the Word becomes flesh within the bride, to bear fruit in love, joy, peace, patience, kindness, trustfulness, gentleness, goodness, and purity.

The Spirit without whom we cannot pray "Jesus is Lord" fills us with wisdom, faith, instructions, the powers of prophecy, miracles, healings, tongues, preaching, discernment of spirits, and the gift of interpretation. We need His abiding presence in prayer.

Christian prayer for St. Teresa is ecclesial. I never pray alone. The entire mystical Body prays in me, and I pray within that mystical Body. The whole Christ prays, as millions say "Our Father." The community supports me. We listen together to the word and respond as one. Prayer is the highest expression of human friendship. I become those I pray for. Present to the Lord together, we become more present to one another. Reverence is the criterion.

"One who has no love for the brother he has seen cannot love God, he has not seen." (I John 4:20.)

Mother Teresa of Calcutta taught that it is not possible to engage in the active apostolate without being a soul of prayer. She told her sisters to take trouble to pray, take time to pray, so that Christ may live His life fully in us. Teresa of Avila taught the very same doctrine five hundred years earlier. A deep prayer life renews the church and every member in it. We try to reform people by preaching, teaching, and contemplation; the only decision and reform that lasts is the one born in the still deep waters of contemplation, where we listen to the infallible quiet voice that speaks from our center.

In a century of psychology and introspection, Teresa shows

us how to look within, to know ourselves, love ourselves, and contemplate and enjoy the Three Persons of the Blessed Trinity who love to live and communicate with us. Our mystical psychologist of the superconscious dives far deeper than Freud, Adler, Jung, or Frankl into the mysterious waters of the spirit where the divine touches the human and weds it. Teresa teaches us how to live life at the depths, to leave the periphery where the problems are, and she holds out a ray of hope and light to all serious thinkers of the twentieth century who are seeking for authentic religion and union with God. Thousands of our young people are searching in vain for a leader and a guide they can trust. Fascination with the mystical and the real, a return to the simple and the essential is a sign of our times.

Tired of an empty, superficial, and completely external materialistic, pragmatic, and utilitarian form of life, many desperate and hungry people have recourse to drugs and drink to turn them on, when in fact, they want to find a person who will lead them inward on the long, lonely journey to God. They escape from the grey world of reality for a few hours, to be deluded in a colored world of their own fancy, built up fantastically by chemicals, hypnosis, rock music, lights, or orgiastic dancing.

The picture Teresa draws for us of the inner world is far richer, far more beautiful, more healthy, more divine, and real. The psychedelic world of chemicals may destroy a man, take away his freedom, while Teresa's nurtures a man. The former can sicken a man, the latter always heals him. The former may bring out the demonic, the latter ultimately manifests the divine. On a bad trip, the one may reveal and let loose the devils, the vipers, the rats within the sick psyche of the drugged, the inspired draws aside the curtain to show man that his soul is the living shrine of the Blessed Trinity. If only we could persuade the youth in our colleges today to turn from their psychedelic literature and read the works of Teresa of Jesus. The cultists of the drug seek chemical ecstasy. Teresa leads us to supernatural ecstasy.

Every religion has rational and nonrational elements. We must not confuse the nonrational with the irrational. Esthetic experience is primarily a nonrational form of knowledge; but it is not irrational to contemplate a beautiful sunset or listen to a symphony orchestra. The rational saves religion from fanatical emotionalism, while the nonrational or the supernatural saves it from mere logic and legalism. Teresa, the mystic with her feminine gifts of intuition and feeling, combined with her respect for revelation, the teaching of the church and the opinions of learned theologians provides that rare balance. She can therefore appeal to the modern set who have grown tired and bored of an over-rationalized, overlegalized religion. Western religion over the past three hundred years has tended to emphasize reason. Today, there is a turning to the mystical. We need good teachers to lead us.

The word mystic must not frighten us. The modern press moves us to conjure up strange images of weird psychics, or phenomenal yogis performing feats that blow the mind. An older literature portrays a desert father standing afloat on top of a Simon stylite tower, a stigmatized woman who oozes blood every Friday, a Carmelite nun behind dark grilles, an emaciated friar flying through the air. We may admire them, but we don't want to imitate these extraordinary feats or extraordinary people.

The authentic Christian mystic does not go in for the extraordinary. In fact he hides and fears it. Teresa and John of the Cross warn us against these external manifestations. The mystic has a direct intuition of ultimate reality and is convinced of his divine intimacy with God through faith, hope, love, and the gifts of the Holy Spirit. Many people enjoy mystical experiences, but they cannot be called real mystics. Experimental attempts have been made to induce mystical experiences by means of drugs, and even if the sensory and emotional states they produce bear some superficial resemblence to the really spiritual, they are in fact worlds apart. The experiences of Teresa surpass any natural peek experience known to Abraham Maslow. Precious and essential distinctions must be made.

William Braden in his book, *The Private Sea LSD and the Search for God*, writes:

> The point often is made that religious ascetics traditionally have promoted their mystical states of consciousness by employing techniques that rival LSD in their probable impact in biochemical balance. These include fasting, yogic breathing, exercises, sleep deprivation, dervish dances, self-flagellation, and monastic isolation. Even in the pews of the pious, religious contemplation may be supported by such trance inducing aids as organ music,

stained glass windows, repetitive chants and incense, prayers and flickering candles (Bantam edition, 1968, p. 24.)

Teresa, like all great mystics and masters of prayer, recognized the danger centuries before. When she diagnosed that her sisters were suffering from defective adrenal metabolism, which manifested itself in general languor, visions, locutions, faintings, raptures, *arrobamiento,* which according to her was in fact *abobamiento* or "foolishness," she speedily ordered them to bed, fed them on good food and meat, saturated them with wine, declared an end to penances, and drastically cut down prayers. Then she watched and waited. Her attention and a few extra pound's weight usually put an end to raptures and ecstasies. A dehydrated brain can play havoc on a woman's vivid imagination, especially when she is cloistered. The down-to-earth-common-sensed Teresa could not be deceived. In any case, she knew all the psychological and diabolical tactics that the subconscious or the devil can play from her own personal and often bitter personal experience.

The real mystic walks with God at a much deeper level. His experimental knowledge of God is a ray of the beatific vision, but not the beatific vision itself, for he still walks by faith, a faith enlightened by love and the gifts of the Holy Spirit. The mystic is the living, knowing, loving, listening, joyful experiencing shrine of God's presence. The awareness takes place in the depths of the spirit. This direct union and communion with God at the heart of the spirit fills the faculties with a feeling of peace, joy, and tranquility—the peace promised by Christ, a peace the world cannot give. Love has eyes and the mystics peer into eternity.

The genuine mystic is known by the fruits of the spirit. St. Paul mentions them in his letter to the Galatians, as, "love, joy, peace, patience, kindness, goodness, trustfulness, gentleness and self-control. (Gal. 5:23.)

People like that are not bound by law. They are a law unto themselves, as they sail their spiritual boat out in the deep, wide open waters of the spiritual Pacific, driven and guided by the breath of the Spirit. This is a case of "love and do what you will." This is freedom. Teresa enjoyed a woman's liberation. The mystic will never do evil, as his soul is tested in the furnace of heroic virtue. The devil can never feign love, joy, or goodness, without leaving a clue sooner or later. If we are really in union and living in the presence of the good God, we must be good ourselves, and forget self in our service of others.

St. Teresa never thought that we must be Carmelites behind grilles to be mystics. Deep prayer is possible, as she says, among the pots and pans in any kitchen in any field. The gift is offered to married people and single people in the world. Today many of our good laity are blessed with the gift. Don Francisco de Salcedo enjoyed it, and he was an ordinary layman. Her own father practiced it when Teresa had lost it. These men did not attain the mystical plateau that Teresa did, but she teaches any Christian who is faithful and generous may enter the fourth mansion. Laypeople falsely believe Teresa is not for them. God has raised her up for all Christians. Many non-Christians find inspiration in her works; it is also interesting to note that Allison Peers, the man who translated all her writings into English, was an Anglican.

At this point, I would like to share with the reader the teaching of St. Teresa on the foundation of prayer as found in *The Way of Perfection.* In Chapter 16, she compares prayer to a game of chess, and the queen that captures the king is the virtue of humility. We must be soft, gentle, passive, open, listening, little, and poor in spirit, as the Mother of Jesus was. Contemplation may not be necessary for everyone, but humility and solid virtue are.

> The King of glory will not come to our soul, and be united with it, if we do not make the effort to gain the great virtues. (*The Way of Perfection* 16, p. 6.)

We must prepare ourselves to enjoy the gift of contemplation by a life of detachment, heroic, fraternal charity, and humility. Mystical phenomena, spiritual delight, tears, raptures, consolation, an almost magical mentality toward God's love are not the foundation on which the Interior Castle of prayer is built. We need a holy daring, a mad determination to keep our eyes fixed on the Lord. A holy simplicity of life and a singlemindedness of purpose guide us along the road of prayer. It amazes me to note the number of times St. Teresa calls for courage, fortitude, holy daring, perseverance in these chapters. Her contemplatives are men and women who are prepared to battle and fight in the war against demons, principalities, and evil powers. We have to be tested in the desert of fire. The testing brings the best out of us, and the soldiers of Teresa will always be found at their post in vigilant prayer.

"Why desire to serve the Lord in a doubtful way, when you have so much that is safe." (*The Way of Perfection*, Ch. 18, 9. p. 105.)

St. Teresa counsels prudence. There is no virtue without balance, and a terrible zeal can burn people up and consume them with a suicidal death wish. Impulsively the fanatic neglects health, drives himself beyond the limits of discretion, becomes mentally deranged, and under demonic instigation may lose all interest in living and continuing the good fight. So our Saint advises:

> The time of prayer should be shortened, however delightful the prayer may be, when it is seen that the bodily energies are failing or that the head might suffer harm. Discretion is very necessary in all. (*The Way of Perfection*, Ch. 19, 13. p. 113.)

True friends are helpful. We must surround ourselves with a support group of resurrected Christians, because too many of the people around us are predominantly negative. They envy the free and the dreamers. We need to breathe in an atmosphere and community of peace and tranquility.

Again and again our mystical doctor warns us against fear.

> Don't be frightened, daughters, by the many things you need to consider in order to begin this divine journey which is the royal road to heaven. (*The Way of Perfection*, 21, 1, p. 117.)

Fear is the favorite tool of the devil and the Sacred Scriptures warn us against the prevailing presence of this dark power. I am sure that if God Almighty were to call in Satan and say to him, "I am going to take away from you all the powers, tools, tricks, and instruments with which you tempt and fool my people and leave you with one," I am certain that Satan would hold on to fear. Fear is the muddy marsh out of which so much sickness, immorality, and sin grows. What we fear, we believe in, and one day we will do. The golfer that is afraid of driving the ball into the water will drive the ball straight into the water.

Fear, anger, guilt, worry, depression are the most horrible

and crippling negative and demonic forces along the path of prayer. They are so prevalent and so subtle that they escape detection.

There are dangers along the way to contemplation, but fear, anger, guilt, worry, and depression are not going to remove them. There is a treasure at the end of the road, and no criticism, no imaginary fear, no false friendship, no silly gossip or pusillanimity must prevent us from possessing it.

> The devil has invented these fears. Therefore, Sisters, give up these fears, never pay attention in like matters to the opinion of the crowd. Behold: these are not the times to believe everyone: believe only these whom you see are walking in conformity with Christ's life. (*The Way of Perfection* 21, 8, 10, p. 121.)

At the center of the garden rests the well of the water of life and prayer. Beginners draw water from the deep well in buckets. This is hard work, for it demands discipline, courage, perseverance, determination, and the recollection of the five senses, solitude, sorrow for sin, constancy in spite of aridity and a readiness to carry the Cross of Christ. A period of desert testing is needed. We meditate on the life of Christ, battle with distractions of the imagination, quieten the mind, endure poverty of thought and spirit and are content with the honor of spending time in the presence and the garden of the Emperor of paradise. This calls for faith. Temptations come, as we become aware of our own worthlessness and misery: we drink the chalice of suffering. We must now trust the goodness of the Lord, rely on the virtue of hope and never question the ways of God or seek to base our prayer life on mere pleasure, sentiment, consolation, or emotion. The temple of prayer must have a solid foundation: will power, determination, discretion, and respect for physical fitness. The body is the temple of the living Lord. We are one—body, mind, and spirit. Bodily indisposition hinders prayer. If you doubt me, try to pray with a toothache. St. Teresa took great care of the physical health of her sisters. She altered the hours of prayer to suit the health of her daughters and advises that there be times when the soul must serve the body for the love of God, enjoy recreation, go on a country walk, have a good chat with a friend, and avoid all depression. The yoke of the Lord is sweet and He leads us gently.

The beginner in prayer must foster special devotion to the Sacred Humanity of Jesus, meditate on the passion and resurrection, imitate His virtues, and learn to live and love as He did. By many acts of resolution we awaken love. Imagination and picturing really help. Just picture Jesus beside you, speak to Him, listen to Him, ask Him for what you need, and complain to Him in time of trial and rejoice with Him in joy. Let words flow to suit the situation. There is no need for a set formula. Jesus is part of life. Prayer makes His presence conscious. Don't force experience. The consolations will flow out of a good life and good prayer in God's own time.

Be humble and trust the Lord. "When His Majesty so wills, He can teach everything in a moment, in a way that amazes me." (*Life*, Ch. 12, p. 73.)

His Majesty is the teacher of prayer, and we must let Him lift up our spirits. There is a limit to human effort and technique.

Learn to relax. Take it easy. Be happy and be free. It is sad to see how tense and serious people become in prayer. The Lord loves and favors happy, courageous souls.

There's a time to dream the impossible dream, think big, imagine bravely and become an eagle. The Christian is called to climb the dizzy heights and fly free. Everything is possible to God. St. Augustine prayed, "Give me, Lord, what Thou commandest and command what thou will." We are created to soar like eagles, not to crawl like toads. False humility is Satan's tool.

Teresa herself was hindered by overcautious directors. Fear is a demonic force. We're afraid to fast, afraid to work, afraid of our health, afraid to dream, afraid of human respect. We are frightened by our own thoughts and images. Teresa countered her fear. "Even if I die, it is of little consequence. Rest, indeed. I need no rest: what I need are crosses" (*Life*, Ch. 12, p. 76.)

There is another subtle temptation that beginners fall into. They take their eyes off of the Lord and start to judge and compare their companions. They suffer from an unholy zeal, lose their own peace of soul, as they force others to become as spiritual as they are. They want to teach.

11.

Contemplation

Contemplation is the manna in the desert of the spiritual journey. It is a gift infused by God, a light divine that enables us to see the real, a spiritual fire of love that flames up within us, and opens us up to a new way of enjoying God, people, ourselves and the beautiful world around us.

Vatican II teaches:

> It is of the essence of the Church that she be both human and divine, visible and yet invisibly endowed, eager to act and yet devoted to contemplation, present in this world and yet not at home in it. She is all these things in such a way that in her the human is directed and subordinated to the divine, the visible likewise to the invisible, action to contemplation, and this present world to that city yet to come." (*Constitution on Sacred Liturgy*, par. 2.)

Here it is clear that contemplation is essential and primary to the life of the church. Action is important, but it is directed and subordinate to contemplation. St. Thomas taught that contemplation is the end of education, and contemplation is that time of holy leisure that helps us enjoy God. We are meant to enjoy God.

One of the urgent problems today in a scientific and technological culture is to preserve among men the faculties of contemplation and wonder that lead to contemplation.

> As special branches of knowledge continue to shoot out so

rapidly, how can the necessary synthesis of them be worked out and how can men preserve the ability to contemplate and to wonder, from which wisdom comes. (*The Church Today*, par. 56.)

In the decree on the missions.

> Working to plant the Church and thoroughly enriched with the treasures of mysticism adorning the Church's religious tradition, religious communities should strive to give expression to these treasures and to hand them on in a manner harmonious with the nature and the genius of each nation. Let them reflect attentively on how Christian religious life may be able to assimilate the ascetic and contemplative traditions whose seeds were sometimes already planted by God in ancient cultures prior to the preaching of the Gospel. . . . The contemplative life belongs to the fullness of the Church's presence, and should therefore be everywhere established. (*Missions*, par. 18.)

St. Teresa anticipated the teaching of Vatican II, and her own life, and reform contributed immeasureably to the new life of the church after the Council of Trent. Here she follows a rich, mystical tradition that is rooted in the Old Testament in Abraham, the prophet Elijah who has inspired Carmelites through the centuries. The prophet who cried, "I am filled with jealous zeal for Yahweh Sabaoth." (1 Kings, 19:10.) When he entered the cave at Horeb, he did not hear the Lord in the earthquake, or the mighty wind, or the fire, but in the whisper of a gentle breeze. This whisper was silence.

In the New Testament Jesus is the mystic. Mary was a mystic. St. John and St. Paul were mystics. Down the golden pages of Christian mysticism, we have Ireneaus, Clement of Alexandria, Augustine, Jerome, Dionysius, the Areopagite, the Dialogues of John Cassian, Gregory the Great, the Irish Monks, John Scotus Erigena, St. Benedict and his Benedictines, the monastic reformers, Romuald and Bruno, Bernard of Clairvaux, Hugh of St. Victor, Francis of Assisi, Bonaventure, Thomas Aquinas, Dante, Ramon Lull, Meister Eckhardt and the German mystics, Tauler, Suso, Ruysbroeck, Thomas a Kempis, the English school of mystics, Walter Hilton, "The Cloud of Unknowing," Aldred, Margery Kempe, Julian of Norwich, Bernardine of Siena. There were schools of Mysticism in Egypt, Italy, France, Ireland, England, Germany, Spain, and Belgium.

Then we have all the great women mystics, Gertrude, Elizabeth Mechthild, Hildegarde, Angela of Foligno, Bridget of Sweden, Catherine of Siena, Catherine of Bologna, Colette, Joan of Arc, Catherine of Genoa.

Contemporary mystics of Teresa were Peter of Alacantara, Luis of Granada, Luis de Leon, Ignatius Loyola and the greatest of them all, St. John of the Cross.

Teresa was at the center of that mighty stream of Western mysticism. The greatest periods of mystical activity historically correspond with the great periods of cultural, political, and religious renaissance. Certain epochs produce a tremendous outpouring of human spirit and creativity that find their zenith in the spiritual conquests of the mystics. They are our tainted nature's greatest boast. They have sung the sweetest notes, composed the finest melodies, seen the greatest, climbed the highest mountains, and dreamed the lasting dream. They touched the Absolute, contemplated the Real, savored the Truth, and conquered Love. They report back to us what they saw. Their evidence is scientific and historical, well documented and open to scrutiny. They prove that the graced spirit of man is capable of immediate communion with God. They don't theorize. They have tasted and seen how good the Lord is.

St. Paul writes on this new spiritual knowledge. It is not taught the way philosophy is taught. It is taught spiritually. It is taught by the Holy Spirit Himself. The unspiritual think it is nonsense. The Holy Spirit reaches the depths of God and the depths of the human spirit. He is the Master and teaches from within.

> We have a wisdom to offer those who have reached maturity, . . . The hidden wisdom of God which we teach in our mysteries is the wisdom God predestined to be for our glory before the ages began. . . We teach what scripture calls: the things that no eye has seen and no ear heard, things beyond the mind of man, all that God has prepared for those who love Him. . . . The Spirit that comes from God teaches us to understand the gifts that He has given us. . . . As scripture says: 'Who can know the mind of the Lord, so who can teach him?' But we are those who have the mind of Christ.
>
> —1 Cor. 2: 6–16.

As we study St. Teresa, our mystical doctor clearly teaches that contemplation is a gift infused by God. We don't merit it. It is a loving knowledge of God and God's world. We intuite the "real," take a long, loving, listening look at the real that flows into delight. This gift is the beginning of beatitude, the supernal activity of the gods, as Aristotle said. The act itself emanates from the apex of the spirit. It is knowledge by connaturality, the science of love rooted in truth. Contemplation, as John of the Cross wrote, is a loving knowledge of God, with more love than knowledge. Love unites us directly to the object. We become one. Lovers see. A new world vista is opened up. The scales are removed from our eyes, and we are given a sagacious knowledge of the divine and the human. This leaves us with a wise and sound judgment on God, self, people, and the world. The contemplator of the real becomes a realist. There is no one more realistic than the mystic and the dreamer. St. Francis was a dreamer. Teresa was a dreamer.

The experience is direct, spirit to spirit. It is immediate, by contact, by touch. There is no medium. "How good Yahweh is—only taste and see." (Psalm 34.)

We look towards Him and become radiant.

The knowledge infused is deep, delicate, confused, and general. It is called apophatic, knowing by unknowing: the cloud of unknowing. This new mode of learning is far superior to any knowledge through sense, image, concept or abstraction. It is super-scientific. The superconscious wakes up. We fly in a mental jet far higher than any telescope or microscope can reach. This is a lover's knowledge, the science of the heart, in a world of poets and artists. The inner eye opens up to a vision that gives certainty. The mystic has no doubt about his experience. He will die for his conviction. There is no hallucination here, no invention by the subconscious, no wishful thinking or a mushy thought. He thinks clearly, believes radically, and writes and speaks translucently.

Contemplation is an idle pleasure in serene glancing. It is enjoying God, the ground of our being: holy leisure. There I discover the sacred and the beautiful, as I allow the Spirit to breathe through me and fill me with His song of love. In deep silence I listen to the Word, not just with my ears, but with my whole person. I just don't listen to words, I listen to the Word to a person, who loves me, and lets me know I am good, lovable and precious in His eyes. I begin a journey into God, which is paradoxically a journey into my deepest self, and once I learn to listen to self, I discover I can listen to God, and then I am ready to listen to people and the myriad musical sounds of nature without.

I respond to the good integrally at all levels mystically, spiritually, morally, intellectually, aesthetically, emotionally, sensually, and at a body level. As the resurrected life of Christ flows into me, I become alive. I'm in harmony. Then I think and see clearly. The thoughts we conceive are conceived, as Yeats said, in the marrow bone. Without this inner vision, people perish. Without this vision and visionaries, the church perishes. The mystic is the pioneer. He leads the boat of Peter into new still waters, to the blessed islands of awe, admiration, amazement, and wonder. He is a man of mighty mirth, humor, playfulness, and folly. He is a little crazy, God's clown. Like a happy child he lives in a world of joy. He travels in purity and poverty under the pure, serene light of God's own star, never impeded by forms, figures, fantasies, or feelings.

Contemplation calls for the gift of time and presence. It is a response to Him who said, "I am who I am and I am here now loving you." Mary gave the perfect response, when she said, "I am the handmaid of the Lord, let what you have said be done to me." (Luke, 1,38.) I don't have to do anything or have some lofty experience or healing. I am. I offer the Lord the gift of my being. In this quiet silence, the Lord manifests Himself as risen and present.

On that day
You will understand that I am in my Father
And you in me and I in you . . .
And anybody who loves me will be loved by my Father,
And I shall love him and show myself to him.
—John 14:21.

St. John of the Cross describes contemplation in Book II, Chapter 14 of his, *Ascent of Mount Carmel.*

> It flows from the soul that has grounded itself in meditation. Through many acts of meditation we come to know and love God. The habit of loving knowledge is formed. God rewards the

generous soul with contemplation, the habit and substance of loving knowledge of a general kind, and not distinct or particular as before.

The water is carried to it and the soul drinks peacefully without any effort or labour as soon as the soul comes before God, it makes an act of knowledge, confused, loving, passive and tranquil, wherein it drinks of wisdom, love and delight.

The mystical doctor continues to give us an image so dear to Teresa. The contemplative is like a baby at its mother's breast. All we have to do now is to drink and grow strong. We don't have to work; we enjoy the fruit of work. We don't have to prepare the meal; we eat and drink. We don't have to serve; we rest and relax. We don't give, we accept, open, and receive. We allow God to act upon us. We suffer the onslaught of the divine. The Lord unites our soul in pure intelligence. The intellect cannot observe what is going on, and can very well become frustrated in this gentle idleness. The mind of an is very selfish. It wants to control, survey, and understand all that is going on. While the will goes out in love, the intellect wants to take in. Divorced from the spirit, the human intellect is luciferous and destructive. The mind is the villain. It is so difficult to quiet the mind. The will receives love passively. The fire is felt, but the knowledge and love are communicated in a very general, confused manner. The higher and more sublime the divine light is, the darker it is to our understanding. That is why the mystical experience itself is so ineffable. This wonder is the basis of purest worship. When the mind lets go, the spirit takes over. Deep insight is given. Great perspicacity is needed.

So contemplation may be a ray of darkness, loving, confused, simple, subtle, pure, and spiritual. It is of a supernatural origin, heavenly intelligence granted passively to a tranquil spirit. But since the object of contemplation is so transcendent, I can only stutter my explanation in metaphor, symbol, analogy, and poetry.

Metaphysics studies God as the First Cause through effects. Theology studies God as revealed. In Faith we see God as He formally reveals Himself. The mystic experiences God as formally believed. He has knowledge by loving union. His is not a knowledge by abstraction or concept. It is knowledge by interpenetration, the way the lovers know the beloved.

The divine weds the human as the *Song of Songs* sings:

Let him kiss me with the kisses of his mouth,
Your love is more delightful than wine . . .
My Beloved is mine and I am his.
He pastures his flock among the lilies . . .
His left arm is under my head
and his right embraces me.

The ordinary person lives in a world of imagination, making God to his own image and likeness. He constructs a theology in his own mind to suit his mind. He is not necessarily in touch with reality. The great poets, artists, and mystics—men and women who are still childlike and innocent—are still in touch, aware, and mystified by the awesomeness of it all. They are ready to leave the museum and the libraries to climb the mountains and encounter the real. The mind of the scientist is analytical. He divides and in doing so often destroys. The eye of the mystic is synthetic. He listens to heavenly symphonies, and so he is sympathetic and compassionate with every created thing. He will not exploit, use, grab, or destroy. He has learned the art of simplicity. He goes from multiplicity to unity, from the external to the internal, from the human to the divine, from the symbol to the sacred in a flash of vision. He knows how to collect all our scattered forces and center on the real. He knows the truth and the truth makes him free. He is a united, unified man in harmony with all that is, and so he can communicate from the depths of communion. His highest feelings far transcend the loftiest ideas. As the Spirit indwells in him, he interdwells in all that he loves. We are all one.

The contemplative has learned to use the right hemisphere of the brain, the part that is artistic, musical, intuitive, poetic, and mystical. The left hemisphere is rational, philosophical, analytical, technological, logical, and verbal. Unfortunately, today we are trained more in the left side than in the right.

As already mentioned, knowledge cannot unite me directly to God. Love does unite me directly and immediately to the Lord. It is the teaching of St. Thomas that the love of charity has for its object that which is already possessed. Love unites, transforms, harmonizes, deifies, and helps me see and sing. Beloved and lover sing the same song. Two spirits unite in one act of love. I feel God's presence. I experience His love. I know that I know that God is one with me in love. I can't describe it or understand it, but I know it. I experience this vital union, this divine, ineffable intimacy. I intuit what Jesus meant, when He said, "If anyone loves me he will keep my words, and my Father will love him and we shall come to him and make our home with him." (John 14:23.)

Love is infused, poured in. We bathe in the living fountain of love itself. The love is indwelling, agape love, trinitarian, Christian, and spiritual. We feel we belong to a sacred family. We live in a home where there is caring and sharing, and deepest communication. This love is intimate.

> On that day you will understand that I am in my Father, and you in me and I in you.
>
> —John 14:20.

It is Abba's love.

> As the Father has loved me so I have loved you.
>
> —John 15:9.

It is mystical.

> I am the vine, you are the branches. Whoever remains in me, with me in him bears fruit in plenty.
>
> —John 15:5.

It is friendly.

> I call you friends.
>
> —John 15:15.

It is self-revelatory.

> I have made known to you everything I have learnt from my Father
>
> —John 15:16.

It is ecclesial,

"Love one another as I have loved you."

(John.15:12)

It is spiritual,

"The Spirit comes to help us in our weakness." (Rom.8:26)
"Anyone who is joined to the Lord is one spirit with him."

(1 Cor. 6:17)

It is vital,

"He who eats my flesh and drinks my blood lives in me and I live in him."

(John.6:56)

It is joyful,

"I shall see you again, and your hearts will be full of joy and that joy no one shall take from you."

(John.16:22)

It is uniting,

"May they all be one, Father, may they be one in us, as you are in me, and I am in you."

(John.17:21)

This love is eternal. It is the only thing we will take with us across the grave. The love that Teresa speaks of is a very personal, mysterious love. It is not a matter of a subject studying an object, it is the truth of the small 'I' in union with the great 'I am.' Our capacity for love expands. We receive a new heart. The Lord takes from our breasts hearts that can be as hard as stone, and fills them instead with His own merciful love. A new fountain springs up within us, a new fire inflames, a new power explodes.

> "The Spirit and the Bride say, 'Come'. Let everyone who listens answer, 'Come'. Then let all who are thirsty come: all who want it may have the water of life, and have it free."
>
> (Rev.22:17)

From the infusion of loving knowledge flows a great delight to the soul. When St. John of the Cross sketches his picture of Mr. Carmel and the summit of contemplative prayer, he writes at the very top,

> "Here there is no longer any way because for the just man there is no law, he is a law unto himself."

This is the utter freedom promised to the children of God. At the very core of the summit, we find the words,

> "Only the honour and glory of God dwells on this mountain."

and

> "I brought you into the land of Carmel to eat its fruits and the good things."
>
> (Jer.2:7)

The contemplative enters the land of Carmel and eats the fruits of the trees in the garden of paradise. These are peace, joy, happiness, delight, wisdom, justice, fortitude, charity and piety. We rise above the clouds of human illusion,

"Glory matters nothing to me. Suffering matters nothing to me." We are free from all the terrible cravings and passion that torment, blind and confound. I am together again, all one, body, mind and spirit. The Spirit is in control. I have a centre, a divine center. From that center I relate to God, myself, people and things. Peace and serenity reign inside my house.

> I am not concerned with great affairs or marvels beyond my scope. Enough for me to keep my soul tranquil and quiet like a child in its mother's arms, as content as a child that has been weaned. (Ps. 131)

I rest and relax. The Lord continues to pour in the light, love and delight. The bride enters the castle of repose, that still point, the ocean of tranquillity. Here she is quiet and peaceful, free from fears and desire, free from the terrible driving compulsions to do and have and control. She enjoys life, its poetry, its music and its wine as she becomes passionately alive and alert, as attentive as a sparrow on a tree top. She is wide awake in mind, memory, imagination, emotion and sense. Energy flows through the body,

> "Set your hearts on his Kingdom, and these other things will be given you as well. There is no need to be afraid for it has pleased your Father to give you the Kingdom." (Lk.12:31)

As we move towards a more complete union with the Transcendent, the dualism ends, between the human and the divine, action and contemplation, Martha and Mary, anima and animus, inner and outer, active energy and passive energy, law and freedom, the yin and the yang of life.

"Peace I bequeath you
my own peace I give you
a peace the world cannot give,
This is my gift to you." (John.14:27)

Contemplation is enjoying God: We offer God the greatest sacrifice of all, the sacrifice of joy.

> "I shall see you again, and your hearts you will be full of joy, and that joy no one shall take from you." (John.16:22)

> "My heart exults, my very soul rejoices, my body, too, will rest securely, you give me unbounded joy in your presence and at your right hand everlasting pleasures." (Ps. 16)

Contemplation does not lock a person up within the close confines of his own soul. The real mystic contemplates and gives to others the fruit of his contemplation. The church has been more enriched by contemplatives than by any other group. Contemplation expands our personality and dynamism, and expresses itself in fraternal charity and the apostolate. Scholars may dispute in theory about the relationship between contemplation and action, but the authentic contemplative does not separate. Contemplation flows into action. Action finds rest and power in contemplation. The contemplative is a man generous in virtue and on fire with charity. He will not be cribbed, cabined, and confined within a cell of cement. Four walls do not make a castle. The contemplative lives life to the fullest—wild and free in the castle of the spirit. Action does not distract him. He is centered even in action. Automatically, with a silent prayer he returns to the inner cathedral as spontaneously as the bee returns to the hive carrying more honey as the fruit of labor. Contemplation is the science of love and must express itself in action. It is the highest form of action.

Jacques Maritain, in his book, *The Degrees of Knowledge*, calls it a practico-practical science, far superior to mathematics, physics, science, philosophy, metaphisics, or theology. At the peak of the various degrees of human knowledge stands St. John of the Cross, the master of the mystical, singing his songs on this incommunicable wisdom. Maritain places him above Aquinas. Aquinas is the great doctor of the highest communicable wisdom. He seeks to know no longer for the sake of knowing, but for the sake of acting. He synthesizes and gathers together everything he already knows and prepares for a concrete act. The passion of things divine and contemplative union with God is the most eminent of all human actions.

John of the Cross and Teresa are not so much interested in telling us what perfection is as in leading us to it. The final end of human life is to become God by a gradual, gentle participation in His divine life through the beatific vision and love in the next life, and through grace, faith, hope, love, and the gifts of the Holy Spirit in this life.

We find descriptions of the various forms and stages of contemplation in the writings of St. Teresa.

1. Semi-Passive
    a. Recollection
       Life, Ch. 14
       Way of Perfection, Ch. 28 and 29.
       Interior Castle, the 4th Mansion.
    b. Prayer of Quiet
       Life, Ch. 15 and 16.

Way of Perfection, Ch. 31.
Interior Castle, 4th Mansion
2. Passive
   a. Prayer of Union
   Life, Ch. 18–21.
   Interior Castle, Mansions 5 and 6.
   b. Spiritual Marriage
   Interior Castle, 7th Mansion.

Many good Christians remain all life long in meditation and vocal prayer, stuck in the third mansion because there is no one ready to lead them across into the more passive waters of contemplation, or because they don't recognize the signs the the Lord is calling them.

St. John of the Cross gives three clear signs by which we may diagnose when we are called into contemplation.

1. *Sense Pleasure*. The time comes, when we no longer enjoy sense pleasure in meditation. We feel no fervour, taste no sweetness, sense no sorrow and shed no tears. The Lord is developing new powers and tastes within us. He wishes to purge and purify our soul of these sensual emotions, so that we may ascend higher on the tree of life.

At the same time we do not indulge in sinful sensual pleasures that might take us away from God. Therefore the aridity is not caused by immoral behaviour or tepid laxity. We must not panic when this aridity strikes. We must learn to wait in the Advent of the spirit. It may very well presage better things to come.

2. *The Memory*. Although we constantly live in the presence of God, and practise prayer and recollection, we can no longer find sweetness and fervour there. We have somehow emptied all the honey there was in this section of the hive. The memory of past graces, insights, knowledge no longer fires us.

At the same time we are worried and afraid that we are not serving God generously enough. We dread the thought of backsliding and do our best to practise virtue. Hence, the aridity is not due to lukewarmness. The Lord wants to withdraw us from the manna of the past and guide us to the Eucharist of the future.

3. *Imagination*. We can no longer use our imagination and powers of reflection with the same facility as of yore. God speaks now spirit to spirit, through an act of simple contemplation, that is secret, general and obscure. He will not be confined to an image, concept, fantasy or form. The images and concepts that helped us in the early stages of prayer are no longer helpful.

The time for waiting patience has arrived. We must not force ourselves to imagine, meditate, or think. The water will flow from a more profound depth. There must be no violence, no noise. Listen and be still and know that the Lord is taking over. We must learn to rest content with a peaceful and loving attentiveness towards God. He has His own ways to infuse knowledge and love.

> Contemplation is naught else than a secret, peaceful and loving infusion from God which if it be permitted enkindles the soul, with the spirit of love.
>
> (*Dark Night*, I, 10, p. 358.)

St. Teresa calls contemplation "the gift of living water," and she holds that the Lord invites us all to drink.

> Remember the Lord invites us all. Since He is truth itself, we cannot doubt Him. If His invitation were not a general one, He would not have said, 'I will give you to drink.' He might have said, 'Come all of you, for after all you will lose nothing by coming, and I will give drink to those whom I think fit for it.' But, as He said, we were all to come, without making this condition. I feel sure that none will fail to receive this living water unless they cannot keep to the path (*The Way of Perfection*, Ch. 19, p. 85.)
>
> His mercy is so great that He has forbidden none to strive to come and drink of this fountain of life. . . . He calls us publicly, and in a loud voice, to do so. Yet, as He is so good, He does not force us to drink, but enables those who wish to follow Him to drink in many ways so that none may lack comfort or die of thirst. For from this rich spring flow many streams—some large, others small, and also little pools for children, which they find quite large enough, for the sight of a great deal of water would frighten them. By children, I mean, those who are in the early stages. (*The Way of Perfection*, Ch. 20, p. 86.)

We may receive the grace of contemplation while fervently reciting vocal prayers. Many have experienced this while reciting the Rosary.

> In case you should think there is little gain to be drived from

practising vocal prayer perfectly, I must tell you that while you are repeating the Pater Noster, or some other vocal prayer, it is quite possible for the Lord to grant you perfect contemplation. In this way His Majesty shows that He is listening to the person who is addressing Him, and that in His greatness, He is addressing her, by suspending the understanding, putting a stop to all thought, and as we say, taking the words out of her mouth, so that even if she wishes to speak she cannot do so, or at any rate not without great difficulty.

Such a person understands that without any sound of words, she is being taught by this Divine Master, who is suspending her faculties, which, if they were to work would be causing her harm rather than profit.

The faculties rejoice without knowing how they rejoice; the soul is enkindled in love without understanding how it loves; it knows that it is rejoicing in the object of its love, yet it does not know how it is rejoicing in it. It is well aware that it is not a joy which can be attained by the understanding; the will embraces it without understanding how, but in so far as it can understand anything, it perceives that this is a blessing which could not be gained by the merits of all the trials suffered on earth. It is a gift of the Lord on earth and Heaven, who gives it like the God he is. This, daughters, is perfect contemplation. (*The Way of Perfection*, Ch. 25, p. 104.)

12.
Prayer of Recollection

In *The Way of Perfection*, St. Teresa studies the prayer of recollection in chapters 28 to 30.

Prayer is a journey into God and God dwells within the heaven of the human spirit. Contemplation is a journey inward. This is an all-important truth, as St. Augustine discovered:

> Late have I loved you, O Beauty ever ancient, ever new, late have I loved you! You were within me, but I was outside, and it was there that I searched for you. In my lovelessness I plunged into the lovely things which you created. You were with me, but I was not with you—You called, you shouted, and broke through my deafness. You flashed, you shone, and you dispelled by blindness. You breathed your fragrance on me; I drew in my breath and now I pant for you. I have tasted you, now I hunger and thirst for more. You touched me, and I burned for your peace. (*Confessions*, Bk.7.)

In Him we live, we move, we have our being. He is near. However quietly we speak, He hears us. All we need is a sacred place and space and time, where we can be alone with Him and give Him the gift of our presence. Enter within:

> Collect the faculties
> Look upon Him present within:
> Ask Him for things as a Father
> Tell Him your troubles
> Delight in His presence
> Accept His gifts

> Speak to Him as a Father, Brother, Lord and Spouse
> He will teach you.
> Ask Him to treat you as His Bride
> Enter the life of the Trinity
> Offer the Son to the Father
> In the little heaven of the soul, we are free from sin.
> The small spark of Divine love is set aflame
> We are aware of our dignity
> Our bodies are palaces of priceless worth
> Tabernacles of precious stones and gold
> A building beautiful
> And at the very core lives and loves
> Our Heavenly Father seated on the throne of our heart.
> The Holy of holies is within us now
> We may enter any time we will.
> We must not take with us the junk of the world, junky thoughts, images, emotions, memories, or preoccupations.
> Rest at the still point, the ocean of tranquillity.
>   He is there.
> He loves to be with us, to comfort us
> This is Heaven on Earth.
> A great Joy comes over us
> Deep peace bathes us
> A mystic tranquillity embalms us
> And a quiet vision makes us aware of God's love.
>   It is in this way, that we have heaven within ourselves since the Lord of heaven is there. —His Majesty will make us conscious that He is there. We shall be able to say the Pater Noster and whatever other prayers we like with great peace of mind and the Lord will help us not to be tired. (*The Way of Perfection*, Ch. 29, p. 121.)

We must never be bashful with God. Complete confidence in His merciful love is needed. We can never exaggerate His goodness and His intimacy. He seeks union with the soul more than the soul seeks union with Him. God wants to enrich us, to divinise us, and lead us gently to mystical marriage.

> Speak to Him as with a Father, a Brother, a Lord and a Spouse. He will teach you what you must do to please Him. Do not be foolish; ask Him to let you speak to Him, and as He is your spouse, to treat you as His Brides. Remember, how important it is for you to understand this truth—that the Lord is within us and that we should be there with Him (*The Way of Perfection*, Ch. 28, p. 115.)

Teresa now tells us why she calls this kind of prayer Recollection: "It is called recollection because the soul collects together all the faculties and enters within itself to be with God." (Ibid)

As the golfer centers his body and focusses all his faculties on that little white ball, the person of prayer centres and focusses the senses, the emotions, the imagination, the intellect, the memory, and the will of God within. Within the cathedral of the spirit we can relive the paschal mysteries of Jesus Christ. There is no need to return to an historical instant or a geographical spot.

> Hidden there within itself, it can think about the Passion, and picture the Son, and offer Him to the Father, without wearying the mind by going to seek Him on Mount Calvary, or in the garden, or at the column. (Ibid)

Teresa continues to draw us in to the palace of her favorite image:

> Let us imagine that we have within us a palace of priceless worth, built entirely of gold and precious stones—a palace, in short, fit for so great a Lord. Imagine that it is partly your doing that this palace should be what it is. There is no building so beautiful as a soul that is pure and full of virtues. The greater these virtues are, the more brilliantly do the stones shine. Imagine that within this palace dwells this great King, who has vouchsafed to become your Father, and who is seated upon a throne of supreme price—namely, your heart. (*The Way of Perfection*, Ch. 28, p. 117.)

This is an excellent way to pray.

> Those who are able to shut themselves up in this way within this little Heaven of the soul, wherein dwells the Maker of Heaven and Earth, and who have formed the habit of looking at nothing and staying in no place which will distract these outward senses, may be sure they are walking on an excellent road, and will come without fail to drink of the water of the fountain. They will journey a long way in a short time. (Ibid.)

As we close the outer senses, the eyes of the spirit open.

> It withdraws the senses from all outward things and spurns them so completely that, without its understanding how, its eyes close and it cannot see them and the soul's spiritual sight becomes clear. (Ibid, p. 116.)

It takes some effort to close the eyes at first, but this simple, ascetical exercise pays rich dividends. The soul soon masters the body and the senses. If we persevere, then, "The soul and the will only have to make a sign to show that they wish to enter into recollection and the senses will obey and allow themselves to be recollected." (Ibid, p. 116.)

Since no hindrance comes from outside, we are more detached, and free to concentrate on the fire within. Any small spark of Divine Love will burst into flame. The Living Flame of love burns, purifies, and enlightens the soul. It becomes easier and more pleasant to live in there.

> The bees are coming to the hive and entering it to make the honey, and all without any effort of ours. . . . When the will calls them afresh they respond more quickly, until, after they have entered the soul many times, the Lord is pleased that they should remain there, altogether in perfect contemplation. (Ibid.)

God reveals Himself gradually. If He is to communicate with us in the sanctuary of the heart, we must empty out the other false idols. The pure of heart see God.

> If we fill the palace with vulgar people and all kinds of junk, how can the Lord and His Court occupy it? When such a crowd is there, it would be a great thing if He were to remain for even a short time. (Ibid, p. 118.)

Teresa continues to comfort us with the example of her own ignorance:

> I knew perfectly well I had a soul, but I did not understand what the soul merited, or who dwelt within it, until I closed my eyes to the vanities of this world. I think, if I understood then, as I do now how this great King really dwells within this little palace of my soul, I should not have left Him alone so often. I should have stayed with Him and never allowed His dwelling place to get so dirty. (Ibid, p. 118.)

The indwelling grace He bestowed on Mary, He grants us. The Christian is the womb of God.

> How wonderful it is that He whose greatness could fill a thousand worlds, and very many more, should confine Himself within so small a space, just as He was pleased to dwell within the womb of His most holy mother. (Ibid.)

The Almighty fashions Himself to our measure.

Mary, the Mother of Jesus, is the model of the contemplative who would find Her Son within. We carry Jesus, as Mary did. The Advent season, the period between the Annunciation and Nativity, is a very sacred time for the contemplative. Like Mary we wed the Spirit and conceive the Word. For nine wonderful months, Mary's body was the first Christian chalice, the first Christian cathedral, the first temple, the shrine of the Christ Child. God was within a woman's skin. He knows what it is to be a woman. The Holy Spirit filled the centre of her Interior Castle. He inspired her, moved her, controlled her, and she listened and obeyed. "I am the handmaid of the Lord, let what you have said be done to me." (Luke 1:38.)

The Word became flesh in Mary and made His home within her. She became the seed, the chalice, the nest of God. The Immaculate one, the reed through whom the Word was to sing His favorite song, was free of all the stain and sin that taints us. Her inner center was not clogged with the mud of fear, guilt, anger, worry, depression. She let the Father work on her; she let the Spirit shape her; she let the Word fill her. She accepted the father, she listened to the Word. She opened to the Spirit. God's will was done in her. His kingdom came and she hallowed His name in the temple of her heart. Divinity wed her humanity. The union was complete in her between the transcendent and the imminent; the divine and the human, the anima and the animus, contemplation and action. Mary is the fertile mother, impregnated by the Spirit—pregnant with the Word. Mary has a center, a divine center, and she above all others, can pray with Paul: "Now I can live for God, and I live now, not with my own life but with the life of Christ who lives in me." (Gal. 2:19–20.)

The Prayer of Recollection is the door to contemplative prayer. It is not what Teresa calls "supernatural" prayer. We must play our part, practice virtue and prepare ourselves to enter the holy of holies, where we may enjoy "the holy companionship with the Holiest of the Holy."

Often during the day, we must learn to stop, look, listen, and retire within ourselves. Holy recollection is concomitant with the Prayer of Recollection. The mischief is done when we imagine God as far away, when in fact, He is within us.

We must learn. . . .

> Abide with the person with whom we are speaking, and not turn our backs upon Him. . . . How is it Lord that we do not look at Thy face, when it is so near us. We do not think that people are listening to us, when we are speaking to them, unless we see them looking at us. And so we close our eyes so as not to see that Thou art looking at us? (*The Way of Perfection*, Ch. 29, p. 121.)

Relaxed familiarity with the Lord is now noted in prayer. We do not fuss over details. We center:

> We have heaven within ourselves since the Lord of heaven is there. If once we accustom ourselves to being glad that there is no need to raise our voices in order to speak to Him, since His Majesty will make us conscious that He is there. . . . The Lord Himself will help us not to grow tired. . . . He loves to save us worry. . . . Like any Father, He loves to be with us, and comfort us. He has no wish for us to tire our brains by a great deal of talking. (Ibid, pp. 121–122.)

This kind of prayer is restful, peaceful, and therapeutic. It is a treasure of great price that brings us deep satisfaction. We gain gradual mastery over ourselves. Teresa prays, "May the Lord teach this to those of you who do not know it." (Ibid, p. 122.)

The Lord can do more in a short time in this form of prayer than we can do in many years. Keep it up, and within six months to a year He will steer you into the still waters of contemplation.

Fourth Mansion

In the Fourth Mansion of *The Interior Castle*, Teresa still insists that the Prayer of Recollection "begins to touch the supernatural." It is a more passive, more contemplative form of prayer. We are becoming more interior. More light comes from the center. The Holy Spirit gradually and gently steers the little boat. The winds are stronger and the ocean calmer. New worlds appear:

> We are now getting near to the place where the King dwells. They are of great beauty and there are such exquisite things to be seen and appreciated in them that the understanding is incapable of describing them accurately without being completely obscure to those devoid of experience. (*The Interior Castle* IV, 1, p. 230.)

The poisonous creatures seldom enter, and if they do, they are harmless. The darkness cannot overpower the light. There are temptations to test us, but grace does more abound.

St. John of the Cross wrote one of his most beautiful passages on this theme:

> Oh, then thou soul most beautiful of all the creatures, that so greatly desirest to know the place where thy Beloved is in order to seek Him. Now, that thou art told that thou thyself art lodging wherein He is hidden and that it is a matter of great contentment and joy for thee to see that all thy good and thy hope are so near as to be within thee, or so to speak, more exactly, so near that thou canst not be without them. Behold, says the Spouse, "the Kingdom of God is within you." and the servant, St. Paul says, "You are the temples of God." (*Spiritual Canticle* I. 7, p. 189.)

The Prayer of Recollection calls for a twofold movement of the faculties. The will centers and concentrates on God, or rather is captivated and occupied by God. The light becomes brilliant. Automatically the soul is attracted, detached and freed from creatures. Teresa teaches a positive form of detachment. Too often we are instructed to become negatively detached and then God will appear. When the Lord comes with His dazzling light and burning love, creatures lose their overwhelming appeal and are put in proper perspective. The craving within us grows quiet. Creatures are but crumbs in comparison with the banquet the Lord provides.

Since the Prayer of Recollection is still partly active, progress depends on our generosity. However, we could never bear by our own personal exertions the fruits and fragrance that now invade and flourish in the garden of the soul.

Our Saint now shares one of her glorious insights:

> If you would progress a long way on this road and ascend to the mansions of your desire, the important thing is not to think much but to love much. (*The Interior Castle* IV, 1, p. 233.)

Meditation has to do with concepts, ideas, images. Contemplation has to do with symbols and love. Lovers see God. "Everyone who loves is begotten by God and knows God. Anyone who fails to love can never have known God, because God is love." (1 John 4:8.)

This love is not sentimental romanticism. It is based on a firm will to please God in everything, do good, avoid sin, pray for the glory of His Son, and work hard to advance the church.

Teresa gives us good advice on how to cope with distracting thoughts and images. We must never despair. She suffered herself.

> I have sometimes been terribly oppressed by this turmoil of thoughts and it is only just over four years ago that I came to understand by experience that thought (or to put it more clearly, imagination) is not the same thing as understanding. . . . For as the understanding is one of the faculties of the soul, I found it very hard to see why it was sometimes so timid; whereas, thoughts, as a rule, fly so fast that only God can restrain them; which He does by uniting us in such a way that we seem in some sense to be loosed from this body. It exasperated me to see the faculties of the soul, as I thought, occupied with God and recollected in Him, and the thoughts, on the other hand, confused and excited. O Lord, do Thou remember we have to suffer on this road through lack of knowledge. (*The Interior Castle* IV, 0, p. 233.)

Teresa laments we suffer so much from lack of a good psychological self-knowledge in prayer. We worry needlessly over what we think is bad, when in fact, it is good. We often imagine we are not in prayer, when in fact we are. Distractions in the imagination and myriad thoughts do not lessen our depth of prayer. I have seen people wrapped in prayer, while they imagined they were wasting their time. Images and thoughts may come and go and the prayer go on forever.

In an article in the book, *Finding Grace at the Center*, Thomas Keating OCSO, has a very helpful teaching.

The key to concentration is a relaxed posture. Then choose a sacred word that centres. The Jesus Prayer is very helpful. "Lord, Jesus Christ, Son of the Living God, have mercy on me, a sinner." I use, "Jesus, Mercy" or simply "Jesus." This word is your defense in the hour of conflict. As you fish deep down in the still waters of the superconscious, the demon will drop his own bait in the form of alluring thoughts or images. Don't be fooled, don't bite, don't grab, don't surface, let go, and just breathe the name of Jesus. Return to the quiet. The senses and the mind which are greedy, will not be frustrated in their idleness. They must do and have. They hate the hunger of emptiness.

The various kinds of thoughts and what to do with them:

Superifical thoughts. Pay no attention to them. In spite of their honking stay in conversation with your heavenly guest.

Interesting thoughts. They call for a reaction. Don't reflect on them. Don't be annoyed. Return to your sacred word. Call on Jesus.

Brilliant thoughts. You may get a brilliant theological or psychological insight. Have ascetical discipline. Let go. Don't be attached. Don't even pray for yourself or another. Return to silence and the sacred word.

Reflective thoughts. You go deep. Time flashes past. Peace is deep. You reflect; how did I get here? Let go reflection. Contemplate in faith. Don't possess. Enjoy the presence. Rest in naked intent disinterested. Contemplate the present reality. Reflection on Joy is an attempt to possess it. Then you lose it. Have peace and don't think about having peace. Return to the sacred word.

Divine Psychotherapy thoughts. In prayer we become aware of our deep wounds, evil tendencies, tensions, motivations. In consciousness a healing takes place. There is a catharsis and purification going on. Accept; let go, and return to the sacred word.

Finally, there is a "blind stirring of love," the "living flame of love," enkindled by the Holy Spirit. We feel the charity infused. Rest and enjoy. (Cf. "Finding Grace at the Center," St. Bede Publications, Still River, Massachusetts. Article, "Cultivating the Centering Prayer," by Thomas Keating, OCSO)

Teresa tells us not to worry over these thoughts and images. Worry is worse than distraction. In her own wonderful way, she describes the danger.

> Hence, proceed the afflictions of many people who practise prayer, and their complaints of interior trials. Their health declines and they even abandon prayer altogether, because they fail to realize that there is an interior world close at hand.
>
> Just as we cannot stop the movement of the heavens revolving as they do with such speed, so we cannot restrain our thought and then we send all the faculties of the soul after it, thinking we are lost, and have misused the time that we are spending in the presence of God. Yet the soul may be wholly united with Him in the mansions very near His presence, while thoughts remain in the outskirts of the castle, suffering the assaults of a thousand wild and venomous creatures. From this suffering it gains merit. This must not upset us, and we must not abandon the struggle, as the devil tries to make us do. Most of these trials come from the fact that we do not understand ourselves (*The Interior Castle* IV, 1, p. 234.)

These distractions come from our weakness. Don't worry. The will and intellect may be peacefully centered, while images and thoughts flash all over the screen of the mind. Rest in tranquil love, be patient, sleep, eat, and drink, learn to relax and return to the still water of peace. The prayer is meritorious, if we persevere. Never abandon the struggle. Compassionately, she adds. "We should take proper measures and learn to understand ourselves, and not blame our souls for what is the work of our weak imagination and our nature and the devil. (*The Interior Castle* IV, 1, p. 236.)

The Lord in His own good time comes to the rescue if we are available.

> A person involuntarily closes his eyes and desires solitude. Without the display of any human skill there seems gradually to be built for him a temple in which he can make the prayer already described. The senses and all external things seem gradually to

lose their hold on him, while the soul, on the other hand regains its lost control." (*The Interior Castle* IV, 3, p. 240.)

The senses and faculties may have been distracted and wandered outside the castle, then:

> The great King who dwells in the Mansion within this castle perceives their good will, and in His great mercy desires to bring them back to Him. Like a good Shepherd with a call so gentle, that even they can hardly recognize it. He teaches them to know His voice and not to go away and get lost but to return to their mansion. So powerful is this Shepherd's call that they give up the things outside the castle which led them astray, and once again enter it. (Ibid.)

As we progress in prayer the Recollection becomes more and more passive, as the Lord takes the initiative.

> These people are sometimes in the castle before they have begun to think about God at all. I cannot say where they entered or how they heard their Shepherd's call. It was certainly not with their ears, for outwardly such a call is not audible. They become markedly conscious that they are gradually retiring within themselves. Anyone who experiences this will discover what I mean. I think I have read that they are like a hedgehog or a tortoise withdrawing into itself. . . . It happens only when God is pleased to grant us this favor. (Ibid, p. 241.)

When this gift is granted we should be very grateful. As the outer sense close, the inner senses open. This is the beginning of a new chapter and stage of your life of prayer. Beware the reasoning. The mind is the villain. Engage in vertical thinking.

> "We should not contrive to use our reasoning powers. Be intent upon discovering what the Lord is working in the soul. (Ibid.)

Teresa gives four reasons why we should remain passive and not exert our senses of thought and reasoning.

> 1. The person who does most is he who thinks least and desires to do least. (Ibid, p. 242.)

We cannot by human thought or action win this favour. We

must learn to wait like humble beggars, silently watching for the sign, when the Emperor within may call us to His presence and permit us to be near Him. The gift of presence and listening attention.

2. Recollection is a gentle and peaceful activity. It cannot be forced or hurried. No artificial yoga techniques or painful asceticism can induce it. We must simply resign ourselves to the will of God. He has His time.

3. The very effort to stop thinking becomes a distraction in itself.

4. We give the greatest glory to God by forgetting ourselves. Let us give, concentrate on the Lord.

In the desert, we have the oasis; from the darkness comes the light; the nada is filled with the todo.

When His Majesty wishes the working of the understanding to cease, He employs it in another manner, and illumines the soul's knowledge to so much higher a degree than any we can ourselves attain. He leads it into a state of absorption, in which, without knowing how, it is much better instructed than it could ever be as a result of its own efforts, which would spoil everything. (Ibid, p. 243.)

Let the will enjoy the loving presence of God. However, she adds, if nothing happens, don't hypnotize or cast a spell over the other faculties. It may be necessary to return to meditation.

All the will has to do now is to enjoy the banquet of love and "It should not labor except for uttering a few loving words." (Ibid.) Just return to your favourite manthra or the Jesus Prayer.

When Teresa treats of the Prayer of Recollection in her *Life*, she imagines the soul as a beautiful garden planted with trees and flowers and well watered and fertile by the water of grace. It gave her great delight to imagine the Lord walks in this garden. The garden of paradise is within her. There the good Lord lavishes His gifts, prunes the branches, and gives the soul the self-knowledge of its helplessness. We cannot of our own accord make the flowers of virtue grow. The Lord is the best gardener, and at this stage we must learn to let Him work while we are passive and receptive. To the religious enthusiast, who believes in the power of the human will, human initiative and asceticsm the art of listening comes difficult. He does not subscribe to the superiority of passive power over active power, of passive virtue over active virtue. Remaining passive under the working of a higher power is the superior activity. We need faith to believe that God can do more in a short time in this form of prayer, than we can achieve in many years. As the Lord pours down His rain and sunshine, the garden softens, warms, and grows more beautiful. It is more refreshed, fertile, and fragrant after one such shower than if we had worked away for many years with our spades, shovels, forks, and buckets.

We must not be bashful with God. We must never underestimate His infinite love and gracious goodness. He delights to be with us. Sometimes we imagine we are under a compliment to Him. We suffer from such a poor self-image. We falsely feel we are not worthy, too weak and too sinful to share these heavenly delights. God made us for joy. Contemplation is enjoying God, already here on earth.

"We are already children of God." —1 John 3:2.

Union with the God of love, truth and joy can never mean sadness, sorrow, and gloom.

Teresa sings of the "great delights of the soul," of "rejoicing in Thee," "words of comfort," "marks of love." (*Life*, Ch. 14, p. 83.)

> The water is now higher and thus much less labour is required than for the drawing of it from the well. The water is nearer, for grace reveals itself to the soul more clearly. This state is a recollecting of the faculties within the soul, so that its fruition of that contentment may be of greater delight. The faculties are not lost nor do they sleep. The will alone is occupied, in such a way that, without knowing it, it becomes captive. It allows itself to become imprisoned by God, as one who well knows itself to be the captive of Him whom it loves. Oh, my Jesus and Lord how much Thy love now means to us! It binds our own love so straitly that at that moment it leaves us no freedom to love anything but Thee. (*Life*, Ch. 14, p. 83.)

The meeting with the Lord in the garden of the soul brings its own sweet satisfaction. This is a gentle and general experimental knowledge of His presence and goodness. This conviction woos the soul away from the creatures, who no longer attract or distract as of old. There is inner freedom. Softened by compassion the soul is freed from any form of compulsion and control. In this new-found love, delight, and peace, we rise above every other created pleasure and satisfaction. The lust for power, riches, fame, honor, and pleasure have lost their grip. We no longer crave them inordinately. We will not sin to have them. Let go, let God.

> Even if we wear ourselves to pieces with penances and prayers and all kinds of other things, we can acquire but little if the Lord is not pleased to bestow it. God, of His greatness desires the soul to realize that His Majesty is so near it that it need not send Him messengers, but may speak with Him itself. It need not cry aloud, because He is so near that if has only to move its lips and He will understand it. (*Life*, Ch. 14, p. 85.)

Our God is very understanding. He fills the void caused by our sins.

> This satisfaction resides in the most intimate part of the soul. The soul cannot tell whence or how it has come to it. Often it knows neither what to do, nor to wish, nor to ask. It seems to find everything at once, yet not know what it has found. (Ibid.)

We judge any form of prayer by its fruits. The Prayer of Recollection leaves us with a new and more adoring appreciation of God. This loving knowledge weans us away from the created pleasures. We develop higher and loftier faculties to taste and savor the divine. Sin loses its hold. Cravings are lessened. We are free. Life has a center, a divine center. Virtue grows, as the Lord prunes and waters the plants in His own sweet way. We are spiritualized by the Holy Spirit, enlightened by the Word, Goddified by the Father. Humble self-knowledge is granted us so that we recognize our nothingness and yet attain an inkling of our greatness. We learn to live in hope and self-confidence. We rely on the Divine Guest within. He gives Himself to us when we open ourselves to receive. He is a gentle master and has His time.

Problems do not disturb us. We do not let them in. The inner cathedral is filled with the glory of God. It is no longer a marketplace. We lead a life of peaceful intimacy and friendship with God. Deep peace ensues. Prayer is far more effective and enjoyable. The soul is filled with hope and courage.

New regions of the spirit are opened:

When a soul sets out upon this path, He does not reveal Himself to it, lest it should feel dismayed at seeing that its littleness can contain such greatness. Gradually He enlarges it to the extent requisite for what He has set within it. He has perfect freedom and power to make the whole of this palace great. . . . If we fill the palace with vulgar people and all kinds of junk, how can the Lord and His Court occupy it? (*Life*, Ch. 28, p. 118.)

13.

The Prayer of Quiet

The Prayer of Quiet according to St. Teresa is "the beginning of pure contemplation." (*The Way of Perfection*, Ch. 30, p. 125.) We may enter the world of the supernatural through prayer, a world of new lights, delights and some ineffable experiences. To the inexperienced it will all seem confused.

Teresa treats of the Prayer of Quiet in her *Way of Perfection*, under the words, "Thy Kingdom come," of her commentary on the Our Father. God's Kingdom is in heaven, and heaven is within the soul. There the good contemplative will retire to recollect his scattered forces, center in and enjoy the peace of the Lord. The good Shepherd will lead him to the meadows of green grass and to the waters of repose, there to revive his drooping spirit. This is the house of God, and here there is nothing but goodness and kindness—it lasts forever. This is where the Holy Grail is hidden. Here the quest ends. The Lord now reveals the wealth and splendor of this Kingdom. The revelation is not as perfect as in the next life, but already on earth the mystic shares "the glory, the joy, the peace, the satisfaction, and the tranquillity of the blessed." (Ibid). Heaven begins on earth. Teresa teaches the earthly mystic. This is eternal life. The world painted by our mystical artist in these pages is one of light, love, and joy. The fruits of the Holy Spirit ripen.

We do not primarily pray for our own perfection and holiness. This would be selfish. The basic motive is the honour and glory of God. This is the highest sacrifice. Jesus' greatest sacrifice was to give praise, honor, and glory to God. "He begins to give us His Kingdom on earth that we may truly praise Him and hallow His name and strive to make others do so likewise." (*The Way of Perfection,* Ch. 31, p. 127.)

Prayer is a means. Contemplation is a means to greater love of God and our fellowman. We search for love and not enlightenment. That love emanates in good done to ourselves and others. We learn compassion. Teresa retains a hierarchy of values.

The Prayer of Quiet is a gift from God. It cannot be acquired by human methods, efforts, or techniques. These may prepare us. They do not open the door. The light and love come from inside.

> This is a supernatural state. However hard we try, we cannot reach it for ourselves. It is a state in which the soul enters into peace, or rather in which the Lord gives it peace through His presence. (*The Way of Perfection,* Ch. 31, p. 127.)

God draws the soul closer to Himself. He reveals His face in a new manner. He awakens our awareness and consciousness. He removes the cataracts from our spiritual eyes. This is a process of loving knowledge and sapiential love never tasted or experienced before. God does not have to use the roundabout way of sense, imagination, emotion, active intellect, ideas, logic, and judgment to instill knowledge and love. He infuses His loving knowledge direct and one small spark or ray can do more to enkindle the will in a few moments than years of discursive reasoning and meditation. God is nearer to us, or rather more immanent than we are to ourselves. He is the soul of our souls. We plunge into our depths and His depth through vertical thinking.

Teresa, like all great mystics, stresses the immanence of God, but she never denies His transcendence. In fact, she lauds the power, the glory, the infinity of His Majesty. She retains that delicate balance, as St. Thomas and St. Augustine did centuries before her. Many other cultists of the immanent ended up teaching a form of pantheism or monism. Teresa of Jesus can never be justly accused of that heresy.

Today there is an interest in the immanent. It is so easy, however, to confuse the spiritual with the psychological, the mystic with the psychedelic, the methaphysical with the magic.

The authentic mystic seeks the love, the honor, and the glory of God, while the magician wants power and knowledge. The mystic seeks the glory of God. Magic wants the glory of self. The followers of the psychedelic claim to have a direct encounter with the God within. They induce what they call mystic states with the help of drugs, music, incense, light, hypnosis, yoga, or transcendental meditation. Christian mysticism is the flower of faith and love based on the word of God.

The interior world that Teresa describes and the God whom she loves and adores cannot be reached with L.S.D. and five dollars. The direct means of union with God are the theological virtues of faith, hope, and charity enlightened by the special light of the Holy Spirit.

> In this state all the faculties are stilled. The soul in a way which has nothing to do with the outward senses, realizes that it is now very close to its God, and that, if it were but a little closer, it would become one with Him through union. . . . It cannot understand how it knows Him, yet it sees that it is in the Kingdom (or at least near the King who will give it the Kingdom). It feels such a reverence that it dares to ask nothing. It is, as it were, in a swoon, both inwardly and outwardly. The outward man (body) does not wish to move, but rests, like one who has almost reached the end of this journey, so that it may the better start again upon its way, with redoubled strength for its task. (*The Way of Reflection*, Ch. 31, p. 127.)

The body experiences the greatest delight and the soul is conscious of deep satisfaction. The joy of the spirit overflows into the body. We are integrated body, mind, and spirit. The body is the temple. We are as spiritual as the body is. The body becomes our best ally or our worst enemy. We must treat it with reverence and care. It is difficult to pray within a sick and tired body. I believe many of our difficulties in prayer are due to tired and tense bodies. We do not know our bodies.

To illustrate somewhat the Prayer of Quiet, Teresa draws on her favorite element, water. Water fascinated her. She was, with all her supernatural gifts and graces, a naturalist. She discovered the deep-down freshness of things and found God at the heart of everything. At the center all become one. There is no separation. God did not create things. He created prayer. Everything is a prayer, a sign, a symbol, calling us like a bell peal to a presence and act of adoration.

"I believe that in every little thing created by God, there is more than we can realize, even in so small a thing as a tiny ant." (*The Interior Castle* IV, 2, p. 26.)

She now imagines the soul as two large basins. They are to be filled with the living water through prayer, meditation and the Prayer of Quiet. Meditation is laborious. A little water has to come a long distance and dribble in through the pipes of much labor and human skill as it rumbles along making much noise as it passes through the senses, imagination, memory, intellect, and will.

In the Prayer of Quiet the basin is at the very source of the water. Water enters immediately and enters direct. Here the water is abundant, flows deep and still; flows all the time and makes no noise. Prayer is accompanied by peace, quietness, and sweetness within. This delight is felt in the depths of the spirit. There are times when it overflows into the faculties and inundates the body. The source is God Himself. He gives us to drink.

A dilation of heart follows. Teresa explains:

> I do not think that this happiness has its source in the heart at all. It arises in a much more interior part like something of which the springs are very deep. I think this must be the center of the soul. . . . I certainly find secret things in ourselves which often amaze me . . . in ourselves there are deep secrets which we cannot fathom . . . This heavenly water begins to flow from this source, from our very depths. It proceeds to spread within us and cause an interior dilation and produce ineffable blessings so that the soul itself cannot understand all that it receives there. (*The Interior Castle* IV, 2, pp. 237–238.)

A delicate fire and heat is felt.

> The fragrance is as if in these interior depths there were a brazier on which were cast sweet perfumes. The light cannot be seen, nor the peace where it swells, but the fragrant smoke and heat penetrate the entire soul, and very often, as I have said, the effects extend even to the body . . . no heat is felt, nor is any fragrance perceived. It's a more delicate thing than that . . . This is not a thing we can fancy, nor, however hard we strive, can we acquire it. It is clear that it is a thing made, not of human metal, but of the purest gold of Divine Wisdom. (*The Interior Castle,* IV, 2, p. 238.)

Like the other great mystics, Teresa mentions the center of the soul that lies deep below our conscious life. That center is in a region deeper than what our faculties of sense, imagination, intellect, will, and feeling with their empirical acts can reach. Even Teresa cannot penetrate those ultimate depths. The center is God. This is the core. The surface waters may be ruffled by the storms of life, or the play of powers, concepts, ideas and images and desires. Deep down there is peace and unity. Here the search ends. We find our true self. From this center flows a new kind of knowledge that is mystical, contemplative, intuitive, and certain. This is the ground of my being and ideals and convictions nursed here endure. Synthesis and synergism take place. Divinity weds humanity, and the Word becomes flesh and dwells among us.

In that precious little book, *Mister God, This is Anna*, the author brings out the point:

> I have a toy . . . two circles of heavy copper wire linked together like two links of a chain. I play with them so often that at times I am quite unaware that I have it in my hands. Anna pointed to one of the circles and said, "I know what that is—that's me. And that's Mister God," she said pointing to the other. "Mister God goes right through my middle and I go right through Mister God's middle." Anna had grasped that her proper place was in God's middle and that God's proper place was in her middle. (*Mister God, This is Anna*, by Fynn, Ballantine Books, New York p. 50).

And Anna like Teresa discovered this true reality because she was empty, and "cos I ain't frightened."

God has made man in His own image and likeness, not in his intelligence, eyes, ears, body or soul but in "this total inwardness" God's love is different.

> Fynn you can love better than any people that ever was, and so can I, can't I. But Mister God is different. You see, Fynn, people can only love outside and can only kiss outside, but Mister God can love you right inside, and Mister God can kiss you right inside, so it's different. Mister God ain't like us. We are a little bit like Mister God, but not much yet. (Ibid, p. 27.)

In her *Way of Perfection*, Teresa has a more beautiful illustration.

> The soul is like an infant still at its mother's breast. Such is the mother's care for it that she gives it its milk without its having to ask for it so much as by moving its lips. That is what happens here. The will simply loves, and no effort needs to be made by the understanding. It is the Lord's pleasure that, without exercising its thought, the soul should realize that it is in His company, and should merely drink the milk which His Majesty puts into its mouth and enjoy the sweetness. The Lord desires it to know that it is He Who is granting it that favor and that in its enjoyment of it He too rejoices. (*The Way of Perfection*, Ch. 31, p. 130.)

The will loves. Like a little babe we rest on a mother's breast, trusting, warm, little, passive, open, ready to receive. We rejoice. We must not try to understand what is going on. That is to pass from the passive to the active, from the anima to the animus, from the deeper to the superficial. While we are happy, we make God, the heavenly mother happy. Contemplation is a holy leisure. We enjoy God.

The Psalmist sings of the same experience.

> Lord, I have given up my pride and turned away from my arrogance. I am not concerned with great matters or with subjects too difficult for me. Instead I am content and at peace as a child lies quietly on its mothers's arms, so my heart is quiet within me. Israel, trust in the Lord now and forever.
>
> —Psalm 131.

The image Teresa has of God is that of a loving mother always ready to nourish, give life, understand, help, forgive, and sustain the children. He is happy when we are gracious receivers.

We may imagine we can merit the Prayer of Quiet. We cannot. We cannot even prolong it, once it begins.

> They imagine that they can prolong it and may even try not to breathe. This is ridiculous. We can no more control this prayer than we can make the day break, or stop night from falling. It is supernatural and something we cannot acquire. (*The Way of Perfection*, Ch. 31, p. 129.)

Humble self-knowledge is still needed. There are secret labyrinths within the soul. Teresa laments the ignorance of religious. She cried:

> O Lord, do thou remember how much we have to suffer on this road through lack of knowledge! The worst of it is that as we do not realize we need to know more, when we think about Thee, we cannot ask those who know. Indeed we have not even any idea what there is for us to ask him. So we suffer terrible trials, because we do not understand ourselves." (*The Interior Castle* IV, 1, pp. 233-234.)

The passage from meditation to contemplation is a very delicate one and we need guidance. Many tragedies happen on account of ignorance. It is the devil's favorite hiding place and his best commandos lurk around here. Sad to relate, many directors keep their protegees forever in the Third Mansion and will not let them enter the Prayer of Quiet.

Some knowledge of psychology and spiritual theology is needed. We must be able to distinguish the various faculties and emotions, and diagnose the difference between natural and supernatural causes. We are passive to their invasion, and we must be able to distinguish. People imagine they are going through the dark night of the spirit described by St. John of the Cross, when in fact their symptom has a purely natural biological or psychological cause. They feel they are victims for Christ when they are just depressed. Quite often their aridity and dryness is due to moral tepidity and lack of fraternal charity. Without this fraternal charity, authentic prayer is impossible. It is easy to tell Jesus in the tabernacle that we love Him, but it is not quite so easy to tell another fellow human being who is temperamentally different and gets on our nerves.

In the Prayer of Quiet the will is captivated by God's goodness and love. The intellect, imagination, and memory may roam free. However:

> Since the will is in union with God for as long as the recollection lasts, its quiet and repose are not lost. The will gradually brings the understanding and memory back to a state of recollection again. Although the will is not yet completely absorbed, it is so well occupied, without knowing how, that, whatever the efforts made by the understanding and memory, they cannot deprive it of its contentment and rejoicing. Indeed without any labour on

> its part, it helps to prevent the little spark of love for God from being quenched." (*Life*, Ch. 15, p. 89.)

The will may be lovingly centered on God, while the imagination is restless. When the intellect does not understand what is going on, it becomes frustrated.

> It roams about all over the place like a demented creature, and can settle down to nothing. The will is fixed so firmly upon its God that this disturbed condition of the understanding causes it great distresses, but it must not take any notice of it, for if it does so it will lose a great part of what it is enjoying. It must forget about it, and abandon itself into the arms of love. His Majesty will teach it what to do next. Its whole work is to realize its unworthiness and to receive such great good and to occupy itself in thanksgiving. (*The Interior Castle* IV, 3, p. 244.)

The tug o'war goes on. We must keep loving in spite of distractions. God will pour a loving knowledge into us. Wisdom will be infused.

Many souls reach this state and remain here. We cannot blame God. It is lost through carelessness. Teresa herself had attained this degree of prayer and then lost it for years. If received we must be humbly grateful for the gift and not fall into the sin of presumption. Above all, never give up prayer. Even if we do fall, prayer will enlighten us and keep us out of danger. Prayer keeps the spark of true love for the Lord enkindled. This divine spark is a prelude and preparation for greater things.

What are we to do?

> At these seasons of quiet the soul is merely to go softly and make no noise (with words and reflections) . . . The will must be calm and discreet and realize that we cannot treat effectively with God by the might of our own efforts. These are like great logs of wood heaped up indiscriminately so that they will quench the spark . . . Let us utter any words of love which come to its mind, with the firm and sure knowledge that what it is saying is the truth. Let it take no notice of the understanding which is merely making itself a nuisance. (*Life*, Ch. 15, p. 91.)

God's love and gifts are gracious mysteries. We don't have to understand them. Let the will enjoy the favor, and make little acts of love. Let the soul repose in its rest. Come aside awhile and rest. The more we relax, the better. This is the time for love and not for knowledge.

Teresa keeps harping on the need for humility.

> When the Spirit of God is at work, there is no need to go about looking for ways of inducing humility and confusion. The Lord Himself reveals these to us in a very different manner from any we can find by means of our puny reflections which are nothing by comparison with a true humility proceeding from the light given us in this way by the Lord. Through this knowledge given by God we may learn that we ourselves have nothing good. (*Life*, Ch. 15, p. 95.)

When the Lord sheds the searchlight of His Wisdom into the murky caverns of our subconscious, we soon earn humility of heart. One such flash carries more humbling knowledge than years of self-appointed ascetical practices.

All servile fear is taken away. We speak in silence.

> They are so close to God that they know they can make themselves understood by signs. They are in the palace, near to their King, and they see that He is already beginning to give them His Kingdom on earth. . . . Nothing distresses them—as long as this state lasts, they are so overwhelmed and absorbed by the joy and delight that they can think of nothing else to wish for, and will gladly say with Saint Peter: Lord let us make here three mansions. (*The Way of Perfection*, Ch. 31, p. 128.)

When all our faculties work together in harmony the experience is wonderful. There is peace in the house. Martha and Mary work together. Minimal effort is required. Teresa has a beautiful illustration as we use a simple manthra or prayer word.

> The most we should do is occasionally, and quite gently, to utter a single word, like a person giving a little puff to a candle, when he sees it has almost gone out, so as to make it burn again. If it were fully alight, I suppose the only result of blowing it would be to put it out. I think the puff should be a gentle one, because, if we begin to tax our brains by making up long speeches, the will may become active again. (*The Way of Perfection*, Ch, 31, p. 130.)

We might well wonder how a person in this state can carry

out her ordinary work and duties. Teresa replies that although the will is absorbed, the other faculties and powers are free. In fact, they may be more alert. Service does not suffer. Compassion is no less. Martha and Mary combine. The greater and loftier our prayer, the greater and richer our apostolate becomes. The history of the saints proves that. We grow in charity. Heroic charity is the test.

Teresa gives a warning. It is easy to grow lax and less vigilant. We may presume that we have a strength and a virtue that we don't really possess, and walk into the occasion of sin. We are still unweaned children in the spiritual life and we must be careful not to walk where angels fear to tread. Since people in this state attract others, the devil is all the more envious and will do his utmost to cause their downfall. Counterfeiting is possible. Pride, presumption and vainglory precede a fall.

Here's another peril that women more than men may fall into, although men are not exempt.

> Because of prayers, vigils, and severe penances and also for other reasons, some women have poor health. When they experience spiritual consolation, therefore, it is too much for them, and as soon as they feel any interior joy there comes over them a physical weakness and langour. They fall into a sleep, which they call "spiritual," and which is a little more marked than the condition that has been described. Thinking the one state to be the same as the other, they abandon themselves to this absorption. The more they relax, the more complete becomes this absorption, because their physical nature continues to grow weaker. So they get it into their heads that it is arrobamiento, or rapture. But I call it abobamiento, foolishment. They are doing nothing but wasting their time and ruining their health. (*The Interior Castle* IV, 3, pp. 245–246.)

The experience may be so lofty that it takes a good healthy, physical, and psychological nervous system to sustain it. Teresa pokes fun at one Sister who was in this foolish state for eight hours. She was not conscious of God at all. Nor was she unconscious. Teresa cured her by giving her more food, sleep and less penance. Self-deception is easy. Wishful thinking may make us hallucinate. If the state really comes from God, there will be no langour in the soul. Nearer to God, it will be energized by joy. Any physical weakness does not last. If it does.

> See that they sleep and eat well, until their physical strength, if it has become exhausted, comes back again. If their constitution is so weak that this does not suffice, they can be certain that God is not calling them to anything beyond the active life. . . . Let anyone of this kind be kept busy with duties, and let care be taken that she is not left alone very much, or her health will be completely ruined. (*The Interior Castle*, IV, 3, p. 246.)

This is good advice.

There's another group of people who may easily stray. These are persons with sickly imaginations and intellects.

"They believe they actually see all they imagine." (Ibid.)

Effects of Prayer of Quiet

The genuiness and authenticity of the Prayer of Quiet are to be tested not by some strange phenomena but by the effects and actions that follow. We must learn to relax and not overstrive. The Lord is conquered by humility. Teresa gives reasons why we should not strive too much.

> (1) Love God without any motive of self interest
> (2) It is lack of humility to think that we deserve anything so great because of our miserable service
> (3) The best preparation to receive these gifts is a desire to suffer and imitate Our Lord—not to seek consolations
> (4) We serve Christ crucified. His Majesty is not obliged to grant favours
> (5) It is labour in vain. This water is a gift. It is given only to the person God chooses, and often, when the soul is not thinking of it at all. (*The Interior Castle* IV, 2, pp. 238–239.)

When God grants the Prayer of Quiet, certain effects or signs are to be seen. There is, first of all, what Teresa calls a dilation or enlargement of the soul. The world of inner space opens up. We have an infinite capacity to receive. As the Lord floods the inner world with water, He enlarges the reservoir.

> The water proceeding from the spring had no means of running away, but the fountain had a device ensuring that the more freely the water flowed, the larger became the basin. (*The Interior Castle* IV, 3, p. 244.)

God works many wonders, so the soul retains all the gifts He gently gives it.

We enjoy more inner freedom here. There is less fear of hell. Instead, we enjoy a firm confidence that we will go to heaven. We are not afraid to really live or do penance. There is no hypochondria about health. In God we can do anything. We face the trials of life bravely, and with faith endure the sacrifice entailed. Earthly goods lose their attraction as we contemplate the majesty of God. We praise more and grumble less. We become captains of our own souls, as we regain mastery over sinful cravings and passions. There is a deep inner peace, harmony in the house. The virtues grow strong. We fly like the eagle to the top of the mountain. Courage and patience develop, and a power of determination and perseverance drives the spirit onward. Although we are aware now more clearly than ever, how weak and miserable we are, this knowledge does not dampen our spirits, but rather boosts our morale, because we rely confidently on the river of God's grace flowing profusely within. A loving gratitude fills the heart.

"This prayer is the beginning of all blessings." (*Life*, Ch. 15, p. 95.)

The Sleep of Powers

The sleep of powers is a more advanced form of the prayer of quiet. Teresa treats of this form of prayer in Chapter Sixteen of her *Life*, where she deals with the third way of watering the prayerful soul. It is a more passive form.

The Lord provides water from a river or spring to irrigate the garden of the soul, so that the flowers of virtue may open, blossom and give forth a sweet fragrance to the glory and praise of God. This prayer of praise is the goal. His Majesty is now the Chief Gardener. He does most of the work. All we need do is to prepare ourselves, open up in faith and love and drink the water of grace which is there in abundance. We can rest. The Holy Spirit is active within us. Let us abandon ourselves into the arms of God and trust His providential generosity.

It no longer belongs to itself. It is given wholly to the Lord. It can

> cease to worry altogether. The soul realizes that He is doing this without any fatiguing of its understanding . . . He does not desire the soul to undertake any labour, but only to take its delight in the first fragrance of the flowers. . . . The Gardener being as He is, the creator of the water gives the soul water without limit. (*Life*, Ch. 16, p. 101.)

The Lord grants more water now than it could attain itself in twenty years' work. The experience lasts a short time. There is no need to devise any method of prayer, or use any techniques to quiet the faculties. We are gripped and held captive by God's light and love. Nothing can distract us.

> Here we are all asleep and fast asleep to the things of the world, and to ourselves. In fact, for the short time that the condition lasts, the soul is without consciousness, and has no power to think, even though it may desire to do so. There is no need now for it to desire any method of suspending the thought. Even in loving, if it is able to love, it cannot understand how or what it is it loves nor what it would desire. In fact it has completely died to the world so that it may live more fully in God. This is a delectable death . . . a death full of delight, for in order to come closer to God, the soul seems to have withdrawn so far from the body that I do not know if it has still life enough to be able to breathe. (*The Interior Castle* V, 1, p. 248.)

We share the paschal mystery of Christ, death, and resurrection. We are dead to self and the world around us and alive only to God. Our entire being, for a short period, is centered and focused on the Lord. None of the faculties dare stir. This is true especially of the will and to a lesser extent of the understanding.

The hands or feet can't move. The body falls into a swoon as if dead. It cannot see nor hear. The understanding counts for nothing. The will has only to consent to the favors which it is enjoying and submit to all that true wisdom may be pleased to accomplish in it. The imagination and memory offer no obstacle to the blessings bestowed on the soul. The devil cannot enter and do any harm. This form of prayer is too secret for the devil.

> I shall venture to affirm, that if this is indeed union with God, the devil cannot enter or do any harm. His Majesty is in such close contact and union with the essence of the soul that he will

not dare to approach, nor can he even understand this secret thing. Great are the gains which come to the soul with God working in it and neither we ourselves nor anyone else hindering Him. (*The Interior Castle* V, 1, p. 249.)

Yet Teresa adds, in this prayer Mary and Martha may work together. The soul may be occupied in the contemplative and active lives at one and the same time. It may carry on its business and do works of charity.

> Those in this state are not wholly masters of themselves, and they know very well that the better part of the soul is elsewhere. It is as if we were speaking to one person while someone else was speaking to us. We cannot be wholly absorbed in either the one conversation or the other. (*Life*, Ch. 17, p. 102.)

Teresa has no time for some timid, half-learned men who think God cannot grant these favors. We must never close the door. Be open.

The most decisive indication of this prayer is:

> God implants Himself in the interior of the soul in such a way that when it returns to itself, it cannot possibly doubt that God has been in it and it has been in God. So firmly does this truth remain within it that, although for years God may never grant it the favor again, it can neither forget it nor doubt that it has received it. This is quite apart from the effects which remain within it, and of which I will speak later. This certainty of the soul is very material. (*The Interior Castle* V, 1, p. 251.)

This certainty is put there by God Himself. After such an experience, Teresa herself was convinced that God was in her by presence, power, essence, and grace, even though a half learned man tried to prove the contrary.

It is the beginning of the Prayer of Union. The King brings the soul "into the cellar of wine." This is His Will. We cannot enter it by any effort of our own.

> His Majesty must put us right into the centre of our soul, and must enter there Himself. In order that He may better show us His wonders, it is His pleasure that our will, which has entirely surrendered itself to Him, should have no part in this. Nor does He desire the door of the faculties and senses which are all asleep,

> to be opened to Him. He will come into the centre of the soul without using a door, as He did when He came into His disciples, and said, Pax Vobis, and when He left the sepulchre without removing the stone. Later on you will see how it is His Majesty's will that the soul should have fruition of Him in its very centre. (*The Interior Castle* V, 1, p. 252.)

This form of prayer brings sublime delight. It is a delectable death. We do not know what to do. We never know whether to be silent or to speak, whether to laugh or to weep.

> This state is a glorious folly, a heavenly madness, in which true wisdom is acquired, and a mode of fruition in which the soul finds the greatest delight. (*Life*, Ch. 16, p. 96.)

We may speak some words to God in praise, love, and gratitude, but they are without order, and perhaps, without meaning. They are words of love.

> It would fain be all tongue so that it might praise the Lord. It utters a thousand holy follies, striving ever to please Him Who thus possess it. (*Life*, Ch. 16, p. 98.)

The soul is possessed by a holy madness ready to dance, play and sing as David did before the Ark.

The prayer of the Sleep of the Powers carries its own graces with it. As to be expected, we grow in virtue. The flowers open. We advance in self-knowledge, courage, and humility. We enjoy a loftier knowledge and appreciation of God. This in turn frees us from the false fascination of all earthly pleasures, satisfactions, and thus we grow in freedom and mastery over sinful passions. We enjoy a state of restful quiet and solitude. The refreshing water overflows on to the body. "The glory and repose of the soul are so great that the body shares in the soul's joy and delight." (*Life*, Ch. 17, p. 104.)

The devil could never feign this peace and joy.

"Let us all be mad, for the love of Him who was called mad for our sakes." (*Life*, Ch. 16, p. 99.)

14.
Prayer of Simple Union

Teresa treats of the Prayer of Union in her *Life*, in the chapter on the fourth way of watering the garden. The Lord now lets the rain come down. There is an abundance of water. Washed clean and completely saturated the soul enters a kind of swoon of sweet delight. It is completely dead to the world. This is heavenly bliss.

> In this state of prayer to which we have now come, there is no feeling, but only rejoicing, unaccompanied by any understanding of the thing in which the soul is rejoicing . . . In this rejoicing all the senses are occupied, so that none of them is free, or able to act in any way, either outwardly or inwardly. (*Life*, Ch. 18, p. 105.)

Joy, praise, thanksgiving are the highest form of prayer. Contemplation is enjoying God, as God enjoys us.

The soul can barely breathe. The eyes close, it cannot move its hands, the intellect cannot reason, the tongue cannot speak. In this union of all the faculties, we cannot communicate what is going on. All outward strength vanishes, because the power of the soul is concentrated on God within. We cannot read.

The suspension lasts a short time, but the will maintains the contact with God.

> If it were to last for half an hour, that would be a long time. I do not think it has ever lasted so long as that with me. As the soul is not conscious of it, its duration is very difficult to estimate, so

I will merely say, that it is never very long before one of the faculties becomes active again (*Life*, Ch. 18, p. 109.)

The will remains calm. When the three faculties—will, intellect, and memory—rejoice together in this prayer, there is inebriation. They are inebriated with the taste of divine wine. They are completely lost for a short period. Even the imagination is completely. For as long as the rapture lasts, there is no distraction.

The experience is ineffable and indescribable.

What really happens: "It is quite clear what union is—two different things becoming one. O my Lord, how good Thou art." (*Life*, Ch. 18, p. 106.)

There is death and resurrection. As the Lord explained to Teresa:

> It dies to itself wholly, daughter, in order that it may give itself more and more to Me. It is no longer itself that lives but I. As it cannot comprehend what it understands, it is an understanding which understands not. . . . (*Life*, Ch. 18, p. 110.)

Here we enter the cloud of unknowing, *docta ignoratia*, a learned ignorance.

> I can only say that the soul feels close to God, and there abides with it such a certainty that it cannot do other than believe. All the faculties now fail and are suspended in such a way that it is impossible to believe they are active. (*Life*, Ch. 18, p. 110.)

The will is fully occupied in loving. The understanding cannot understand how it understands. The memory has burned its wings.

Teresa herself enjoyed this gift of presence, until an unlearned person disturbed her. She admits.

"I did not know that God was in all things, and when He seemed to me to be

> So very present, I thought it impossible. I could not cease believing that he was there, for it seemed almost certain that I had been conscious of His very presence. Unlearned persons would tell me that He was there only by grace. I could not believe that. He seemed to me to be really present. (*Life*, Ch. 18, p. 111.)

The good Fr. Bañez, O.P. freed her from her dilemma.

> This rain from Heaven often comes when the gardener is least expecting it. Yet it is true that at first it almost always comes after long mental prayer. As one degree of prayer succeeds another, the Lord catches this little bird and puts it into the nest where it may repose. Having watched it flying for a long time, striving with mind and will and all its strength to seek and please God, it becomes His pleasure, while it is still in this life, to give it its reward. (*Life*, Ch. 18, p. 108.)

This prayer leaves us with a great tenderness. Tears of joy flood the soul. Courage grows. Faith is deepened. Love is inflamed and trust is confirmed. No vainglory or vanity is possible. We humbly admit this is a gift. Self-knowledge is granted. We become free and detached. We know we are forgiven. Then we are really free to praise God, as divine wisdom is infused and heavenly secrets are revealed.

Teresa gives her teaching on the Prayer of Union in the fifth mansion of her *Interior Castle*. This prayer brings riches, treasures, and delights beyond all description.

Teresa admits that many persons of prayer enter this far into the castle. This is true especially of Carmelites.

> They are called to prayer and contemplation, because that was the first principle of our Order. We are descended from the line of those holy Fathers of ours from Mount Carmel, who sought this treasure, this precious pearl of which we speak, in such great solitude and with such contempt for the world (*The Interior Castle* V, 1, p. 247.)

The rest of us do not prepare ourselves as we ought. This preparation is not a matter of external acts, customs, habits, mortifications, or services. We dare not neglect these. But the preparation goes much deeper now. It is a matter of preparing ourselves to communicate with God in a new manner and in a new atmosphere beyond methods and means, beyond and above rites and rubrics. Instead of waiting on God, we wait for God. When we wait on God, we serve God; when we wait for God, God serves us. God does the work for us. Unfortunately, we are too insecure and feverishly proud to permit this. We refuse to be like little children. We don't want to be carried in the eagle's wings. We shun the heights, unless we are allowed to climb there ourselves in our own preconceived ascetical way. We panic before Christian mysticism.

> To some extent it is possible for us to enjoy Heaven upon earth. . . . May we dig until we find the hidden treasure, since it is quite true that we have it within us. (*The Interior Castle* V, 1, p. 248.)

We must be generous and brave here. Literally let go, let God. Our faculties and powers have reached their limits here. We now rely on grace, faith, and the gifts of the Holy Spirit. God implants Himself in the center of the soul and from there He bestows His blessings. A great delight and peace floods the soul. This delight cannot be feigned by Satan or counterfeited by nature. "It penetrates to the very marrow of the bones." (*The Interior Castle* V, 1, p. 250.)

There can be no doubt as to the authenticity of the source of this experience. Certainty is a characteristic. Teresa comes back to the theme: "We can do nothing to make His Majesty grant us this favour, we can do a great deal to prepare ourselves for it." (*The Interior Castle* V, 2, p. 253.)

Prayer cannot be divorced from life and the prayer of union helps us to integrate and harmonize our lives. It integrates us more quickly in our moral, psychological and prayer life. Then the body and our social action benefit.

> We cannot attain to the heights I have spoken of if we are not sure that we have the union in which we resign our wills to the will of God. (*The Interior Castle,* V, 3, p. 260.)

To do the will of God is the goal. Then nothing can disturb the inner boat, neither poverty or sickness, success or failure. This is genuine union, the safest union, the union we must all acquire. We need not strive for other forms of delectable union. Union of wills is essential.

Teresa builds her prayer castle on the solid foundation of morals. This resignation to the will of God carries delight and psychological peace.

To describe the metamorphosis that takes place, Teresa makes use of the silkworm allegory. The silkworm is the soul.

> Silk comes from a kind of seed which looks like tiny peppercorns. . . . When the warm weather comes, and the mulberry trees begin to show leaf, this seed starts to take life. Until it has this sustenance in which it feeds, it is as dead. . . . People put down twigs, and with their tiny mouths, they start spinning silk, making themselves very tight little cocoons, in which they busy themselves. Then finally the worm, which was large and ugly, comes right out of the cocoon a beautiful white butterfly. (*The Interior Castle* V, 2, p. 253.)

We are that ugly fat little worm, that must be buried in the cocoon, the tomb of selfishness and sin. We rise and grow up under the warm light of the Holy Spirit, by making use of the general helps Christ has left us in the church, sacraments, prayer, books, meditation, and sermons. These are our spiritual food. We thus grow in grace and virtue, build ourselves up as temples of the Trinity, beautiful silken cocoons of God, shrines where we live with the Father in a new life of intimacy, awareness, and love.

> God will take this tiny achievement of ours, which is nothing at all, unite it with His greatness and give it such worth that its reward will be the Lord Himself. . . . He will unite our small trials with the great trials which He suffered, and make both of them into one. (*The Interior Castle* V, 2, p. 254.)

We must renounce our self-will, self-love, our attachments to earthly things. Let us practice penance, prayer and mortification, obedience, and all the other good works. This means death to the ugly little worm. Then we are ready for resurrection. "When it is in this state of prayer, and quite dead to the world, it comes out a little white butterfly." (*The Interior Castle* V, 2, p. 255).

Now the soul flies free in the realm of spirit continuously praising God.

This experience lasts a very short time perhaps half an hour. The results are marvelous. We feel much more courageous, ready to suffer trials, detached from the world, desiring solitude, full of zeal and free in the spirit. The little white butterfly can fly now and will never again be content to crawl. Crosses may come and go, but we can take them with courage and contentment. We are resigned to the will of God. We have attained union. Our will becomes one with the will of God.

God shares His love with us, and He expects us to share that love with others. The heat of charity must warm and soften the lives of the people around us. In this we share the passion of Christ. We suffer for sin.

The bride becomes like soft wax in the hands of God.

> His will is that without understanding him, the soul shall go thence sealed with His seal. The soul in that state does no more than the wax when a seal is impressed upon it. The wax does not impress itself. It is only prepared for the imprint; that is, it is soft. And it does not even soften itself so as to be prepared. It merely remains quiet and consenting. . . . Thou dost require only our will and dost ask that thy wax may offer no impediment. (*The Interior Castle* V, 2, p. 257.)

Teresa keeps calling us back to essentials. Love God and love our neighbor.

> Here, the Lord asks only two things of us: love for His Majesty and love for our neighbor. It is for these two virtues that we must strive. If we attain them perfectly we are doing His will and so shall be united with Him. (*The Interior Castle* V, 3, p. 261.)

The surest sign is the love we have for our neighbor, and the greater our union, the more heroic will our fraternal charity be. Charity is the greatest moral miracle and the surest sign of the presence of the Holy Spirit and the resurrected life of Christ within us. This effective charity is tested on the anvil of action, and the realist Teresa advises us:

> Not to take notice of all the fine plans which come crowding into our minds when we are at prayer. . . . If our later actions are not in harmony with these plans, we can have no reason for believing that we should have ever put them into practice. I say the same of humility. . . . The wiles of the devil are terrible. He will run a thousand times around hell if by so doing he can make us believe that we have a single virtue which we have not. (*The Interior Castle* V, 3, p. 262.)

It is easy to dream on a soft padded predieu. Imaginary virtue is an illusion, a dangerous waste of time.

Watch the imagination:

> The devil makes good use of the imagination in practicing his surprises and deceptions, and there are many such which he can practice on women, or on unlettered persons, because we do not understand the difference between the faculties and the imagination, and thousands of other things belonging to the interior life. (*The Interior Castle* V, 3, p. 262.)

Psychological balance and knowledge are still requisites for the life of prayer. Diligence about prayer is not the all-important criterion of holiness. Teresa laughs at people who are so wrapped in prayer that they scarcely dare breathe or stir. They are forever wondering in what Mansion they are. They are afraid to lose the smallest degree of tenderness and consolation. They are generally lost in their own little emotional world. "What the Lord desires is works." (*The Interior Castle* V, 3, p. 263.)

Teresa gives a practical example. If we see a sick person who really needs our help, then we should be prepared to leave our prayer and go to her aid. Take pity on her, and if necessary, fast so that she may have food. "That is true union with His will. Believe me, if you find you are lacking in this virtue, you have not yet attained union." (Ibid.)

There must be no envy, jealousy, or censoriousness among us. Rejoice when others are praised.

15.

Spiritual Betrothal

> God is love and anyone who lives in love lives in God, and God lives in him.
>
> —1 John 4:15.

Our Divine Spouse lives, loves, shares, and communicates Himself to us. In Mary, our model, the Holy Spirit wed humanity. The fruit of the union, is the Word, who prays in us "Abba," Father. To express this love, the Holy Spirit uses the allegory of the Bride and Bridegroom. Sacred Scripture is full of the symbol.

> I am going to lure her
> and lead her out into the wilderness
> and speak to her heart . . .
> She will call me, 'my husband' . . .
> I will betroth you to myself forever,
> betroth you with integrity and justice
> with tenderness and love;
> I will betroth you to myself with faithfulness
> and you will come to know Yahweh.
>
> —Hosea, 2:14–22.

> You ravish my heart,
> my sister, my promised bride,

you ravish my heart . . .
She is a garden enclosed,
my sister, my promised bride . . .
open to me, my sister, my love,
my dove, my perfect one.

—Song of Songs, 4:9–12.

Many Christian mystics, foremost among them St. John of the Cross, have made moving commentaries on the Canticle of Canticles. Teresa makes use of the symbol of betrothal to portray the mystic life of the spirit in the sixth mansion.

> You will often have heard that God betrothes Himself to souls spiritually. . . . It is all a union of love with love, and its operations are entirely pure, and so delicate and gentle that there is no way of describing them. The Lord can make the soul very conscious of them. (*The Interior Castle* V, 4, p. 264.)

The pages in St. Teresa's works which deal with Betrothal are among the most difficult. Teresa herself spent from ten to sixteen years in the state of betrothal. If we admit that the betrothal begins with the first ecstacy, then it must have begun for our saint at the convent of the Incarnation, in 1556. Other Teresian scholars date it 1562. As we have already seen, Teresa suffered a great deal from 1556 to 1572. Much of the material treated here is studied by St. John of the Cross under the passive night of the spirit.

The Lord grants many extraordinary graces and experiences to some people. Teresa mentions locutions, visions, raptures, ecstacies. It is also a period of excrutiating pain. Suffering is sacred. The pearls of the spiritual life, like the pearls of the ocean, come out of the conflict between alienating forces striving for possession of the inner temple. We have to be tested. We must go through the desert. The struggle helps us transcend ourselves.

There has to be a period of preparation before betrothal. During this time, His Majesty visits the beloved.

> It seems to me that this union has not yet reached the point of spiritual betrothal, but is rather like what happens in our earthly life, when two people are about to be betrothed. (*The Interior Castle* V, 4, p. 264.)

The two lovers spend a lot of time together. They meet, visit, discuss and dialogue. They express their love and pledge fidelity, and so they get to know and appreciate each other more.

> They shall meet together, and He shall unite her with Himself. We can compare this kind of union to a short meeting. . . . In a secret way the soul sees who this Spouse is that she is to take. By means of the senses and faculties she could not understand in a thousand years what she understands in this way in the briefest space of time. . . . The soul after one visit is worthier to join hands with Him, becomes so fired with love that she does her utmost not to thwart this Divine betrothal. (*The Interior Castle* V, 4, p. 265.)

However, we must not be presumptuous. It is not yet all sunshine. People have fallen from this dizzy height. The real battle has only begun. The devil will marshall all the powers of hell to destroy one such saintly soul. Lucifer deceives under the form of light. He is the meridian devil. The sun at midday is at its zenith and casts no shadow. Then it falls. The presumptuous soul that reaches its meridian zenith and is not conscious of its own shadow will fall. The devil uses good to divide. There is no cloister so secluded, no oratory so quiet that he cannot enter. He was present at the Last Supper, and entered the heart of Judas. So we must never grow lax or less vigilant. We must continue in our search for true humble self-knowledge and practice fraternal love. When we stray a little, the Lord will give a warning. Trials now await, as we leave Tabor and face Jerusalem. Even though we are determined to choose no other spouse or lord, there are other spirits that try to thwart the marriage. We need courage.

Teresa speaks from her own personal experience. During this stage of her spiritual journey, all hell broke loose. Friends deserted her, people clamored against her, enemies accused her

> She is going to perdition,
> Obviously being deluded,
> This is the devil's work,
> She takes in all her confessors,
> She is going the way of So-and-so,
> They ruined their own lives and dragged

good people down with them.

Fear sets in. Confessors would not listen to Teresa. Self-confidence is shaken. We are more aware of our sinfulness. Condemnation comes easy; praise can't be accepted. The Inquisitors threaten to destroy. Yet this suffering is sacred and sanctifying, because we share in the paschal pains of Christ, and serve to save our neighbors. Moreover, we grow in the wisdom of the ways of God and man, as we learn patience and perseverance.

Quite often bodily health begins to break down. The strain is too much.

> Acute pain affects the soul both outwardly and inwardly, till it becomes so much oppressed as not to know what to do itself, and would much rather suffer any martyrdom than these pains. . . . God gives us no more than we can bear, and He gives patience first. (*The Interior Castle* VI, 1, pp. 271–272.)

Then Teresa courageously adds, "I should always choose the way of suffering, if only to imitate Our Lord Jesus Christ." (Ibid. p.272)

The external sufferings are nothing in comparison with the interior and spiritual ones. It is terrible not to be able to find an understanding confessor, who can make a truthful diagnosis. So many conclude that the experience may be an hallucination or a wile of the devil. Many confessors are intolerant, and expect the penitent to be angelic, when she is still human, sinful, and weak. Then he may say it is due to melancholy or depression.

> The world is so full of melancholy and the devil makes so much use of it to work harm, that confessors have very good cause to be afraid of it and to watch for it carefully. (*The Interior Castle* VI, 1, p. 272.)

Then since the experience is ineffable, it is a torment to describe it to a confessor. The only thing to do is to wait upon the mercy of God.

To add to our woe, mental prayer is impossible, solitude tiresome and study out of the question. The best thing to do is to get involved with external things and fraternal charity. Don't pine away doing nothing.

Mystical Graces

While travelling through the dark and passive night of the spirit, the soul does not see her Spouse. She believes that He rests in the depths of her spirit. However, the Lord at times grants some extraordinary favors. These favors compensate for the trials and at the same time lead the soul forward to betrothal. God awakens the soul.

Visits

Before the soul is fully one with Him, the Divine Spouse fills it with fervent desires. The touch is so delicate that we cannot understand it. We learn here by experience.

> Often when a person is quite unprepared for such a thing, and is not even thinking of God, he is awakened by His Majesty, as though by a rushing comet or a thunderclap. No sound is heard, but the soul is very well aware that it has been called by God. . . . It is conscious of having been most delectably wounded. (*The Interior Castle* VI, 2, p. 276.)

There is pain in the experience, for the Lord does not reveal Himself fully. This is again the agony and ecstasy of love. The joy is more satisfying than that felt during the Prayer of Quiet, but the pain of absence is likewise experienced. A fire burns within the Spirit. The living flame of love is doing its purifying work.

> My God could be described as the fire in a lighted brazier, from which some spark will fly out and touch the soul, in such a way that it will be able to feel the burning heat of the fire. As the fire is not hot enough to burn it up, and the experience is very delectable, the soul continues to feel that pain and the mere touch suffice to produce that effect in it. (Ibid, p. 277.)

The impulse is not yet permanent, and does not completely enkindle the soul, and when the spark dies, the yearning pain returns. While it lasts there is a clear consciousness of the Lord's presence, and a consuming fire of desire. So strong is this awareness that the senses, imagination, or intellect do not stir.

No deception is possible. This loving impulse cannot possibly come from some psychological form of depression or be a concoction of the imagination. The devil cannot counterfeit it. There is no doubt, but it has its origin in the Lord. The joy is too intense. There is security because:

1. The devil cannot unite pain and peace in the soul at the same time. The devil's pain is restless.
2. The soul is determined to suffer any trial, withdraw from unduly pleasure.
3. The devil has no authority over the region from which this delectable tempest comes.

If there is any doubt you can be certain the impulse is not authentic.

Enkindling of Love

God communicates with the soul in another way during the preparatory phase before union. Teresa described the enkindling of love.

> Quite unexpectedly, when engaged in vocal prayer, and not thinking of interior things, it seems in some wonderful way to catch fire. Suddenly a fragrance so powerful diffuses itself through all the senses, . . . The soul is moved by a delectable desire to enjoy Him and this disposes it to make many acts and to sing praises to Our Lord, . . . There is nothing here that causes pain. . . . There is no reason to fear. One must endeavour to receive this favour and give thanks for it. (Ibid, p. 278.)

Locutions

God also awakens the soul through locutions or spiritual words. "This may be more perilous." There are many kinds.

> Some of them seem to come from without; others from the innermost depths of the soul; others from its higher part; while others again are so completely outside the soul that they can be heard with the ears, and seem to be uttered by a human voice. (*The Interior Castle* VI, 3, p. 279.)

Teresa, therefore mentions three kinds of locutions:

Corporeal. These locutions are actually heard by the physical powers of hearing.
Imaginary. These are received in the imagination. Words are not heard with the ear. Yet its impossible not to hear and understand them.
Spiritual or Intellectual. God imprints what He says in the depth of the spirit. God reveals great truths and mysteries in this way. The soul may find itself learned about the Trinity, in a way no theologian can teach.

Teresa warns us that some locutions may be mere fancy, especially in people who have sick imaginations or suffer from melancholic depression. We should humor such people and pay no heed to them. Give them less time to pray and fancy. They are convinced they have heard God speak.

So locutions may come from four sources: God, the devil, oneself, or the imagination. How can we discern a divine locution?

1. A locution that comes from God has the stamp of power, certainty and authority. Peace follows. When the Lord says, "It is I, fear not," a marvelous comfort follows.
2. The soul desires to sing the praises of God, with a tranquil, peaceful, and recollected spirit.
3. We remember the words for a long time. We may never forget them. If there is a prediction, the soul is certain it will come true.

Locutions that are concoctions of a sick imagination don't bring this peace, certainty or confidence. The devil's locutions are to be feared more, but the same criteria may be used.

We should never, never act on these locutions without consulting a confessor or a reliable third person. Deception is only too possible and too frequent.

"I consider it very dangerous for a person to do anything but what he has been told to do." (Ibid, p. 283.) The Lord has told us to put the confessor in His place.

We may judge the authenticity of a locution from the effects.

1. The genuine locution is very clear. Every syllable and phrase is understood. When created by the imagination the voice and words are indistinct and dreamy.
2. The locution comes unexpectedly and refers to things never thought of as possible. The imagination could not invent them.
3. In a genuine locution the soul hears something. The imagination composes bit by bit what it wants to hear.
4. In a genuine locution one single word contains such a world of meaning that the understanding alone could never be put into human language.
5. Much more will be understood than the words convey.

Humble self-esteem follows an authentic locution. When the Spirit speaks we cannot but listen.

Rapture and Betrothal

Once the preparation period is over and the soul has gone through the dark night of sense and a great part of the night of the spirit, the grace of spiritual betrothal is granted. Teresa herself was introduced to this blessed state through a rapture.

> I spent the greater part of the whole day in prayer: and then beseeching the Lord that He should help me to please Him in everything, I began the hymn (Veni Creator)—while I was reciting it, there came to me a transport so sudden that it almost carried me away. I could make no mistake about this, so clear was it. This was the first time that Our Lord had granted me the favour of any kind of rapture. I heard these words: I will have thee converse now, not with men, but with angels. (*Life*, 24, 5.)

These raptures bring strength and enlightenment. They carry the soul out of its senses, Union takes place.

> One kind of rapture is this. The soul though not actually engaged in prayer, is struck by some word, which it either remembers or hears spoken by God. His Majesty is moved with compassion at having seen the soul suffering so long through its yearning for Him, and seems to be causing the spark of which

> we have already spoken to grow within it, so that like a phoenix it catches fire and springs into new life. One may piously believe that the sins of such a soul are pardoned . . . when it is thus cleansed, God unites it with Himself, in a way which none can understand save it and He. The soul does not understand this in such a way to be able to speak of it afterwards, though it is not deprived of its interior senses. It is not like one who suffers a swoon or a paroxysm so that it can understand nothing either within itself or without. (*The Interior Castle* V, 4, p. 287.)

The grace takes place in the very center of the soul. The faculties and senses are enraptured and so they cannot understand what takes place. The spouse learns marvelous truths that can never be forgotten. We wake up and become alive and conscious.

> The soul becomes one with God. It is brought into this mansion of the empyrean Heaven, which we must have in the depths of our souls. Since God dwells in them, He must have one of these mansions, although while the soul is in ecstasy, the Lord will not always wish it to see these secrets. He is sometimes pleased that it should emerge from this absorption, and then it will at once see what there is in this room. Then after coming to itself, it will remember the revelation of the great things it has seen. It will not, however, be able to describe any of them. (*The Interior Castle*, VI, 4, p. 289.)

The Divine Spouse now takes the entire soul of His Bride to Himself. She is now His property. He takes her joyfully to His home, and shows her part of the Kingdom He has stored up for her. The door of the mansion is closed and the Bridegroom and bride remain there in deepest serenity and peace undisturbed by the faculties. Here, He communicates in silence. The soul seems to part from the body. The bride cannot breathe or speak. The body and hands grow momentarily cold. The will and understanding may be transported for days, grasping nothing that does not awaken the will to love. Complete ecstasy does not last long.

Teresa exclaims:

> Oh, my sisters, what nothingness is all that we have given up, or all that we are doing, or can ever do for God who is pleased to communicate Himself in this way to a worm. (*The Interior Castle* VI, 4, p. 290.)

Essentially the grace of betrothal consists of the immediate union of the substance and powers of the soul with God in its very center or substance. The substance enjoys the fruitful touch of God in union. The understanding contemplates the truths of God. The will is immersed in a sea of delight as it basks in the sunshine of its Beloved's embrace.

Fervour and ardent desire follow:

Such a soul would gladly have a thousand lives so as to use them all for God. It would like everything on earth to be tongue so that it might praise Him. (*The Interior Castle* VI, 4, p. 291.)

The union of betrothal is not habitual or permanent as in the state of spiritual marraige. The lovers are here united, but also separated.

> We might say that the union is as if the ends of two wax candles were joined so that the light they give is one. The wicks and the wax and the light are all one; yet afterwards the one candle can be perfectly well separated from the other and the candles become two again, or the wick may be withdrawn from the wax. (*The Interior Castle* VII, 2, p. 335.)

The soul is now the pledged spouse of Christ. A new life begins for her. He will protect her.

> Our Lord wants everyone to realize that such a person's soul is now His and that no one must touch it. People are welcome to attack her body, her honour and her possessions . . . but her soul they may not attack (*The Interior Castle* VI, 4, p. 292.)

Visits—Flight of the Spirit

God now exalts the soul through more mystical phenomena and graces. Courage is needed here. The flight of the spirit is a kind of rapture

> Sometimes the soul becomes conscious of such rapid motion that the spirit seems to be transported with a speed, which, especially at first fills it with fear. (*The Interior Castle* VI, 5, p. 293.)

Resistance is impossible. The Divine Spouse sweeps His

bride away, while in complete possession of her senses. He is Lord.

> This great God who controls the source of the waters, has loosed the sources whence water has been coming into this basin; and with tremendous force there rises up so powerful a wave that this little ship—our soul—is lifted up on high. And if the ship can do nothing, and neither the pilot nor any of the crew has any power over it, when the waves make a furious assault upon it and toss it about at their will, even less able in their interior part of the soul to stop where it likes, while its senses and faculties can do no more than has been commanded them. The exterior senses, however, are quite unaffected by this. (*The Interior Castle* VI, 5, p. 294.)

The experience leaves us with a terrible sense of unworthiness and humility.

An out-of-body experience follows.

> The soul really seems to have left the body. . . . He feels as if he has been in another world. . . . In a single instant he is taught so many things all at once that, if he were to labour for years on end trying to get them all into his imagination and thought he could not succeed with a thousandth part of them (*The Interior Castle* VI, 5, p. 295.)

This new knowledge and light help to give us a balanced appreciation of created things, a clearer understanding of ourselves, a new insight into the greatness of God, and a deep feeling of peace and tranquillity. We can now carry the cross with greater equanimity. We are ready to serve.

> These meetings with the Spouse remain deeply engraven in the memory, so that I think it is impossible for the soul to forget them, until it is enjoying them forever. (Ibid., p. 297.)

Intellectual Visions

The Lord grants the favor of intellectual visions during the state of betrothal. The object of the vision may be the Sacred Humanity of Jesus, Mary His mother, the angels or the saints. At times they may attain to the Godhead and Blessed Trinity.

When they take place in the midst of an ecstasy they are very special.

> When the Lord so wills, it may happen that the soul will be at prayer, and in possession of all its senses, then there will suddenly come to it a suspension in which the Lord communicates most secret things to it, which it seems to see within God Himself. These are not visions of the most sacred Humanity. Although I say that the soul "sees" Him, it really sees nothing, for this is not an imaginary, but a notably intellectual vision, in which is revealed to the soul how all things are seen in God, and how within Himself He contains them all. Such a vision is highly profitable because although it passes in a moment, it remains engraven upon the soul. (*The Interior Castle* VI, 10, p. 321.)

It leaves us with a horror of sin that we commit within God Himself. As He is merciful, we too must be merciful and humble. Then follows one of Teresa's famous passages on the relationship between truth and humility. God loves humility.

> Because God is Sovereign Truth and to be humble is to walk in truth, for it is absolutely true to say that we have no good thing in ourselves, but only misery and nothingness. Anyone who fails to understand this is walking in falsehood. (Ibid, p. 323.)

These graces come when we least expect them. They are completely gratuitous, and we know with certainty that Jesus is really present, although we do not "see" Him. We know He cares and He loves. We lose fear. We habitually think of God.

> She felt that He was always looking at her. . . . She felt that He was so near that He could not fail to hear her. . . . She was conscious that He was walking at her right hand. (*The Interior Castle* VI, 8, p. 311.)

This is a very deep and subtle form of knowing that is ineffable and indescribable, but it leaves the soul with a burning desire to serve God. Our conscience becomes very sensitive to any form of evil. The soul is flooded with a wave of gratitude and praise. At the same time Teresa warns us again, lest we go running after the accidental and miss the essential:

> Let none of you imagine that, because a sister has had such experiences, she is any better than the rest. . . . Sometimes it is the weakest whom the Lord leads by this road. . . . We must base our judgments on the virtues. The saintliest will be she who serves Our Lord with the greatest mortification and humility and purity of conscience. (*The Interior Castle* VI, 8, p. 314.)

Imaginary Visions

The Lord communicates Himself also through imaginary visions. We must be careful because the devil can interfere. However, "When they come from Our Lord, they seem to me in some ways more profitable because they are in closer conformity with our nature." (*The Interior Castle* VI, 9, p. 314.)

> When Our Lord is prepared to bestow greater consolations upon this soul, He grants it a clear revelation of His Sacred Humanity, either as He was when He lived in the world, or as He was after His resurrection. Although He does this so quickly that we might liken the action to a flash of lightening, this most glorious image is so deeply engraven upon the imagination that I do not believe it can possibly disappear until it is seen where it can be enjoyed to all eternity. (Ibid, p. 315.)

Sometimes Our Lord may speak and reveal great secrets. He is really alive and present. The soul cannot gaze on this brilliancy for long. The light is so bright that it hurts, just as the midday sun hurts the naked eye. It does not last long.

> Almost invariably the soul on which God bestows this favour remains in rapture, because its unworthiness cannot endure so terrible a sight. (*The Interior Castle* VI, 9, p. 315.)

The imagination cannot invent this vision. It comes as suddenly and as unexpectedly as Paul's vision of Jesus on the road to Damascus. A complete certainty, calm, and serenity follow:
Yet, Teresa adds, that we must never desire or pray for these favors:

1. It would show a lack of humility.
2. Such a person will be deceived by the devil.

3. The imagination may see what it desires to see.
4. It is presumptuous to chose one's path to God.
5. We may not be able to bear the trials.
6. The very thing you expect to give you gain may bring you loss, as happened to Saul, when he became King.

Many saintly people have never received these favours, and many people who received them are not saintly. We must follow the will of God and practice the virtues.

Jubilations

Jubilation is another favor described to Teresa.

> Our Lord sometimes bestows upon the soul a jubilation and a strange kind of prayer, the nature of which it cannot ascertain. . . . The faculties are in close union; Our Lord leaves both faculties and senses free to enjoy this happiness, without understanding what it is they are enjoying and how they are enjoying it. That sounds nonsense but it is certainly what happens. The joy of the soul is so exceedingly great that it would like not to rejoice in God in solitude, but to tell its joy to all, so that they may help it to praise Our Lord. . . . Such interior joy in the depths of the soul's being, such peace and happiness that it calls upon all to praise God cannot possibly have come from the devil. (*The Interior Castle* VI, 6, p. 301.)

Saint Francis enjoyed this ecstatic form of prayer and was thought mad. "What a blessed madness."

Joy is the highest form of prayer, and the sacrifice of joy gives great glory and delight to God. God is joyful. We must enjoy Him, too.

Suffering That Sanctifies

It would be a great mistake to conclude that the soul enjoys these mystical graces continuously. Clouds still appear amid the sunshine.

The first source of suffering is the mystical grace itself, because under the power of its marvellous light appears the sinfulness of the soul. We become cognizant of our ingratitude, lack of reverence, the foolish mistakes we made in the past, and the possible offenses we may easily commit in the future. We may suffer shame and confusion in the presence of others. People who complacently live in the third mansion do not understand the enthusiasm and experience of a mystic who lives in the sixth. The latter's freedom of spirit may easily be interpreted as nonsense and downright disobedience. The mystic like the imperial eagle flies free at these lofty heights and knows what he is doing and where he is going. To the mouse living in the soft down of the third mansion, it all seems crazy. Criticism is certain. Persecution is inevitable. Gossip circles. The mice want to ground the eagle.

There is still a certain amount of personal insecurity in betrothal. We are not used to these dazzling heights and we fear we may go astray. This is a new world of adventure, unmapped, never pioneered before and there are not roads or signs to follow. We are all alone. We fear it may be just a dream, a mystical illusion, a trick of the evil one, one great mistake. It can be lonely up there.

The soul desires complete union, but is frustrated. The time has not yet come. "Life becomes sheer though delectable torture."

> It has the keenest longing for death, and so it frequently and tearfully begs God to take it out of this exile. Everything in this life that it sees wearies it. (*The Interior Castle*, VI 6, p. 297.)

Very often the confessor may not understand or be sympathetic. He may demand too much of her, and even blame her for having these raptures, as if she could control them.

The betrothed is not impeccable. But like St. Paul she discovers the split between the spiritual and unspiritual within her.

> I cannot understand my own behavior. I fail to carry out the things I want to do, and I find myself doing the very things I hate. . . . The will to do what is good is in me, the performance is not. Instead of doing the good things I want to do, I carry out the sinful things I do not want.
>
> —Rom. 7:15–19.

This makes us wretched.

> She would not intentionally commit so much as a venial sin, even were she to be cut in pieces; and thus she is greatly distressed to find that, without being aware of the fact, she cannot avoid committing a great many. (*The Interior Castle* VI, 6, p. 298.)

The soul suffers the terrible pain of unrequited love. The visions have given the betrothed a new appreciation of the Truth and Holiness of God, and she now suffers all the more at the sight of so much sin in herself and in the world. It is excruciating to feel so unworthy of one we love. This fills her with a spirit of apostolic zeal and compassion, and she would give a thousand lives, if only one soul could be saved, and more people praise God. These fervent desires are in their turn frustrated and only add to the suffering of the soul.

Contrary to what we might expect, prayer itself can be arid and distracted. This can be very painful. A burning desire consumes the soul. She yearns for complete intimacy. An arrow of fire penetrates her very being. The soul keenly feels the absence of God.

> The suffering resembles that of souls in purgatory, . . . She is absent from her Good and why should she want to live? She in conscious of a strange solitude, since there is not a creature on the whole earth who can be a companion to her, save Him whom she loves. All earthly companionship is a torment to her. . . . She is parched with thirst, yet cannot reach the water. (*The Interior Castle* VI, 11, p. 325.)

The sanctifying suffering endured in preparation for mystical marriage is far more radical and absolute than that felt at any other period of the spiritual life. Moral, psychological, and bodily fitness are expected at the peak of holiness. Integration takes place. The soul is tested and refined in the fire of suffering. On the top of Mount Carmel, the soul and all its faculties, and even the body itself, are capable of breathing the pure air of heaven and of receiving the most sublime communications without swooning or stumbling. The climb was hard, but the view now is majestic. The contemplative soul basks in the sunshine of God's glory; and when the cloud covers the view, the absence is lonely. She may yearn for death. The undulation between the agony and ecstasy of betrothal continues to cause so much pain. When the pain is most intense the Beloved sends relief.

> By granting her a deep rapture or some kind of vision, in which the true comforter comforts and strengthens her so that she can wish to live for as long as He wills (*The Interior Castle* VI, 11, p. 327.)

Sanctifying suffering has one wonderful characteristic. It is always accompanied by resignation and joy. Christ was joyful on the Cross. We lose all fear of any other form of suffering. Tremendous courage controls the soul. We are finally free and detached.

> Now, sisters, you will see if I was not right in saying that courage is necessary for us here and that if you ask the Lord for these things He will be justified in answering you as He answered the sons of Zebedee "can you drink the chalice?" I believe sisters, that we should all reply, "We can." (*The Interior Castle* VI, 11, p. 328.)

The Sacred Humanity

There is a subtle temptation, when we reach these high forms of prayer to forget and neglect devotion to the Sacred Humanity of Our Lord Jesus Christ. Heretics down the centuries have taught that we concentrate on the divinity and ignore the humanity. Teresa teaches that we must continue to celebrate and meditate on the mysteries of Christ's Life, Passion, Death, and Resurrection. We contemplate the goodness of God revealed in the Passion.

> Some souls imagine that they cannot dwell upon the passion, in which case they will be able still less to meditate upon the most sacred Virgin and the lives of the saints . . . I cannot conceive what they are thinking of. Although angelic spirits, freed from everything corporeal may remain permanently enkindled in love, this is not possible for those of us who live in this mortal body . . . our greatest help and blessing is the most sacred Humanity of Our Lord Jesus Christ . . . I can assure them, they will never enter the last two mansions. If they lose their guide, the good Jesus, they will be unable to find their way . . . The Lord Himself says that He is the Way, He is the Light, and that no one can come to the Father save by Him. (*The Interior Castle* VI, 7, p. 305.)

We cannot enjoy the possession of perfect contemplation forever. The fire of love needs fuel, and the flames will not come down from heaven to us, as they did for Elias. Christ is the fuel. We cannot excuse ourselves from meditating on the mysteries of Christ, especially during these times of the year, when the church liturgically celebrates them. A loving and grateful heart can never fail to remember the loving acts by which God intervened in Salvation history. "They are living sparks which will enkindle the soul more and more in its love for Our Lord." (*The Interior Castle* VI, 7, p. 307.)

However, Teresa adds, that the soul will understand them in a more perfect way. We contemplate Jesus with a simple regard, and the will is inspired by a deep emotion of love.

The teaching of Teresa proves her burning love for the Sacred Humanity of Jesus Christ. Teresian prayer is Trinitarian and Christological. Christ is at the heart of Carmelite prayer. The Holy Spirit draws us to Jesus, and Jesus leads us to the Father

> God has sent the Spirit of his Son into our hearts: the Spirit that cries, 'Abba, Father.'
>
> —Gal. 4:17

Christ is our Mediator with the Father, and through Him we are divinized and sanctified. He is in us. We are in Him. In prayer we become aware of this tremendous mystery and through our knowledge and love we grow more Christlike. This dialogue is transforming. When we really listen to the Word we change radically. In Christian prayer, we live our Baptism. We learn to die to self and live to Christ. We grow in Faith, Hope and Love. The painful purgation is part of our immersion in the paschal mysteries of Jesus Christ. Then, "It is not longer I who live, but Christ who lives in me." (Gal.2:10.)

What is begun at Baptism is perfected by the Blessed Eucharist and Teresa warns us, "We must not allow the devil to 'cause us to lose our devotion to the Most Blessed Sacrament.' " (*The Interior Castle* VI, 7, p. 309.)

In Chapter 22 of her *Life,* Teresa explains her own historical difficulties. Books and teachers had advised her to put all corporeal imagination aside and approach the contemplation of the Divinity. They falsely taught that even Christ's Humanity would impede perfect contemplation. Teresa responds:

> It will be all right, I think, to do this sometimes, but I cannot bear the idea that we must withdraw ourselves entirely from Christ and treat that Divine Body of His as though it were on a level with Our miseries, and with all created things. (*Life*, Ch. 22, p. 136.)

Our saint admits she made a mistake herself, when she gave up meditating on the Humanity of Jesus once she reached the Prayer of Quiet and Union. This is a lack of humility.

> What I should like to make clear is that Christ's most sacred Humanity must not be reckoned among these corporeal objects. . . . We are not angels and we have bodies. . . . As a rule our thoughts must have something to lean upon. Sometimes the soul may go out from itself and be so full of God that it will need no created thing to assist it in recollection. But this is not very usual. (*Life*, Ch. 22, p. 140.)

This entire chapter provides very profitable reading.

Visions and Revelations

When Teresa and John of the Cross teach mysticism they are talking normally about infused contemplation that gradually leads the soul to transforming union with God. Visions, revelations, heavenly visits, and other phenomena are only secondary and accidental. They are not essential. They may even be obstacles to pure faith, love, and trust. There is an overexaggerated esteem for visions and visionaries. The Lord wants our ears. He wills us to listen to His Word in faith. The person who controls our ears, controls us. When we give our inner ear to the Lord, He controls us. Lovers listen. A craving for the marvelous leads many astray and away from the path of ordinary virtue and valor. The extraordinary can be an escape. The mystic may not be a visionary.

The theological virtues of faith, hope, and love lead us directly to God and we must not base our spiritual life on visions and revelations. God has spoken. His final message is the Word. We must be detached from visions.

Mystical contemplation is at the core of the spiritual life and it is granted to a person who is well grounded in virtue, theological and moral, who is humble, loving and ever-ready to do God's will. This is infinitely more important than visions—and far more secure. When visions do come we may not receive them except on the advice of a competent confessor. St. John of the Cross would have us take up a rather negative attitude towards them. We must not desire or esteem them, and we must avoid them as much as possible.

The soul is not united directly and immediately to God through concepts of the understanding, through enjoyment, through imagination, through sense, or through any vision, locution, or revelation. They may be intermediate means of union with God, but they do not unite us immediately to the deity. They belong to the created order. Faith, Hope, and Love are supernatural and unite us directly to God. Distinct concepts, words, and images do not unite us directly with God. Contemplation in obscure and loving faith does.

Let us not be absolute. St. John of the Cross admits that at times God makes use of visions and words to help us. At the heart of the experience is an interior grace that draws us closer to God. The cognoscitive element of the vision by which we learn what is going on is the external rind. We profit by the interior grace and it takes effect whether we cooperate or not. Let us gain by the grace and not become preoccupied with the grind. The interior grace urges us to love God. The external manifestation may rouse curiosity and useless speculation. In any case, leave the judgment to the confessor.

Although inspired by a revelation, Teresa herself would not make a foundation unless she had the permission and blessing of her superior Gracian.

There are certain manifestations of God that appear at the peak of the spiritual life. St. John of the Cross calls them "the intuition of naked truths."

> It consists in comprehending and seeing with the understanding the truths of God. . . . This kind of knowledge comes to the soul in direct relation to God, when the soul, after a most lofty manner, has a perception of some attributes of God—of His

omnipotence, might, goodness, sweetness, etc. . . . This is pure contemplation. (A.Bk.II,Ch.26,p.182)

These manifestations concern the Creator Himself and do not relate to any particular created thing. God gives these divine touches direct to the soul.

Jesus promised.

> Anybody who loves me will be loved by my Father, and I shall love him and show myself to him

—John 14:21.

The manifestation is part of the grace of union and happy is the soul that receives it.

In conclusion, we must not encourage an exaggerated esteem for visions. There are true visions, even on the external and imaginary planes, but here we must follow the advice of a director. Forget the outer covering and relish the interior grace of light and love.

16.
Spiritual Marriage

The mercies and wonders of God are beyond measure. We are made in His image and likeness, and He has given us the grace here on earth to enter into the deepest communication with Him. Most of us are in darkness to the deep secrets contained within the human spirit. The mystics see in the light. When Teresa deals with spiritual marriage, the loftiest form of prayer, her poetic soul breaks into songs of praise. The Bridegroom is ready to share His greatest gifts.

When the bride has been prepared and washed in the waters of suffering and love, the Divine Bridegroom brings her into the very special mansion.

> When the Lord has taken the soul spiritually to be His bride, He brings her into this mansion of His, which is the seventh, before consummating the Spiritual Marriage. He must needs have an abiding place in the soul, just as He has one in heaven. (*The Interior Castle* VII, Ch. 1, p. 330.)

The Sun of Justice now floods the soul with lights and the warmth of love. Here the marriage is consummated, and the bride finds heaven on earth.

The bride is introduced to his heavenly Kingdom through an intellectual vision. Every seal is removed from the inner eye.

> It is brought into this mansion by means of an intellectual vision, in which, by a representation of the truth in a particular way, the most Holy Trinity reveals Itself, in all Three Persons.

> First of all the spirit becomes enkindled and is illumined, as it were, by a cloud of the greatest brightness. It sees these Three Persons individually, and yet by a wonderful kind of knowledge which is given to it, the soul realizes that most certainly and truly all these Three Persons are one substance and one power and one knowledge and one God alone, so that what we hold by faith the soul may be said here to grasp by sight, although nothing is seen by the eyes, either of the body, or of the soul, for it is no imaginary vision. Here all Three Persons communicate Themselves to the soul and speak to the soul and explain to it these words which the Gospel attributes to the Lord—namely, that He and the Father and the Holy Spirit will come to dwell with the soul which loves Him and keeps His commandments. (*The Interior Castle* VII, Ch. 1, pp. 331–332.)

Through this awesome vision the bride has that experiential knowledge of the great truth of uncreated grace, the indwelling Trinity. She receives a loving enlightenment on the most sublime of our Christian mysteries, the Blessed Trinity, Father, Son, and Spirit, living, loving, enlightening, and communicating within the living temple of the Christian soul.

At the Last Supper Jesus promised, "If anyone loves me he will keep my word, and my Father will love him and we shall come to him and make our home with him." (John 14,23.)

There is a mysterious difference between hearing these words and believing them in the center of the seventh mansion. Now the bride knows that she knows they are true. The master who teaches is within. No human master can explain the reality. The experience is ineffable and inexplicable.

Teresa felt within herself the Divine companionship.

> She feels they have never left her, and perceives quite clearly, in the way I have described, that they are in the interior of her heart—in the most interior peace of all and in its greatest depths. (*The Interior Castle* VII, I, p. 332.)

Life is now a perpetual honeymoon, as this life of union, communion, and dialogue goes on between bride and Bridegroom. Separation is now impossible. The Spirit is forever alert. She is in complete possession of her senses. She knows what she is about. This is not a case of auto-suggestion or some form of self-hypnosis. When it comes to her duty and service of God and others, she is wide awake, while at another level she enjoys the Divine companionship. This realization engenders tremendous confidence.

The presence is not always realized to the full!

> This presence is not of course always realized so fully—I mean so clearly—as it is when it just comes, or on certain other occasions when God grants the soul this consolation. If it were, it would be impossible for the soul to think of anything else, or even to live among men. (Ibid, p. 332.)

There may be many trials and worries on the outside, but the essential part of the soul never moves from the dwelling place. The boats of business may be rocked by the surface waves of the world, but deep down the spirit rests in the ocean of tranquillity.

Teresa comments on the difference between soul and spirit.

> We know that there is some kind of difference and a very definite one, between the soul and the spirit, although they are both one. So subtle is the division perceptible between them that sometimes the operation of the one seems different from that of the other, as are the respective Joys that the Lord is pleased to give them. It seems to me, too, that the soul is a different thing from the faculties and that they are not all one and the same. There are so many and such subtle things in the interior life that it would be presumptuous for me to begin to expound them. (Ibid, p. 333.)

Only in the life to come will the whole mystery become clear.

Teresa shares how she herself was introduced to his favor:

> When granting this favour for the first time, His Majesty is pleased to reveal Himself to the soul through an imaginary vision of His most sacred Humanity, so that it may clearly understand what is taking place and not be ignorant of the fact that it is receiving so sovereign a gift. To other people the experience will come in a different way. The Lord revealed Himself (to herself) one day, when she had just received Communion, in great splendour and beauty and majesty, as He did after His resurrection, and told her that it was time she took upon her His affairs, as if they were her own, and that He would take her affairs upon Himself. (*The Interior Castle* VII, Ch. 2, p. 334.)

There's a difference between this experience and other similar experiences at an earlier stage of the journey. It takes place at a more interior part of the soul and carries far more force and uniting power.

Teresa explains the nature of the favor:

> This secret union takes place in the deepest centre of the soul, which must be where God Himself dwells. I do not think there is any need of a door by which to enter it. I say there is no need of a door because all that has been so far described seems to have come through the medium of the senses and faculties. What passes in the union of the Spiritual Marriage is very different. The Lord appears in the centre of the soul, not through an imaginary, but through an intellectual vision (although this is a subtler one than already mentioned), just as He appeared to the Apostles, without entering through the door, when He said to them. 'Pax Vobis.' This instantaneous communication of God to the soul is so great a secret and so sublime a favour, and such delight is felt by the soul, that I do not know with what to compare it, beyond saying that the Lord is pleased to manifest to the soul at that moment the glory that is in Heaven, in a sublimer manner than is possible through any vision or spiritual consolation. . . . The Spirit of this soul is made one with God, who being likewise a Spirit, has been pleased to reveal the love that He has for us by showing to certain persons the extent of that love, so that we may praise His greatness. He has been pleased to unite Himself with His creature in such a way that they have become like two who cannot be separated from one another: even so He will not separate Himself from her. (*The Interior Castle* VII, 2, pp. 234–235.)

During Spiritual Betrothal there were frequent separations. The symbol there is that of two wax candles becoming the light, but they can be separated again.

In Spiritual Marriage the union is deeper and permanent.

> Here it is like rain falling from the heavens into a river or a spring. There is nothing but water there and it is impossible to divide or separate the water belonging to the river from that which fell from the heavens. Or it is as if a tiny streamlet enters the sea, from which it will find no way of separating itself, or as if in a room there were two large windows through which the light streamed in: it enters in different places but it all becomes one. (*The Interior Castle* VII, 2, p. 335.)

We are reminded of this great symbol every day at Mass—"By the mystery of this water and wine, may he come to share in the divinity of Christ who humbled Himself to share in our humanity."

The words of St. Paul now ring true; "He who is joined to God becomes one spirit with Him." (1 Cor.6:17.)

"Mihi vivere Christus est, mori lucrum."

"Life to me, of course, is Christ, but then death would bring me something more." (Ph.1,21.)

The little butterfly now dies and is endowed with new divine life. Christ is now its life and its center. He inundates the Bride with peace. Peace is flowing like a river.

> From these Divine breasts, where it seems that God is ever sustaining the soul, flow streams of milk which solace all who dwell in the castle." (Ibid,p. 336.)

In this state of pure spirituality the soul is united to the uncreated Spirit. The prayer of Jesus is fulfilled.

> May they all be one, Father, may they be one in us, as you are in me and I am in you. May the love with which you loved me be in them, and so that I may be in them.
>
> —John 17:21,26.

Yet, we must walk humbly knowing that the Lord holds us in the palm of His hand. We must be careful not to offend Him.

In this empyrean heaven of the soul there is deep peace. The faculties and imagination can no longer ruffle the still waters. The passions are vanquished, stilled, and quiet.

> A King is living in His palace; many wars are waged in his Kingdom and many other distressing things happen, but he remains where He is despite them all. So it is here. (Ibid, p. 338.)

Peace and tranquillity reign in the house. There is order. Integrity is restored. The disharmony that reigned between the body, psyche, and spirit is now removed. Life is lived from its deepest center, and from there we love God, ourselves, the people around us and the world He has given us.

The little butterfly has died. Full of joy she finds rest in a new life. Within her lives Christ.

The first effect of this prayer is self-forgetfulness. There is no worry. All the bride cares for is the glory of God. "She must take care of His business and He will take care of hers." (*The Interior Castle* VII, 3, p. 339.)

She is ready to die, and give up this world, and yet she does not neglect to eat and sleep and rest.

The bride has a great desire to suffer and carry the Cross bravely. If the suffering comes, she is ready. The only important thing to do now is the will of God.

When persecuted, she has an interior joy and peace. She will bear ill will to no one. She even conceives a special love for every foe and enemy and will constantly commend them to God in prayer. If she can help a soul, she is ready to live on for years and suffer severest trials.

> Their conception of glory is of being able in some way to help the Crucified, especially when they see how often people offend Him and how few there are who really care about His honour and are detached from everything else. (*The Interior Castle* VII, 3, p. 340.)

Detachment is freedom. There are no aridities or interior trials. When the soul is negligent, the Lord Himself awakens it in the interior. The flame of fires proceeds from the center very gently. It is not ignited by thought or a memory. It is inflamed by the Holy Spirit.

The great gain in the prayer is:

> Our realization of God's special care of us in His communicating with us and of the way He keeps begging us to dwell with Him. . . . We enjoy these gentle, yet penetrating touches of His love. . . . He sends it to you like a letter written very lovingly. (*The Interior Castle* VII, 3, p. 340)

This experience takes place in a part of the spirit too deep for disturbance. The senses or faculties cannot possibly produce it and the devil cannot counterfeit the grace. Certainly the divine source removes all forms of fear. Tranquillity reigns

> In this mansion of His, He and the soul alone have fruition

> of each other in the deepest silence. There is no reason now for the understanding to stir, or to seek out anything, for the Lord who created the soul is now pleased to calm it, and would have it look as it were, through a little think at what is passing. . . . The faculties are not lost here; it is merely that they do not work but seem to be dazed. (Ibid, p. 342.)

The amazing thing is that raptures cease, or happen very rarely and never in public. Devotional images, sermons, music no longer lead to a suspension of the senses. The Lord has made them strong. There is no lack of crosses but they pass quickly.

> Here to this wounded heart are given waters in abundance. Here the soul delights in the tabernacle of God. Here the dove sent out by Noah to see if the storm is over finds the olive branch—the sign that it has discovered firm ground amidst the waters and storms of this world. (*The Interior Castle* VII, 3, p. 343.)

These effects are habitually but not invariably present. Maybe for a day His Majesty may leave us in turmoil to keep us humble and alert. He wants our will and praise. We remain free.

> The Lord gives it great determination so that it will on no account turn aside from His service and from its own good resolutions. (*The Interior Castle* VII, 4, p. 344.)

Yet weaknesses remain. We are not immaculate nor impeccable even at this lofty state of the spiritual life. In spite of our vehement desires, we can still fall into venial sins and imperfections. We are free from mortal sin, but not completely proof against it.

Favors abound, but they are not granted simply to give us pleasure. This would be a great error.

> I feel certain, therefore, that these favours are given us to strengthen our weaknesses, so that we may be able to imitate Him in His great sufferings. (Ibid, p. 345.)

That was the road followed by all the great saints.

The fruit of the spiritual marriage between the Divine Bridegroom and the human bride is good works.

> Such works are the sign of every genuine favour and of everything else that comes from God. (Ibid, p. 346.)

The realistic Teresa tells us that it profits little to be recollected in retreat, and making acts of love and promises to the Lord if we do the opposite, when we come out. We must fix our eyes on the Cruicified. Words alone do not suffice. Our love must be real and active.

> If you wish to lay good foundations, each of you must try to be the least of all, and slaves of God, and must seek a way and means to please and serve all you companions . . . you must not build upon the foundation of prayer and contemplation alone, for unless you strive after the virtues and practise them, you will never grow to more and than dwarfs. (Ibid, p. 347.)

The battle goes on on the outside. We must never fall into the sleep of complacency. The divine companionship will give us inner strength, and from this sovereign union between Spirit and spirit a power overflows into the body. This explains the zeal of the saints. Martha and Mary work together.

> We should desire and engage in prayer, not for our own enjoyment, but for the sake of acquiring this strength which fits us for service. (Ibid, p. 348.)

A cloistered Carmelite might be tempted to think that since she cannot preach or teach she cannot bring souls to the Lord. Teresa replies:

> Serve Our Lord in ways within our powers. Apart from praying for people, by which you can do a great deal for them, do not try to help everybody. Limit yourself to your own companions. . . . By your doing things which you really can do, His Majesty will know that you would like to do many more, and He will reward you exactly as if you had won many souls for Him. (Ibid, p. 349.)

We may object that this is converting the converted. Teresa responds:

> If they become better, their praises will be more pleasing to the Lord, and their prayers of greater value to their neighbour. (Ibid, p. 349.)

Teresa concludes:

> I will end by saying that we must not build towers without foundations, and the Lord does not look so much at the magnitude of anything we do as at the love with which we do it. (Ibid, p. 350.)

Conclusion

St. Teresa reached the summit of mystical contemplation and has shown us the way to arrive at that experimental knowledge of love and union with God. She has demonstrated how charity transforms us as it grows, deiforms us, and gradually conforms us to God. We are spiritualized by the Holy Spirit, and this loving transformation has repercussion in knowledge. In this union we are changed, and we know it. We experience the love. With the power of love and the special light of the Holy Spirit, we enter the very depths of God and experience the ultimate life of the Three Persons. This love flows from faith, which unites our intellect to God. There is no need for distinct knowledge, for God in one act communicates light and love together.

In a world grown materialistic and pragmatic; in a world where terrible violence reigns; in a world where survival and all the cultural achievement of centuries is threatened by an all-out nuclear war; in a world where Christianity has watered down its substance and considers contemplation dangerous and superfluous—Teresa comes as a great mystical doctor pointing out the pathway to the summit of Mt. Carmel, where God dwells. The glory and honor of God dwell alone in this mountain top, and there we offer a sacrifice of praise.

The end of the journey is transformation into God. St. John of the Cross teaches more clearly than Teresa does what this transformation entails.

> God communicates to it His supernatural Being, in such wise that it appears to be God Himself, and has all that God Himself has. (*Ascent*, II, Ch. 5, p. 82.)

> The understanding of the soul is now the understanding of

God; and its will is the will of God; and its memory is the memory of God; and its delight is the delight of God. And the substance of the soul, although it is not the Substance of God, for into this it cannot be changed, is nevertheless united in Him and absorbed in Him, and is thus God by participation in God. (*Living Flame*, St. 2, p. 57.)

Teresa, the great contemplative, lived and experienced this transformation. She had to undergo a terrific catharsis and terrifying purification to be united to God in love. It left nothing of herself in her. In slaying her, the Spirit changed her death into life. Teresa heroically prepared herself for the divine marriage, and in His loving embrace, He taught her, illumined her and vivified her and sanctified her. He filled her with a spirit of love, joy, peace, patience, kindness, trustfulness, and chastity.

Our mystical doctor fully spiritualized, and enjoying full liberty of spirit could sing with St. John of the Cross.

> Mine are the heavens,
> and mine is the earth;
> Mine are the people,
> The righteous are mine, and mine the sinners,
> The Angels are mine
> The Mother of God is mine
> And all things are mine;
> And God Himself is mine and for me,
> For Christ is mine and all for me.
> What then, dost thou ask for and seek, my soul?
> Thine is all this, and it is all for thee.
> (*Spiritual Sentences and Maxims*, Peers, III, p. 244.)

Teresa now possessed the peace promised by Christ; the deepest secrets were revealed, she lived in a new garden of paradise, as she was confirmed in grace. Security reigned within her, and so she could fearlessly tackle her life's mission and work. She was sanctified not just for herself but for the entire church—and, in fact, the whole world. She was one of those chosen women, whom God had taken to keep life and love alive. The marriage was fruitful. Without women like Teresa, our world would wither.

Women like Teresa shake society. As Bergson has pointed out, social progress does not take place of itself.

> It is really a leap forward which is only taken, when the society has made up its mind to try an experiment; this means that the society must have allowed itself to be convinced, or at any rate allowed itself to be shaken; and the shake is always given by somebody. (*Toynbee, A Study of History*, abridgement by D.C. Somervell, Oxford University Press, London, New York, Toronto, 1960, p. 212.)

Such shakers of society are more than mere men and they work miracles. They are privileged souls who feel themselves related to all souls, and in their love they stretch forward the limits and boundaries of civilizations. For Bergson, it is the mystics who are the superhuman creators par excellence.

> The soul of the great mystic does not come to a halt at the mystical ecstasy as though that were the goal of a journey. The ecstasy may indeed be called a state of repose, but it is the repose of a locomotive standing in a station under steam pressure, with its movement continuing as a stationary, throbbing while it waits for the moment to make a new leap forward. The great mystic has felt the truth flow into him from its source like a force in action. . . . His desire is with God's help to complete the creation of the human species. . . . The mystic's direction is the very direction of the elan of life. It is the elan itself, communicated in its entirety to privileged human beings whose desire it is thereafter to set the imprint of it upon the whole of mankind and—by a contradiction of which they are aware—to convert a species, which is essentially a created thing, into creative effort; to make a movement out of something which by definition is a halt. (Ibid, p. 212.)

Mystically inspired people are always creative and transforming. They inspire others to imitate them.

> The creative mutation which has taken place in the microcosm of the mystic requires an adoptive mortification on the macrocosm before it can become either complete or secure. (Ibid, p. 213.)

Teresa was a mystical creative genius who brought about in her own milieu, among her own Carmelites and myriad of followers, the change she had achieved in herself. Her creativeness was fruitful, and is still fruitful, more fruitful today than in any other century. The transfigured Teresa made life intolerable for all the static souls around her, and so they tried to destroy her. This what Jesus meant, when He said:

> I have come to bring fire to the earth, and how I wish it were blazing already. . . . Do you suppose I am here to bring peace on earth? No, I tell you, but rather division. From now on a household of five will be divided; three against two and two against three; the father divided against the son, son against father, mother against daughter, daughter against mother, mother-in-law against daughter-in-law, daughter-in-law against mother-in-law.

—Luke 12,49–53.

Teresa united but she also caused division. Although completely outnumbered, she held her ground courageously and her ideas have entered the minds and books of millions. All social changes in the history of civilization have been engineered by a few creative individuals and minority groups. The masses remained in inertia. Our mystical doctor did not force her ideas on anybody; they were accepted for their own inner brilliance and originality.

To have this transformation take place, Teresa herself had to retire into solitude, the physical solitude of her Carmelite monastery, and the mystical solitude of her heart. This withdrawal and return is an historical pattern in the lives of all the mystical leaders of religion. Moses did it, Christ did it, Paul did it, Benedict did it, the Irish monks did it, Francis did it—and Teresa had to do it. She came out of the shadows of the Platonic cave to stand serenely in the light, but unlike the Platonist or Hindu, she returned to the dark cave to share her vision with those who were still in the valley of darkness. There they laughed at her and gave her a hostile reception. People don't like their beneficiaries who open their eyes to a higher light and urge them on to a transcendent greatness. Toynbee sums up brilliantly the difference between the Platonic philosopher and the mystic like Teresa,

> Believing that the ecstasy and not the return was the be-all and the end-all of the spiritual Odyssey on which they embarked, they saw nothing but a sacrifice on the altar of duty in the painful

passage from ecstasy to return which was really the purpose and culmination of the movement in which they were engaged. Their mystical experience lacked the cardinal Christian virtue' of love which inspires the Christian mystic to pass direct from the heights of communion to the slums, moral and material, of the unredeemed workaday world. (Ibid, p. 220.)

Filled with Christian charity, Teresa returned to her workaday world filled with power and glory to transform and transfigure her milieu. Her work continues, and that explains why after the Bible, Shakespeare, Don Quixote, she is the most read and revered writer in world literature. Her achievement is not material, but spiritual. She is a giant in the world of the Spirit.

Teresa entered the deepest thickets of desire, the world of mystery, marvel and wisdom and shares the treasure with the rest of us. To achieve this, she had to pass through trial and tribulation, for the purest suffering brings with it the purest knowledge, and the loftiest joy.

The mystic lover desires to love God as she is loved. How can divine love be equalled? This mystery is difficult to understand, but St. John of the Cross holds that it takes place in the order of love. According to St. Thomas, knowledge unites the object known to the person who knows, and in love the lover loses himself in the beloved. Teresa was lost in her Divine Beloved, in such a way that He became the principle and agent of all her operations. There are two natures in one spirit and love of God.

St. Paul writes, "Anyone who is joined to the Lord is one spirit with him." (1 Cor. 6,17.)

St. John of the Cross sings of this blissful state that Teresa attained:

> In this state, the soul can perform no acts, but it is the Holy Spirit that moves it to perform them. Wherefore all its acts are divine. . . . Although they come from Him, they belong to the soul likewise, for God works them in the soul with its own aid, since it gives its will and consent. (*Living Flame*, St. 1, 5, 1. 3, p. 21.)

Love outstrips understanding, and love causes the transformation. The wood becomes fire; the rain drop becomes the ocean the candlelight is united to the sun and the human becomes the divine.

God is happy, since He knows and loves and rejoices in Himself without the possibility of doing otherwise. He is not, nor can He be, free to forget Himself. Thou wilt not enter into thy rest, my soul, until thou becomest inwardly one with the Highest Good, knowing what He knows, loving what He loves and enjoying what He enjoys. Then shalt thou see the end of the mutibility of thy will; then shall there be an end of mutibility. For the grace of God will have wrought so much in thee that it will have made thee a partaker of His Divine nature, with such perfection that thou wilt neither desire nor be able to forget the Highest Good nor cease to rejoice in Him and in His love. (*Exclamations of the Soul to God*, XVII, p. 420.)

St. Teresa's Bookmark

Let nothing disturb thee:
Let nothing dismay thee:
All things pass:
God never changes
Patience attains
All that it strives for
He who has God
Finds he lacks nothing
God alone suffices.

Bibliography

The Complete Works of Saint Teresa, in 3 vols. E. Allison Peers, London, New York: Sheed & Ward, 1944.
The Letters of Saint Teresa of Jesus, in 2 vols. E. Allison Peers. London: Sheed and Ward, 1980.
The Letters of Saint Teresa. Benedictines of Stanbrook. London: Thomas Baker, 1924.
The Complete Works of Saint John of the Cross, in 3 vols. E. Allison Peers. London: Burns Oates & Washbourne Ltd., 1951.
Handbook to The Life and Times of Saint Teresa and Saint John of the Cross. E. Allison Peers. London: Burns Oates, 1954.

All scriptural references are from The Jersualem Bible, London: Darton, Longman & Todd, 1966.